A survey of

TWENTIETH CENTURY PROTESTANT CHURCH MUSIC IN AMERICA

Talmage W. Dean

BROADMAN PRESS
Nashville, Tennessee

To Frances

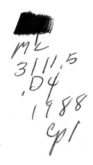

© Copyright 1988 • Broadman Press
All Rights Reserved
4268-13
ISBN: 0-8054-6813-7
Dewey Decimal Classification: 783
Subject Heading: CHURCH MUSIC - HISTORY AND CRITICISM
Library of Congress Catalog Number: 87-35522
Printed in the United States of America

Library of Congress Cataloging-in-Publication Data

Dean, Talmage W., 1915-
  Twentieth-century Protestant church music in
America.

  Bibliography: p. 266
  Includes index.
    1. Church music—Protestant churches—20th century.
2. Church music—United States—20th century. I. Title.
ML3111.5.D4 1988   783'.02'6   87-35522
ISBN 0-8054-6813-7

Acknowledgments

This exploration of some of the major developments in the field of church music during the twentieth century has been a personal and nostalgic experience. During my own extended activities, I have had the good fortune to know so many of the people featured in this study. As a college and seminary professor, I have experienced first-hand these major trends in the music of Protestant worship.

The project could never have been completed except for the resources, facilities, and gracious assistance of the staff of the Richardson Library, the Smith Music Library, and of the School of Music of Hardin-Simmons University. A special acknowledgment is also extended to the staff and extensive resources of the Music Library of Southwestern Baptist Theological Seminary.

The cooperation and encouragement of the music publishers, the media, and the educational institutions have also added a significant value to the study, and will add clarity to the complex expansion of Protestant worship. May the total result be a unanimous *soli Deo gloria!*

Preface

Twentieth-century church music is a phenomenon which has become a major element of our American musical culture. A subject of controversy from its earliest inception, it has been practiced under rigid controls throughout Christian history. But even in the most authoritative liturgical environment, music has always found spontaneous native expressions of faith, hope, and Christian love for one another. Only in America, however, with complete freedom of worship and near total autonomy of each congregation in things musical, did church musicians find the opportunity and resources for such expansive music programs as are produced in our contemporary services of worship, praise, and festive celebrations.

The present base for these productions is a musical literacy inherited from the community singing school, public-school music education, the college music curricula, and, in recent years, programs of music instruction in the church that focus upon all ages from preschool to senior citizens. The current musical base is a conglomeration of musical styles which include our own folk music, the lyric and musical creations of the self-taught singing schoolmaster, a body of familiar historical literature, and intense contemporary settings of great scriptural texts proclaiming our Christian faith and message.

This study of twentieth-century church music is not included as a review of the theological or philosophical writings on church music in this century. It is also, hopefully, not a projection of my own convictions or prejudices. It is, rather, a look at the foundations of our American church music, which can be found in our changing religious, social, economic, and political environments. It has been from the stress of wars, depression, frightening scientific developments, social decay, and theological controversy that much of our native hymnody and church music have been created. It has also been much of this music that has provided a "resting place" for the living faith of each new generation. Our music has also given us a basis for a better understanding of our own heritage of faith and mission.

It is my hope that much of our twentieth-century church music can be better understood when placed in its own environmental context. Then I also hope that this study might encourage others to research and record other aspects of this most active element of our contemporary Christian pilgrimage. But a stronger desire is that we might intensify our efforts to create new and honest musical expressions of our own living faith as members of "one body in Christ."

Contents

Part I:

The Social and Religious Heritage

1

Religious Life
in a Free Society

The year 1900 was not greeted as the mere turn of another century. The Christian world had already experienced many others. This was the dawn of a new millennium. Although America was still struggling with economic reconstruction, the social assimilation of emancipated slaves, and an influx of twelve million immigrants since 1871, the people were filled with hope, optimism, and a concept of "manifest destiny." America was now a "more perfect" union. The new religious freedoms, and the new geographic, academic, and scientific frontiers combined to create the image of a new "Canaan" or Promised Land for all.

Given an unprecedented ethnic mixture, total freedom of religion, and a steady movement toward a vast new Western frontier, America had become the most fertile ground for religious diversity and indigenous expressions of the Christian faith. William James, noted American physiologist, psychologist, and philosopher, attempted to analyze this diversity in his book *The Varieties of Religious Experience*, published in 1902. James described American religious experiences as either institutional (denominational) or personal. He concluded that the basic institutional concerns were the nature of God, proper ceremonies of worship, and organization. The personal concerns were the inner dispositions of persons themselves and their individual acts designed to serve God or to claim His favor. These personal experiences James described as direct "heart to heart" and "soul to soul" between the individual and the Creator. As we examine our nineteenth-century religious and musical heritage, it will be convenient for us to use James's division as a frequent frame of reference and organization. Even though many major Protestant denominations were still divided into "north" and "south" entities, the enthusiasm for America's "manifest destiny" was shared by all. They had founded colleges and seminaries, launched impressive mission programs to evangelize the world, were actively promoting temperance and a prohibition amendment, and were deeply involved (albeit through varying approaches) in the establishment of a godly world society—in effect, a biblical millennium. This religious fervor even influenced high-level political decisions to go to war and to take over certain territories in order to educate and evangelize the native populations. The institutional churches shared, or often adopted, the idealistic goals of many independent Christian organizations which had been pursuing these goals for a large part of the nineteenth century—the YMCA, YWCA, Salvation Army, Student Volunteer Movement, American Tract Society, Women's Christian Temperance Union, American Bible Society, Mission Societies, Sunday Schools, revivalism, and many "utopian" groups who were already busy establishing their own "Promised Land" in America. There was in all of these groups a commonality of evangelistic purpose which was either to *build* a Christian millenium or to *prepare* the people for Christ's second coming, which would then inaugurate His millennial reign on earth.

The problems of organizing and expediting these denominational programs were many. Society in the late nineteenth century remained primarily rural and very mobile. The location and constituency of these rural churches were determined by modes of travel—or walking distance. Within a radius of five miles, one could often find as many as ten small churches. The effectiveness of any centralized organization (or authority) was basically a problem of communication and was increased by the individual freedoms of the landowner or homesteader. The problems were further compounded by the constant westward migration. No longer in covered wagons, the new settlers moved by trainloads on the new transcontinental railroads, equipped with telegraphic communication, and with endless vistas of new land to be settled. The motivations for this mass movement were very diverse—land, free enterprise, freedom of religion, a fresh start for the Southern aristocracy, escape to the anonymity of a new name, adventure, and, always, new freedoms.

Within this fluid society, the autonomous churches flourished under the leadership of a part-time local minister or an itinerant "circuit rider." In many sparsely settled areas of the West, a community church was impossible. In such cases, the camp meeting survived as an annual, and often interdenominational, revival. In some remote areas these still exist. A sophisticated extension of these meetings can still be seen in the form of large denominational and religious conferences which are held in vacation or resort-like facilities throughout America.

Another apparent problem had arisen within the institutional churches in the East near the end of the century—a sharp decline in the number of students preparing for the ministry. Alfred Brown cited the urgency of the problem:

> The Harvard catalogue recently issued shows 551 students in law school, 560 in medical school, and only 26 in the divinity school. . . . At the end of the first century of Yale's history thirty-nine per cent of her graduates turned to the ministry; . . . During the last decade of her second century the number of ministerial students is *seven per cent*. The decline has been comparatively steady, but most rapid during the past twenty years.[1]

Notwithstanding, if one should try to characterize the mood of our institutional religion in 1900, the word would have to be optimism, and its moving force would be *progress*. The primary fuels for these attitudes were education and science. The secondary fuel was a near total confidence in the ultimate world triumph of democracy and the "church militant."

The apparent conflicts between much scientific thought and traditional biblical interpretation brought about many highly publicized debates on religion versus science. The most heated issue grew out of Charles Darwin's theory of "natural selection." This biological theory invaded the academic community in many fields of study and was quickly applied to such diverse areas as sociology, economics, and even religion. Society, via natural selection, was evolving into a world democracy. By the same token, a laissez-faire economy would "select" those who were worthy of financial success. Among religious leaders, many believed that man's educational and spiritual progress would soon eliminate the possibility of another major war.

At the conclusion of a long summary of the scientific, social, economic, and political achievements in the nineteenth century, an editorial in *The New York Times* dated December 31, 1899, concluded that:

> We step upon the threshold of 1900, which leads to the new century facing a still brighter dawn for human civilization. . . . America is facing westward and beginning to take its part in carrying the regenerating forces of popular government to the uttermost parts of the earth. Notwithstanding the bloody conflicts through which some of the steps of progress must still be made, the "vision of the world" grows clearer toward the time when—
>
> > The war-drum throbbed no longer, and the
> > battle-flags were furled
> > In the parliament of man, the federation of
> > the world.
> > There the common sense of most shall hold
> > a fretful realm in awe
> > And the kindly earth shall slumber, lapped in
> > universal law.

This quote from Tennyson's poem *Locksley Hall* would soon seek fulfillment in the League of Nations and again in the United Nations.

While the institutional churches were working toward social equality, Christian community, and a worldwide democracy, the advocates and practitioners of a personal Christianity were directing their efforts toward individual conversions. The basic rationale for their efforts was "Seek ye first the kingdom of heaven and all these things shall be added unto you." The social dynamics of the late nineteenth century suggest a field ripe for such a religious harvest. Elia W. Peattie described the vigorous racial and ethnic mix in Chicago in 1899 as being Jews, Poles,

Icelanders, Swedes, and lots of Germans—a majority of whom
had come from countries with a state church:

> See the mingling of strange peoples, the mob of wild faces from
> less fortunate lands, the old stories on the faces of those born with
> old ideas to new conditions! . . . But the story of the American
> is greatest, for it is his land and his day, and he is drunk with his
> own achievements. He plays at the game of commerce, and is
> satisfied; for losing or winning does not so much matter to him
> as that he have the chance of the game.[2]

The new industrial and scientific revolution had already
brought an expanded rail system, nationwide telegraphic communication, electricity for home use, the promise of electric
automobiles, agricultural machinery, and assembly-line production. It had also created wealth and poverty in staggering
proportions. Workers envisioned the eventual loss of demand
for their skills, and their fears were compounded by the preva-
lence of disease and various forms of discrimination in the job
market.

It was in the midst of this socioeconomic environment that
the revivalism of Dwight L. Moody and Ira D. Sankey had
flourished. People had responded with enthusiasm to this in-
dividualistic Christianity, which they felt to be an inherent element of their own personal freedoms. Sankey was the
songwriter, publisher, songleader, and especially the soloist
who popularized the gospel song. The texts of these songs, in
turn, became the embodiment and living theology of the personal religious experience. In collaboration with P. P. Bliss, Sankey published *Gospel Hymns and Sacred Songs* in 1875, which
was followed by five later editions and culminated in *Gospel
Hymns Nos. 1-6 Complete* (1894), containing 739 hymns. The
revenue from the millions of copies helped to build one of
Moody's Chicago churches and to bring about the founding of
the Moody Bible Institute.

The organization of the churches emphasizing this personal
religious experience was, for the most part, autonomous. Many
were independent and nondenominational. Their clergy was
not necessarily trained in the church's college or seminary.

They were free to preach wherever they could find, or build, a local congregation. Their message was basic—sin, atonement, redemption, and regeneration. Moral practices incorporated a rigid piety and temperance. The beliefs included the virgin birth; biblical authority; substitutionary atonement; the bodily resurrection of Christ; and His second coming.

Doctrinal conflicts were inevitable, however, in both institutional and independent churches. The major factions were usually termed "Modernists Versus Fundamentalists" or "Evolutionists Versus Creationists." The underlying issues were not settled in the nineteenth century, and probably will remain unresolved—in spite of one of the most dramatic confrontations in the religious history of America. In the summer of 1925 the John Scopes trial in Dayton, Tennessee, brought William Jennings Bryan to assist in the prosecution and Clarence Darrow from Chicago to assist in the defense of Scopes, who was accused of teaching evolution in violation of Tennessee law. Bryan was the acknowledged leader of the Democratic party from 1896-1912; the party's nominee for President in 1896, 1900, and 1908; secretary of state under President Wilson; and known as America's "silver-tongued orator." Darrow was equally famous as an avowed agnostic and a criminal lawyer. Probably no trial in American history to this date had received more extensive news coverage. After weeks of debate, Scopes pleaded guilty and was fined one hundred dollars. Both sides could claim a victory and recoup for further encounters. The stress was too much for Bryan, who died before leaving Dayton.

2

The Heritage of Song

Toward the end of the century, most of the large mainline denominations in America had published an "official" hymnal. The Episcopal Church had an American version of *Hymns Ancient and Modern* (1866), *The Church Hymnal* (1892, without music), and a collection of tunes called *Hutchins' Hymnal* (1894). A new Methodist hymnal was in preparation and was published in 1905. Presbyterians already had *The Presbyterian Hymnal* (1874), which was strongly influenced by *Hymns Ancient and Modern*.

If there could be a dominant theme in all of these publications, it would be a commitment to congregational singing as an important element in public worship. And, almost without exception, the desire to "improve" congregational singing was a high priority of the editorial committees. This emphasis upon congregational participation places the hymn tune and its text in a preeminent position in any study of American church music, and "their importance in church history exceeds that of all other musical types in a nation so democratic as America."[3]

Second only to congregational participation among these major denominations was the literary value of the text, its relation to the liturgical year, or its evangelical content. The early romantic English poets Coleridge, Wordsworth, Carlyle, and Byron wrote religious poetry, and from the clergy came an outpouring of hymns. In the year 1827 there "appeared John Keble's *The Christian Year*, Robert Pollock's *The Course of Time*, James Montgomery's *The Christian Poet*, and the posthumous *Hymns* of Bishop [Reginald] Heber."[4] The dominant thrust of these literary hymns was to influence the English move from psalmody to hymnody. The most significant influences were Heber's *Hymns Written and Adapted to the Weekly Service of the Church Year* (1827) and James Montgomery's *The Christian Psalmist* (1825). The strength of this "literary movement" was nowhere felt more strongly than in Reginald Heber's "Holy, Holy, Holy, Lord God Almighty," where, according to Benson, "the poet's is the only voice one cares to hear."[5]

The American implementation of this literary movement was led by Henry Ward Beecher, pastor of Plymouth Church, Brooklyn. With the help of John Zundel, the church's organist, Darius E. Jones, Beecher's music director, published *Temple Melodies* (1851). This was a collection of about two hundred popular tunes, adapted to nearly five hundred favorite hymns. The collection did not satisfy Beecher, however, and he proceeded to prepare a larger collection (1,374 hymns) published in 1855 as *The Plymouth Collection of Hymns and Tunes*, a private venture of the A. S. Barnes & Company of New York. With this new collection,

> he wrought great things at Plymouth Church. The hearty singing of the vast congregation became almost as much of an attraction as his [Beecher's] preaching. Its fame spread far and wide, encouraged countless congregations to emulate it, and carried the *Collection* itself into Baptist and Presbyterian, as well as Congregational churches.[6]

The movement spread rapidly in America. Such poets as Whittier, Longfellow, Holmes, Bryant, Lanier, and Emerson wrote religious poetry which provided texts for many standard hymns of the major Protestant hymnals. An outpouring of hymn texts followed from the American clergy and lesser poets. Foote provided an interesting aspect of the institutional origins of the major writers of these literary hymns in the nineteenth century. The centers for the enormous flow of hymns were Union Theological Seminary; Harvard University and Divinity School; Yale University and Andover Seminary; and Princeton University and Seminary.

> Unquestionably the influence of these educational institutions upon the hymns produced by their graduates was considerable.

It moulded the cultural standards of the writers and helped to formulate their thought and their religious outlook. . . . It was natural that the great missionary movement of the middle period of the nineteenth century should find its fullest utterance in the hymns produced by the graduates of Yale and Andover, for both institutions were profoundly affected by evangelical zeal for foreign missions.[7]

The writers from these institutions crossed well-established denominational lines—Baptists, Congregationalists, Episcopalians, Methodists, Presbyterians, and Unitarians. Foote also mentioned the remarkable influence of Harvard upon American hymnody for a century and a half. As champions of greater religious freedom, "it came about that, throughout the nineteenth century, Harvard produced by far the most notable succession of hymn-writers in the English-speaking world coming from any single institution."[8]

This late-nineteenth-century American hymnody was, for the most part, an assimilation of earlier English hymnody and literary ideals. It was, at the same time, an expression of the religious optimism which pervaded the large urban churches and theological seminaries of the Northeast. Its acceptance and influence were also greatest within the same geographical and educational environment.

Many of the larger churches in the metropolitan areas took advantage of the rapidly growing catalogs of available hymn plates to have special hymnals published for their own congregations. A typical example would be another special publication by the A. S. Barnes Company, *Many Voices; or Carmina Sanctorum, Evangelistic Edition with Tunes* (1891), published for the New Brooklyn Tabernacle, and prepared by the pastor, T. DeWitt Talmage. Termed a combination of "the old classic hymnody and the modern chorus," it all but ignores the gospel-song movement except for "Wonderful Words of Life," "Hold the Fort," and "I Am Praying for You"—perhaps because the Biglow & Main Company possessed the rights to most of the titles. The "modern chorus" obviously referred to the works of Lowell Mason and his followers. Mason's tunes were used forty-nine times. Among the other active American composers featured were William B. Bradbury, I. B. Woodbury, B. C. Unseld, George Root, and George C. Stebbins. The major English composers were Henry Smart, Arthur Sullivan, Samuel S. Wesley, Samuel Webbe, and the most frequent tunes were by Joseph Barnby and John B. Dykes. It was anticipated by the publisher that the hymnal would be used by thousands of other churches and associations.

Another significant element of our hymnic heritage might be called the Reformation Inheritance. The increasing flow of immigrants in the latter half of the century brought more groups seeking religious freedom as well as economic opportunities. Among these were more Lutherans and other reformed groups from Prussia, Saxony, Sweden, Norway, and the Netherlands. They were among the earliest settlers of Pennsylvania; but with transcontinental rail travel now available, they moved into the rich farmlands of the Midwest from Texas to the Dakotas. They were strongly motivated by the desire to retain their own language, music, and religious traditions. They established economically independent communities along the rivers and railroads of the new American frontier and founded educational institutions wherever they settled. Though their ethnic backgrounds were quite diverse, these conservative Lutherans soon organized themselves into synods by states, then later by larger interstate synodical conferences.

A unifying element was the highly developed musical tradition which soon congealed around the desire to preserve the Lutheran chorale, to maintain a conservative theology, and to restore the Lutheran liturgy. They were fairly successful in preserving their native tongue in worship, but the strong anti-German sentiment, which developed during World War I, gradually brought about a near-complete transition to English. The publication of *The Lutheran Hymnal* in 1941 was an important indication of the dominance of English, the preservation of the chorale, and the successful restoration of the liturgy. This musical landmark among Lutherans also marked a fusion of their musical backgrounds with such distinctively American forces as the Sunday School movement, the missions movement, and the singing school.

The direct musical heritage from the nineteenth-century American synods was a body of hymnody and special-purpose songbooks which had been carefully collected and approved for their musical and theological contents. These included a revised *Gesangbuch* (1872) containing 695 hymns; *Hymns of the Evangelical Lutheran Church* for the use of English Lutheran Missions (1866) published by Concordia; *Evangelical Lutheran Hymnbook*, "consisting of 400 hymns without music and printed by H. Lang of Baltimore (1889); and a *Sunday School Hymnal*, which was the first full-size hymnal with four-part settings,"[9] published by the American Lutheran Publication Board, Pittsburgh (1901); and the Missouri Synod's *Evangelical Lutheran Hymnbook with Tunes* (1912), written in four parts, with all liturgical forms, prayers, select psalms, and 567 hymns.[10] Although a major segment of the hymns were translations of earlier chorales, many of the Sunday School and mission hymns were contemporary.

Although this body of published music was already available to Lutherans in America, a more significant influence upon the total growth and style of church music in the twentieth century was the establishment of many Lutheran colleges and seminaries in America.

> Almost from the beginning [1839] choral groups, and in many instances, instrumental groups helped to make the service a better worship service through their aid in the singing or playing of the hymns.[11]

Ethnic conflicts occurred early in Pennsylvania, where various European ties and traditions were strongest. But the forces of amalgamation were at work in this highly publicized atmosphere of religious freedom. The international language of music and its practice was at work in the singing societies and the singing schools. The nondenominational singing societies flourished in all of the cities along the East Coast. In Pennsylvania, eleven mixed and männerchor societies were active in Philadelphia, New York, Lancaster, Reading, and Harrisburg.[12] The names "Haydn Society," "Handelian Society," "St. Cecilia Society," and "Beethoven Society" suggest serious baroque and classical emphases. It is important to note that the meeting places had also moved to the schools or other public buildings, and the participants were somewhat musically literate adults. This musical and cultural community activity precluded any primary religious emphasis, but increased the desire and the capacity for a higher level of performance and literature in these urban churches.

3

The Indigenous Heritage

The singing school movement originated in New England and rapidly took roots in all denominations as a means of teaching the people to read music and thereby improve congregational singing—a need which crossed all theological barriers. The schools spread to Pennsylvania and flourished, particularly in the rural areas and small towns. To many of these groups, the singing school served multiple purposes—language preservation, instruction in the music of the church, and a wholesome activity for the old and young during the winter when outside work was limited or during the late summer when crops were "laid by."

The New England influence was prominent in that *The Easy Instructor* (1807), by Little and Smith, was the text used most often during the first half of the nineteenth century. "With a choice collection of Psalm Tunes and Anthems from the most celebrated authors," *The Easy Instructor* was especially important for its use of shaped notes to represent the syllables *fa,sol, la,* and *mi* from Guido d'Arezzo's (d. 1050) hexachord scale *ut,re,mi,fa,sol,* and *la.*

Another textbook using solmization was *The Sacred Minstrel* by Joel Harmon Carlisle (1828), which contained "a selection of

Psalm and Hymn Tunes in general use. . . . Also, several anthems and set-pieces designed for Worship Assemblies and singing societies."[13]

J. G. Schmauk, organist at Saint Michael's Lutheran Church in Philadelphia, published his *Deutsche Harmonie* "fur Deutsche Singschulen" in 1833. In the same year Henry D. Eyer published *The Union Choral Harmonie*, "consisting of Sacred Music with German and English lines to each tune, adapted to the use of CHRISTIAN CHURCHES OF EVERY DENOMINATION."[14] Eyer also included "lighter songs" to "keep up that necessary excitement which will ensure regular attendance."

Lowell Mason was very important in the growing influence of the singing school, as was his pioneer work in public-school music education. Many of the Pennsylvania teachers attended his music "conventions" and his summer classes in Boston. As church choirs began to assume the leadership of congregational singing, the churches had to depend upon the church-sponsored singing school, and the latter half of the century brought many teachers who were innovative and more effective in their techniques. Among the more successful was John B. McCormick, whose *School and Concert* (1881), published by Biglow & Main of New York, contained solos, trios, quartets, septets, and choruses.

Another was T. R. Weber, whose *Pennsylvania Choral Harmony*, using the shaped notes of Little and Smith, was "Adapted to the use of CHRISTIAN CHURCHES of every denomination."[15] Mason's influence was also continuing through the widespread use of his *The Coronation*, also published by Biglow & Main.

The most successful method of all was introduced by J. B. Aikin in *The Christian Minstrel* (1846). His new system introduced seven shaped notes, *do,re,mi,fa,sol,la,* and *si,* for the octave scale instead of the four shapes based upon Guido's hexachord *ut,re,mi,fa,sol,* and *la.* With vowel changes for chromatic alterations (*do,di,re,ri,* etc.) it became possible for the singer to sightread the entire twelve-tone octave. The system was soon adopted by Joseph Funk of Singer's Glen, Virginia, whose teachers and students would spread their own gospel songbooks throughout the South and Midwest. At this writing, many independent church hymnals are still published in the seven-shaped-note system.

The musical proficiency achieved in these late nineteenth-century singing schools is pointed out in a 1963 interview with John Climenhaga, an elderly retired teacher: "In advanced classes we learned even difficult songs like Handel's 'Hallelujah Chorus' by syllable, singing without the use of an instrument."[16]

Although the small rural churches had to rely upon the independent publishers and composers, this did not forego the development of strong musical traditions within these congregations. Throughout the century, these publishers had issued specialized songbooks for Sunday Schools, temperance societies, mission groups, lay religious organizations, and gospel songbooks for the raging fires of revivalism. All-purpose books were then assembled which incorporated the best (or favorites) from each of these books in order to serve the total needs of the small church. Isaac Watts, Charles Wesley, John Newton, and William Cowper provided the texts for a majority of the standard hymns included, but there were regional preferences for their adapted tunes. Because of the familiarity and wide distribution of many indigenous and folk melodies used in the singing schools, such tunes were more often preferred to the more stately settings of Lowell Mason or the traditional styles of the English Hymns or Lutheran chorales.

Another factor in the dominance of the regional publishers was the availability of their new songbooks. They were rapidly replacing the little hymnals (with texts only) in a more musically literate society. By 1900 a strong assist was given to the gospel songbooks by the mail-order house. The 1900 Sears Roebuck Catalog (#109) advertised the complete Sankey's *Gospel Hymns*, vols. 1-6 in cloth binding for one dollar. Published by the Biglow & Main Company, the book featured the works of William B. Bradbury, Ira D. Sankey, Philip P. Bliss, W. H. Doane, James McGranahan, George C. Stebbins, and, most important of all, Fanny J. Crosby. Crosby produced some nine thousand texts, most of which were set to music. Many of these remain as a significant component of most evangelical hymnals to this day. Other major publishers of the day were Peter P. Bilhorn of Chicago; Edwin O. Excell of Chicago; Fillmore Brothers of Cincinnati; and the Hall-Mack Company of Philadelphia.

An interesting "hit parade" of "Sacred Music" appeared in the same 1900 catalog of Sears Roebuck, in the form of "rollers" to be played on their small roller (barrel) organs. These rollers operated the little hand organs in the same way as the rollers of a music box, and thus could be used at home or to accompany a small congregation. This had been practiced in the small churches of New England a century earlier. The rollers cataloged were all gospel song titles except for a few familiar hymn tunes interspersed between them.

The titles are of such interest that they deserve listing in order: "In the Sweet Bye and Bye"; "Nearer My God to Thee"; "I Need Thee Every Hour"; "From Greenland's Icy Mountains"; "Onward Christian Soldiers"; "Hold the Fort"; "Just As I Am"; "America"; "He Leadeth Me"; "I Love to Tell the Story"; "The Home Over There"; "Almost Persuaded"; "Where Is My Boy Tonight?"; "Bringing in the Sheaves"; "Let the Lower Lights Be Burning"; "Only an Armor Bearer"; "I Will Sing of My Redeemer"; "Pull for the Shore"; "Precious Name"; "Hark, the Herald Angels Sing"; "Abide with Me"; "Even Me"; "Watchman, Tell Us of the Night"; "Come Ye Disconsolate"; "What a Friend"; "We Shall Meet Beyond the River"; "I Am Praying for You"; "Whosoever Will"; "All The Way My Savior Leads Me"; "Rescue the Perishing"; "Follow On"; "Knocking, Knocking, Who Is There?"; "Shall We Gather at the River."

The standard hymn tunes on rollers included: DUKE STREET, ANTIOCH, ITALIAN HYMN, FEDERAL STREET, PLEYEL'S HYMN, OLD HUNDRED, and WELLESLEY. This serves as a reminder that most of the gospel songs remain in circulation, and all of the tunes remain in most worship hymnals.

The twentieth century also became heir to a unique heritage of religious songs which evolved in the camp meetings and singing schools in the South and Midwest. Downey's study of the music of early American revivalism poses the premise that "among rural Separatists and Baptists a vigorous musical activity with its origin in the revival fervor of 1740 did indeed exist in the period 1760-1800."[17] This folk origin was based upon the need for new tunes to accompany the hymns of Watts, which were the chief musical expression of the Separatists. Also, the earliest editions of the nineteenth-century tune books had a strong relation to the folk music of the British Isles. Downey added: "It is reasonable to assume that accretions to the texts of the Separatists were accompanied by the introduction of the new and the adoption of the old tunes."[18]

As the singing schools moved to the West and South, their folk elements were institutionalized in their own regional traditions —emerging as the gospel songs of "free grace" in the Midwest and merging with the Negro spiritual in the South. Downey based these premises upon the work of George P. Jackson and Irving Lowens. Downey classified the folk hymns as the group or social "praise hymn"; the "religious ballad"; and the "revival spiritual." All were typical of the revivals and used patterns of congregational repetition which were characteristic of the Negro spirituals.[19]

The early singing schools adopted the four syllables *fa,sol,la,* and *mi* and their four shaped notes from Little and Smith's *Easy Instructor.* They were used in the same pattern as found in the popular theory textbook of the sixteenth century, *Micrologus,* by the German theorist Ornithoparchus. It was translated into English by John Dowland and used the four syllable sounds with a mutation between two of Guido's hexachords to teach the sound of our descending major scale. This system was used by both the *Southern Harmony* and the *Sacred Harp,* and both books relied heavily upon published "songsters" and hymnals for their texts. The tunes which were assigned to each text might be folk, spiritual, or original. Popular congregational refrains were added freely to almost any hymn and, in many cases, became the "composed" refrain of the gospel songs in the late nineteenth and early twentieth centuries. These arbitrary refrains remain in such twentieth-century settings as Watts' "Alas, and Did My Savior Bleed" and Samuel Stennett's "On Jordan's Stormy Banks I Stand."

The *Sacred Harp* has survived many revisions, additions, and reprints. Regular "classes" are held throughout the South, Southwest, and on the West Coast; in fact, I recently received (1983) the program for a "Sacred Harp Singing" at a major university in New England. These classes might use a recent four-part edition or the recent reprint of the three-part edition of 1911. And many of these tunes are now included in our most recent denominational hymnals.

Joseph Funk's *Harmonia Sacra* (1851) with its new seven-shaped notes brought new life to the singing school in the latter half of the century and spawned a new genre of the gospel song. The leading publishers in this new form and musical style at the turn of this century were A. J. Showalter of Dalton, Georgia, and James D. Vaughan of Lawrenceburg, Tennessee. The most prolific poet for this new market was James Rowe. He wrote about one thousand texts for Showalter alone and claimed to have written nineteen thousand before his death in 1929. Shortly before Rowe's death, a small publisher wrote a new tune and sent it to him. Rowe returned the melody within a week with a custom-written text—for one dollar.

These new gospel songs typically avoided all controversial social and theological issues of the day. Their themes were the more universal concepts of sin, atonement, redemption, the difficulties and brevity of life, the assurance of heaven, motherhood, morality, good works, the second coming, and Jesus as Savior, Shepherd, Pilot, and Friend.

Probably the most indigenous heritage of religious song in America was the Negro spiritual. After the war between the states, black Americans had already established many of their own churches as freedmen in the North. In the South, where many of the slaves had shared a token participation in the segregated worship of their white owners, the move was to their own separate and free churches, but retaining a familiar identification as Baptist, Methodist, and so forth.

Contrary to popular expectations and many studies of the Negro spirituals, the Negroes did not equate the Ohio River with the river Jordan and migrate to the North. Booker T. Washington, noted black scholar and educator, wrote in the

Atlantic Monthly (November 1899) that of approximately ten million blacks in the United States, about eight million remained in the South. Their population had already doubled since emancipation and Washington added:

> I say without hesitation that, with some exceptional cases, the negro is at his best in the Southern States. While he enjoys certain privileges in the North that he does not have in the South, when it comes to the matter of securing property, enjoying business opportunities and employment, the South presents a far better opportunity than the North.[20]

Through the efforts of the American Missionary Association and many Northern philanthropists, segregated colleges were established for blacks in Georgia, Alabama, Mississippi, Virginia, and Tennessee. These schools provided leadership for the black community during the late nineteenth and the first half of the twentieth centuries. Also, it was from these "ethnic islands" that some of America's most significant indigenous music was created and brought to the attention of the Western world. By 1900 the Fisk Jubilee Singers had already traveled for many years in both America and Europe raising money for Fisk University. More important for this study, they established the Negro spiritual as a basic component of Christian song literature.

Even in bondage, the illiterate slaves had learned the basic biblical stories, an inherited modal melodic style, and the refrain structure of the white spirituals. Then they created songs that were uniquely their own. The oral tradition almost dictated a congregational refrain that could be remembered and that embodied the central theme of the song. This, in turn, required a leader who could improvise a stanza or story line in a musical dialogue with the congregation. Because of the literacy problem, it was necessary for George Pullen Jackson to cite the person who sang many of the songs for him. Then he would often add the fact that the singer's parents "had lived and learned it on a plantation" or "as it was sung in camp meetings."

The structure of the spiritual of 1900 was an opening refrain by the congregation, followed by stanzas sung as a learned or improvised solo, each followed by the congregational repetition of the refrain. Both the spiritual and the camp meeting songs used a variety of familiar refrains which might be remotely related to the story or text. The surviving refrains used and published with Stennett's "On Jordan's Stormy Banks" might be "I Am Bound for the Promised Land"; "On the Other Side of Jordan"; "One More River to Cross"; or "We Will Rest in that Fair and Happy Land." These preexisting refrains were attached appropriately to any newly learned text or improvisation.

A common type of text for the spiritual was a biblical story narrated in couplets or a single line ("Were You There?") repeated over and over. Very popular narratives were the crucifixion, death, and resurrection. Some stories used the experiences of Bible heroes—Moses, Joshua, David, Paul, or Peter—to carry the message. Others used a familiar catalog of characters such as brothers, sisters, mothers, preachers, and so forth. Heaven, Hell, Canaan, Promised Land, death, mourning, suffering, and resurrection were dominant themes of these deeply personal experiences to which these former slaves could strongly relate.

In sharp contrast to the rejection of the folk hymns and spirituals by the established denominations, the Negro spiritual was espoused and promoted by the religious and political establishments of the North, Great Britain, and Germany. The group most responsible for this was the Jubilee Singers of Fisk University in Nashville, Tennessee. Established in 1866 in an old Union hospital barracks, Fisk's average attendance during the first year was over a thousand, with the majority learning to read and write. George L. White became a part-time instructor in vocal music, and five years later his "choir" of eleven students set out upon their first tour. After many trying circumstances, they came to New York and sang in the Brooklyn churches of T. DeWitt Talmage and Henry Ward Beecher. Here their offerings were generous and they continued to tour for three months from Washington, D.C. to New England. Their songs were written down and published by Theodore F. Seward and sold at all concerts. The net proceeds for the tour amounted to twenty thousand dollars.

This was the beginning of more extended tours to Great Britain and Germany. While in Great Britain the Jubilee Singers were sponsored by Moody and Sankey, who were in a revival campaign, and by the church of Charles H. Spurgeon. They were received by the royal families of both Britain and Germany and raised enough money to purchase a new site for Fisk and a new "Jubilee Hall" by 1875. In J. B. T. Marsh's account, Fisk had

raised up the Jubilee Singers, who had done great things for their people in breaking down, by the magic of their song, the cruel prejudice against color that was everywhere in America the greatest of all hindrances to their advancement.[21]

For the music world, an important collection of one of America's most important folk contributions to church music was in print and distributed in America, Great Britain, and Germany.

The concert numbers given special note by Marsh were "Steal Away to Jesus"; "Go Down Moses"; "The Lord's Prayer" (sung in traditional English chant); "O Brothers, Don't Stay Away"; "I've Been Redeemed"; "He 'Rose, He 'Rose"; "Roll, Jordan, Roll"; "I'll Hear the Trumpet Sound"; and "Sweet Chariot." Jackson also cited an important performance practice when he quoted a musician who had heard "Miss Jackson, the contralto of the original Fisk Jubilee Singers, sing 'You May Bury Me in the East' without accompaniment of any sort."[22]

The forces which fostered the dynamic growth of America in the nineteenth century also encouraged the development of many independent and indigenous religious groups. One of these, which was to become a major influence upon twentieth-century church music, was the Church of Jesus Christ of Latter-Day Saints. Organized in 1830, the church is distinct in that its founding was based upon a so-called "restoration of the true church" and upon a "new revelation" to its prophet, Joseph Smith. "Among the first official revelations was one given to the Prophet Joseph Smith in July of 1830 instructing his wife Emma to collect hymns to be used in the newly restored church."[23]

These earliest hymns appeared in *The Evening and Morning Star*, an official publication of the church in 1832. Thirty-three more hymns had been published by July 1833, when a mob destroyed their printing presses. In August of 1835 a vest-pocket edition of ninety hymn texts, also selected by Emma Smith, was published in Kirtland, Ohio. Thirty-nine of these had been written by Latter-Day Saint poets.[24] Another hymnal, issued by Emma Smith in 1841, contained 304 hymns and was published in Nauvoo, Illinois.

A strong mission effort in England afforded Brigham Young, Parley P. Pratt, and John Taylor the opportunity to publish *A Collection of Sacred Hymns for the Church of Jesus Christ of Latter-Day Saints in Europe* (1840), which contained 271 hymn texts.[25] This "Manchester Hymnal" and its twenty-four succeeding editions were used officially for eighty-seven years. The later editions were published in Liverpool, England, and Salt Lake City, Utah.

The Latter-Day Saints' strong commitment to church music soon extended far beyond an appropriate hymnody. Their first publication with music was *The Latter-Day Saints' Psalmody*, edited by John Tullidge and published in Liverpool in 1857. It contained thirty-eight easy anthems and many hymn texts set to original tunes.[26] A new *Latter-Day Saints Psalmody*, published in Salt Lake City in 1889, was the first large collection of hymns with musical settings. Scored in three staves, the music was designed for more sophisticated musicians by a young English immigrant and conductor of the Mormon Tabernacle Choir, George Edward Percy Careless. Under his direction, the choir had already performed Handel's *Messiah*, Rossini's *Stabat Mater*, and Mendelssohn's *Hymn of Praise*. George Careless had come to Salt Lake City to fulfill a mission call from Brigham Young "to take the Tabernacle Choir and the theater orchestra and lay a foundation for good music in Utah."[27] His successor as director of the choir, Ebenezer Beesley, also English, had already published *A Collection of Hymns and Anthems* in 1883 for the use of the Tabernacle Choir, which strongly influenced Careless's 1889 *Psalmody*.

The most significant influence of the Mormon (Latter-Day

Saint) musical heritage, and ultimately upon American church music, was not the sectarian hymnody but the choir itself. During the 1880s Beesley took the choir to other cities in the Utah Territory. Under his successor, Evan Stephens (1890-1916), the two-hundred-fifty-member choir went to Chicago to participate in a singing contest. From this point forward, the Mormon Tabernacle Choir became the spearhead of a lasting musical relationship with the American people and began to exert a powerful influence upon the choral music of the church. Expanded tours and, eventually, weekly network radio and television programs and recording contracts with major artists and symphony orchestras, were all destined to establish the three-hundred-voice Mormon Tabernacle Choir as a household musical experience in America. Their anthem literature, in particular, caught the ears of church music directors and became familiar literature in urban Protestant sanctuaries all over America.

4

The Heritage of Musical Romanticism

The productivity of a huge catalog of concert music for the church (or church music for the concert) during the nineteenth century was grounded in the European literary movement known as Romanticism. The first poetic element identified by German poets as "romantic" was a subjective "inexpressible longing" for the ideal, the nonexistent, or a meaning beyond words. Equally strong was the religious yearning for the restoration of the early church, an idealized piety, and the order and authority of the medieval church.

With the rise of personal freedoms, these subjective emotions found expression in poetry, drama, and art, but music was ac-

knowledged to be the supreme expression and understanding
of this "meaning beyond words." The rise of the art song allowed the accompaniment to convey this inexpressible meaning beyond the text. Composers extended this poetic quality of
music to piano music in such works as Mendelssohn's *Songs
Without Words* and large orchestral compositions generally
called *tone poems.* With these continually enlarged resources of
the orchestra, formerly inaccessible aspects of human emotion
were exploited. The individual and private experience of intui-
tion or instinct then acquired a validity and a special religious
appeal through choral and orchestral music. Thus arose an
urban dilettante following of opera and oratorio, the desire for
a piano in every parlor, and the organist and professional quartet in the church choir loft.

This surge of interest in serious music all over America at the
end of the century might be attributed to many factors, but two
were of particular importance: the teaching of music in the
public schools and music as family or social recreation. The 1902
Sears, Roebuck Catalog (#111) contained forty-five pages of
musical instruments of all kinds, available to rural as well as
urban families.

The romantic European penchant for the grandiose, plus the
availability of more literate musicians, made possible such festivals as Patrick Gilmore's "World Peace Jubilee" in Boston
(1872). The Jubilee featured an orchestra of two thousand and
a chorus of twenty thousand. *Dwight's Journal of Music* also
announced Dr. Leopold Damrosch's great festival in New York
City in May 1881 as "featuring an orchestra of 250, chorus of
1,200 voices, besides 1,500 girls from the schools, and 250 boys
from the church choirs." The works performed included Handel's *Dettingen Te Deum;* Rubinstein's *Tower of Babel;* Beethoven's *Symphony No. Nine;* Berlioz's *Requiem;* and "a great
abundance and variety of lesser treasures old and new—all in
four evenings and three afternoon concerts, beginning Tuesday
evening. The hall will seat 10,000 people."[28]

The same issue announced the performance in New York of
J. S. Bach's *Passion According to St. Matthew* on Good Friday
and Mendelssohn's *St. Paul* on Easter. Benjamin Lang had re-

cently conducted a performance with a seventy-five-piece orchestra in his church and featured the works of Beethoven,
Mendelssohn, and Schubert. George W. Chadwick had also
been appointed musical director of the Clarendon Street Baptist Church.[29]

The ultimate vocal and choral expression of musical romanticism was opera. Oratorio already had its role in the larger
churches, but, as in its earlier days, it was a dramatic and musical imitation of opera. Where oratorio was not possible, simplified arrangements of best loved operatic arias or choruses were
common fare, with sacred texts substituted for the original.
Even the independent all-purpose hymnals had "sacred" adap-
tions of Gounod, Rossini, or Cherubini. An American version of
the sacred cantata was already a tradition in the smaller urban
church choirs.

Probably the best-established performance tradition in the
urban denominational church in 1900 was the mixed-quartet
anthem and the sacred solo art song. The organist-director was
thus expected to provide *good* church music, performed by the
best singers available. This practice had fostered an expanding
catalog of anthem literature, sacred cantatas (performed by the
quartet), and especially the sacred art song. Since Dudley
Buck's introduction of his solo art songs in 1869, a genre of
"semi-popular" sacred songs have been a standard element of
Protestant worship in America.[30] An interesting editorial note
in the Lorenz music magazine *The Choir Herald* for May 1901
commented on the popularity of Stephen Adam's "The Holy
City." Emma L. Ashford quoted a Methodist Bishop G_____
who told of the music which all of his city and country churches
performed during his regular visits:

> They usually attempt music beyond their ability, and sometimes
> make a sorry mess of it. But I could stand all that if they wouldn't
> sing "The Holy City" at every church I visit. Last winter I was
> on my way up in the mountains, holding two services every day
> and sometimes three, and every time we collected the offertory
> [sic] some one would start in with "The Holy City."

A few years hence the Bishop might well have been speaking of Mrs. Ashford's own popular art song, "My Task."

If the major established churches in America should lay claim to a native solo and choral literature in 1900, it would doubtless be the works of Dudley Buck (1839-1909). Although his music covers a broad spectrum of hymns, vocal solos, anthems, sacred services, cantatas, organ, piano, orchestra, opera, chamber music, and concertos, Buck was primarily known as a concert organist and church musician. The majority of his music is based upon texts, and his sacred texts include 20 songs, 119 anthems, canticles, and hymns, and 9 services and cantatas. His 18 compositions for the organ could be classified as concert or functional service music, even though many are transcriptions of orchestral overtures.

After thorough European training in theory, composition, and performance, Buck returned to America to church positions as organist/composer in Hartford, Boston, Chicago, and Brooklyn. He served as organist/choirmaster in Congregational and Episcopal churches. A position of particular interest was a brief period at Saint James Episcopal in Chicago (1869-1871), a church that was to become increasingly prominent in American church music under Leo Sowerby. In addition to his church duties, Buck was active as an orchestral composer and conductor during the tenure of Theodore Thomas as conductor of the Chicago Symphony. Buck also became a proponent of American music, helped organize and promote the American Guild of Organists, and emphasized the need for advanced studies in music by refusing an honorary doctorate from Yale University.

While in Chicago, Buck built an organ studio and recital hall (seating two hundred) onto his home and accumulated an enviable music library. He was on a concert tour in 1871 when the Great Fire of Chicago destroyed the entire structure. William Gallo, citing *Dwight's Journal of Music,* stated that he possessed:

> all of the Bach scores published by the Bach and Handel Society of Leipzig, a great deal of organ music, the complete scores of

Beethoven, . . . a large assortment of the best German work on theory, and . . . Topfer's work on organ building.[31]

Buck's most influential church position was at Holy Trinity in Brooklyn. Here he adopted the practice of a special musical service on the first Sunday evening of each month. The format included organ compositions, anthems, and services and favored the choral works of Joseph Barnby and Felix Mendelssohn. According to Buck's correspondence, "these services became so popular that strangers packed the church even to standing room."[32] While at Holy Trinity, his music began to attract widespread attention and was published by some seventeen publishers. These included such firms as G. Schirmer (New York); Oliver Ditson (Boston); Theodore Presser (Philadelphia); Lyon & Healy (Chicago); John Church Company (Cincinnati); Novello (London); and C. A. Klemm (Leipzig). The extensive use of his music at the turn of the century is shown by the *Musical Courier*'s published lists of music which appeared on special church programs for Easter, Christmas, or other special occasions. On almost all of these lists published in 1892-1893, "the music of Dudley Buck constituted at least a fourth of the compositions mentioned."[33]

Gallo's summary of Buck's significance as a composer states:

Buck's music was preeminently for his own age. . . . However, if another view be taken, the view that music is significantly served by a composer whose work was relevant for his own generation and led that generation to an increased musical awareness, then Buck must be ranked much higher than he has been. He was, in his own generation, a sincere, competent musician whose music moved both layman and musically educated alike, and such a man is vital to music at any time.[34]

5

The Creative American Heritage

Other significant indicators of our musical heritage are many collections of choral literature issued by some of the major American publishers. These collections show the continuing influence of our historical European heritage, but they also indicate the enormous production of American composers. The most striking characteristic of their music is its design for the performance abilities of the volunteer choir in an average urban congregation. Another is the characteristic use of texts from familiar hymns or gospel songs and music appropriate for distinctly American holidays and festivals.

The Choir Journal (B. F. Wood, 1899) was "A collection of Anthems, Hymn-Anthems, and Responses" and "Suitable for Quartet or Chorus Choir." Almost all of the works contained solos for various voice parts, and the majority were by English composers. The collection contained a few works by American composers, with Daniel Protheroe listed most often.

G. Schirmer published a collection, *Shepard's Anthem Book,* which relied heavily upon Handel, Gounod, A. R. Gaul, Joseph Barnby, and Mendelssohn. The book also contained thirteen selections by T. G. Shepard and a few works by the Americans G. B. Nevin and H. N. Bartlett.

The vitality of church music in the Midwest found expression in many published collections of anthems. A notable example was *Herbert's Anthems* (Cincinnati: Fillmore Brothers, 1889). This was a collection of sixty anthems by Dr. J. B. Herbert for "Chorus and Quartet Choirs." Anthems for special occasions included Christmas, Easter, Thanksgiving, Dedication, and Advent. Of particular interest was his near-exclusive use of Scripture texts. After joining the Lorenz Company, Herbert compiled *The Harp of David* (1900). This was a special collection which used only texts from the Psalms and was directed toward Presbyterian congregations.

Excell's Anthems, Vols. III and IV (1890 and 1893), were published by E. O. Excell of Chicago and contained Solos, Duets, Trios, Quartets, and Choruses. The index contained more than a hundred entries, over 384 pages, and a list of thirty composers—all of whom are believed to be American. The texts were almost entirely familiar hymn texts. Of special interest in the collection were numerous works by Emma L. Ashford, J. A. Parks, Charles H. Gabriel, William Kirkpatrick, and A. W. Nelson. All of these composers would soon join the Lorenz Company and become editors and regular contributors to the Lorenz music magazines.

A similar publication from Chicago was *Beirly's Regal Choir* (Chicago: Alfred Beirly, 1899) which also contained Choruses, Quartettes, Trios, Duets, and Solos. Anthems for special occasions were for Christmas, Easter, Patriotic, Children's Day, Thanksgiving, and Funeral. All of the music was by Beirly, and the texts were familiar hymns and religious poetry.

The Lorenz Company of Dayton, Ohio was already becoming established as an important publisher of church music. It was founded in 1890 by Edmund S. Lorenz, the son of a missionary pastor who was also active in the Sunday School movement. After graduating from high school in 1870, Edmund taught German in the public schools. In 1874 he became associated with the United Brethren Publishing House in Dayton and edited (or coedited) at least a dozen Sunday School and gospel song books. Through his association with Jeremiah E. Rankin, then president of Howard University, Washington, D.C., he published *Murphy's Temperance Hymnal* in 1878. All of this publishing activity provided support for additional studies at the United Brethren Seminary in Dayton; an M.A. degree at Otterbein in 1881; a B.D. from Yale in 1883; and postgraduate studies at the Universities of Leipzig and Berlin.[35]

Lorenz organized the Lorenz Publishing Company in October 1890 from a borrowed desk in the printing house of the

United Brethren. "Little did he dream that what was intended as a sick man's pastime should develop into [a] large, symmetrical business to which ten thousand churches would look for their regular supply of music."[36] The company first provided music for the Sunday Schools and for festal occasions. These festal days included Christmas, Easter, Memorial Day, Children's Day, Independence Day, Flower Sunday, Missionary Concerts, Harvest Home, and Thanksgiving. As a composer, Lorenz would contribute over 830 Sunday School and gospel songs, writing both text and music for many. He wrote over 725 anthems, more than 40 seasonal cantatas, about 35 solos, and more than 260 calls to worship, responses, and benedictions. He edited more than 70 special collections of music which contained anthems, music for men's and women's voices, and music for primary and junior "classes."[37]

The most significant contribution of the Lorenz Company to church music, however, was the highly successful application of the "magazine" distribution of church music materials. The idea had already been tried by Alfred Beirly (*Beirly's Anthem Serial*) and J. P. Vance (*The Choir Herald*) when Lorenz founded his *Choir Leader* in 1894. The most distinct addition to the *Leader* was special articles designed to help choir directors with their problems of organization, theory, vocal techniques, and so forth. One year after its inception, the *Choir Leader* had eight thousand subscribers, representing one thousand churches. After the death of J. P. Vance (1897), Lorenz acquired *The Choir Herald*. With the same format as the *Leader,* it became a highly successful magazine of less difficult music, containing four or more "Good Anthems by Well Known Composers." A bimonthly magazine, *The Organist,* appeared in 1897 with organ music and articles about organs and organ pedagogy. *The Volunteer Choir,* without articles and containing even easier music, would also appear in 1913 and increase the Company's 1915 mailout to fifty thousand from offices in Dayton, New York City, and Chicago.

The availability of relatively easy music in these magazines allowed the smaller urban churches to attain a remarkable homogeneity of musical style and literature at the beginning of the new century. Lorenz was the editor of both the *Leader* and the *Herald.* Assisting him on the *Leader* was Emma L. Ashford (a former member of Dudley Buck's choir at St. James in Chicago) and J. A. Parks. Charles H. Gabriel and L. O. Emerson (with extensive experience working Lowell Mason's "music conventions") assisted with the *Herald.* In addition to the feature articles for the directors, much space in the magazines was given to advertising solos, octavos, anthem and organ collections, cantatas, and songbooks for worship, Sunday Schools, or camp meetings.

The seasonal cantata was already an established tradition in many of these urban churches. The March copy of *The Choir Leader* (1900) advertised fifteen Easter cantatas (three of them new) composed by Ashford, Baltzell, Florio, Gabriel, Lorenz, Porter, and Prior.

The magazines contained new choral settings of familiar hymn texts and (particularly in the *Leader*) more sophisticated settings of Scripture texts. Also included were choral responses, settings of the major canticles, and original texts and music for each festal day of the year. Many of these festal day settings were for women's voices, men's quartets, or soloists. A catalog of works appearing in Volume III (Oct. 1899—Sept. 1900) of the *Herald* tended more toward hymn and gospel-song texts. Musical settings for thirty-one of the seventy-eight selections were provided by editors Lorenz, Gabriel, and Emerson. Others who made regular contributions to the *Herald* were H. W. Porter, J. A. Parks, J. H. Tenney, Arthur W. Nelson, B. C. Unseld, and Lee G. Kratz. Volume III also contained five responses, four Gloria Patris, four funeral songs, one patriotic song, and one temperance song; the remainder were general or seasonal anthems.

The Organist, edited by Emma L. Ashford, contained thirty-two pages of organ music and two pages of helpful articles. Mrs. Ashford had already published three collections of organ music —*Ashford's Organ Voluntaries, Nos. 1 & 2,* and *The Organ Treasury.* These featured forty-three composers. Her collection of *Regal Anthems* contained fifty-six works by twenty-two composers. *Ashford's Anthems* (1899) contained twelve of her anthems and arrangements of classical composers. Other anthems included were by Lorenz and Parks.

An editorial by Lorenz in the December 1900 issue of the *Herald* calls attention to the musical versatility of Mrs. Ashford. Vanderbilt University had recently commissioned her to write a special *Ode* to commemorate the twenty-fifth anniversary of the founding of the University. At the performance, which was directed by her husband,

> It [the *Ode*] was sung by seventy voices . . . accompanied by an orchestra of twenty-six pieces, and proved a grand success. As Mr. Ashford's baton sank at the close of the rendering, the five or six thousand people present broke out in cheers and huzzas. Mrs. Ashford was led out before the audience by the chancellor of the University, and a spontaneous ovation was given her on that academic occasion, such as falls to the lot of few women. . . . The *Ode* was then repeated, when bishops, doctors of divinity, members of the faculty, and board of trustees crowded about her and overwhelmed her with congratulations and expressions of admiration for her work and of pride that she belonged to their university and city.

The September 1900 *Choir Leader* also paid tribute to another composer and assistant editor of the *Herald*, Dr. L. O. Emerson, on the occasion of his eightieth birthday:

> He has conducted over two hundred and fifty music conventions, which means an impetus to better music in hundreds of cities and towns. The music-books which bear his name as compiler, number more than seventy, of various grades, with divers purposes, the "Harp of Judah" reaching a sale of nearly 50,000 in the first six months. But though not able to *hear* delicate music, his power of composing has not waned with his increasing age, for during the last five years he has written perhaps the most artistically strong of all his works, three masses,—and still the fire burns.

A more detailed look at the contents of the Lorenz magazines reveals a continuing emphasis upon music for festal days. Children's Day brought music for and about children. Special music for Memorial Day services was always a feature in the May issues. The *Leader* for May 1900 contained two anthems: "Droop, Weeping Willows" by E. S. Lorenz and "Soldier, Rest" by Charles Gabriel. The same issue advertised twenty-one Memorial Day octavo anthems and male quartets and three special collections of Memorial Day pieces by Lorenz, Gabriel, and William J. Kirkpatrick. A special notice was given to "The Boys in Blue," described as "the most effective song issued in years."

The June issues of both magazines always featured a patriotic anthem for Independence Day. The June (1901) *Choir Herald* contained an original setting of the text of "America," with the suggestion that the congregation be asked to stand during the performance in order to avoid any outbursts of overzealous patriotism.

The September (1900) issue of *The Choir Herald* carried a very prophetic editorial by E. S. Lorenz on Sunday School music. It was directed toward church and denominational leadership:

> As the Sunday School is the recognized training school for all branches of church work, we hope to see the day when it is recognized as the musical training school as well. . . . Denominational America has sooner or later to learn the value of the material under its control, or else lose it to other fields which are more inviting.

The October and November magazines were characteristically filled with Thanksgiving and Christmas music. They also advertised special cantatas and octavo music. The October (1900) *Leader* advertised twenty-five titles of "Thanksgiving Octavo Music," carefully graded I, II, and III. The November issue advertised twenty-two varied Christmas services and children's cantatas entitled "Christian Praises" and "The King's Crown," designed especially for the Sunday School. A new Christmas cantata, *The Son of the Highest,* was also advertised as containing full choruses, quartets for men's and women's voices, duets, and solos for all parts. Typical anthems included in the same issue were "To Bethlehem Hasten" by Ashford;

"Arise, Shine, for Thy Light Is Come" by Kratz; "Seek Ye the Lord" by Parks; and "Fear Not" by Lorenz.

An interesting regular feature in the magazines was the advertisements for "Humorous" or "Entertaining" cantatas to be performed as a means of raising money for the choir or the church. The Christmas titles were *President Santa Claus, General Santa Claus, Mother Santa's Bicycle Trip,* and *Santa's Surprise Party.* The nonseasonal titles were *American Heroines, Those Good Old Times,* and *In Days of Yore.*

A summary of the solo, anthem, and cantata literature at the turn of the century reveals many common style elements which were adaptations of the European romantic heritage of literature and music theory. The diversity of the indigenous American influences would require some time for assimilation, before composers and congregations could freely develop their own musical styles and worship traditions.

The theoretical analysis of the standard literature of our musical heritage might be summarized as follows:

1. A mastery of the harmonic-progression and part-writing techniques put forth in the German textbooks on music theory. Harmonic modulations were standardized transitions to related keys, but with easily anticipated returns to the main key. At any new section, the tonality might shift directly up or down a third in the manner of Beethoven's "third relationship." These dramatic changes of key occurred most often at a new stanza or verse of text and might introduce a solo passage or the return to the full chorus or quartet. Also used frequently was the change of mode from the major to its parallel minor, or vice versa. The chords of the augmented sixth and diminished seventh were used frequently, and often in their enharmonic relationships, but always in carefully determined part writing.

2. Imitative polyphony was not a major element of form or text development, and phrases were carefully written in four-measure segments. Since the texts were in verse (Scripture) or stanza (hymn) form, the changes of key or mode were common techniques of text interpretation. Sequential repetition of a text and its theme was very common and often incorporated antiphonal effects between voice parts.

3. Intermittent solos, duets, trios, or quartets within choral works also served as a factor in text development. Most composers were alert to the reality of the constituents of most church choirs, where the use of solos was necessary for the individual members of the quartet/choir to have an opportunity to perform. Solo passages with choral background were especially desirable for dramatic effect in the romantic tradition.

4. The total style throughout was almost entirely homophonic. Although great attention was usually given to the relationship between the soprano melody and the thorough bass, often little care was given to the inner voice lines—the proper harmonic doubling of the voice parts apparently being more important than the alto and tenor lines.

5. The major publishers of octavo music relied heavily upon the better-known European composers of choral music, and quite often a new text in English adapted to a familiar classical or operatic melody. These favored composers were Mendelssohn, Beethoven, Haydn, Wagner, and Cherubini. The American composers listed most were Dudley Buck and Harry Rowe Shelley. After these, the Theodore Presser Company cataloged J. T. Walcott, W. H. Neidlinger, R. M. Stults, and George S. Schuler. For the most part, Presser's titles were listed as hymn-anthems for mixed voices. Oliver Ditson featured two complete catalogs of Dudley Buck. One contained thirty-nine works for morning service, evening service, and general anthems. Of these, twenty-seven were for various soloists and mixed quartets. G. Schirmer also had listings of anthems by Buck and Shelley for quartets, choruses, and women's or boy's voices. Other American composers featured by Schirmer were Harker, Berwald, and Clemens. Schirmer's catalog of general anthems also included Bartlett, Vogrich, Rees, Schnecker, Parker, and Warren. After Shelley, the John Church Company had their most listings by Spross.

A most interesting collection of anthems "For use in liberal Churches," and selected by a special committee of theologians and musicians, was published by Oliver Ditson (1905). Some of these anthems would soon become standard repertoire in almost all Protestant denominations—William S. Bennett's "God

Is a Spirit" from his *Woman of Samaria;* Henry Smart's "The Lord Is My Shepherd"; John E. West's "The Lord Is Exalted"; J. V. Roberts' "Seek Ye the Lord"; James H. Rogers' "Still, Still with Thee"; and three selections by Dudley Buck.

6. The accumulated heritage of two centuries of English hymnody was one of the richest and most accessible in all of the history of the Christian church. The clergy had been the most prolific creators and collectors of serious religious poetry. The Oxford Movement found its most significant and lasting expression in its hymns. The Lutherans brought their most treasured heritage, the Reformation Chorale. The followers of John Calvin retained a vast body of metrical psalmody, and their essential theological concepts were retained in the original works of Isaac Watts.

The fires of evangelism had contributed a tremendous body of sacred songs which typified the new religious freedoms and the personal religious experiences expressed by P. P. Bliss, Ira D. Sankey, and Fanny J. Crosby. The people of the rural South and the expanding frontiers of the West created their own body of religious song, classified as folk hymns and spiritual songs. In sharp contrast to the accepted rules of harmony, their meaning and worth were not highly esteemed at the turn of the century. However, its traditions and followers remain, and its musical elements are now assimilated into the more ecumenical hymnody of twentieth-century church music.

Notes

1. Brown, Alfred, "Wanted, A Chair of Tent-making," *The Atlantic Monthly,* Vol. LXXXIV, December 1899 (New York: Doubleday & McClure Co.), p.795.

2. Peattie, Elia W., "The Artistic Side of Chicago," *The Atlantic Monthly,* Vol. LXXXIV, December 1899 (New York: Doubleday & McClure Co.), p.834.

3. Stevenson, Robert, *Protestant Church Music in America* (New York: W. W. Norton & Company, Inc.), p. 112.

4. Benson, Louis F., *The English Hymn* (Richmond: John Knox Press, 1962), p. 436.

5. Ibid., p.442.

6. Ibid., p.474.

7. Foote, Henry Wilder, *Three Centuries of American Hymnody* (Cambridge: Harvard University Press, 1940), p.353.

8. Ibid., p.356.

9. Lehmann, Arnold Otto, *The Music of the Lutheran Church Synodical Conference, Chiefly the Areas of Missouri, Illinois, Wisconsin and Neighboring States* (Ph.D. Diss., Western Reserve University, 1967), p.166.

10. Ibid., p.172.

11. Ibid., p.337.

12. Rosewall, Richard B., *Singing Schools of Pennsylvania, 1800-1900* (Ph.D. Diss., University of Minnesota, 1969), p.94.

13. Ibid., p.58.

14. Ibid., p.60.

15. Ibid., p.121.

16. Ibid., p.146.

17. Downey, James Cecil, *The Music of Revivalism* (Ph.D. Diss., Tulane University, 1968), p.88.

18. Ibid., p.89.

19. Ibid., p.92.

20. Washington, Booker T., "The Case of the Negro," *The Atlantic Monthly,* Vol. LXXXIV, November, 1899 (New York: Doubleday & McClure Co.), p.577.

21. Marsh, J. B. T., *The Story of the Jubilee Singers; with Their Songs,* Revised Edition (New York: Negro Universities Press, 1969), p.75.

22. Jackson, George Pullen, *White Spirituals in the Southern Uplands* (Chapel Hill: University of North Carolina Press, 1933), p.255.

23. Moody, Michael Finlinson, *Hymnody in the Church of Jesus Christ of Latter-Day Saints* (Ph.D. Diss., University of Southern California, 1972), p.7.

24. Ibid., p.8.

25. Ibid., p.10.

26. Ibid., p.11.

27. Calman, Charles Jeffrey and Kaufmann, William I., *The Mormon Tabernacle Choir* (New York: Harper and Row, 1979), p.39.

28. *Dwight's Journal of Music,* Vol. XLI, No. 104, April 23, 1881 (Boston: Houghton, Mifflin & Co.), p.69.

29. Ibid., p.62.

30. Glass, James W., *The Sacred Art Song in the United States,* 1869-1975 (D.M.A. Diss., Southwestern Baptist Theological Seminary), 1976.

31. Gallo, William K., *The Life and Church Music of Dudley Buck* (1839-1909) (Ph.D. Diss., The Catholic University of America, 1968), p.17.

32. Ibid., p.105.

33. Ibid., p.98.

34. Ibid., p.216.

35. Stewart, Roger D., *The Contributions of Edmund S. Lorenz to American Church Music* (M.C.M. Thesis, Southwestern Baptist Theological Seminary, 1967), p.6.

36. Lorenz, E. S., "Editorial Notes," *The Choir Herald,* October 1915, p.2.

37. Ibid., p.11.

Part II:

External Twentieth-Century Influences

6

Social and Economic Influences

The story of church music is normally a study of institutionalized churches—their hymns, anthems, oratorios, composers, and worship practices. But when one looks at any aspect of church music in the twentieth century, the most prominent element throughout has been change. The strongest forces of change, for the most part, have been beyond the control of any established denomination, yet have affected almost every musical standard and practice of Christian worship.

External forces have always been active catalysts of change since the beginnings of Christianity. At various periods they might have been political, military, theological, or scientific. Dogmas, creeds, rituals, and liturgies have been subject to modification by regional and native cultures and have found their most immediate expression in music. These external forces have been most active in this century and have exerted influences equal in strength to all previous centuries combined. None of these has been instigated for the purpose of religious reform. Some have been espoused by the churches. Others have created stressful conditions for the churches and brought about many changes in the direction and character of our Christian ministries.

One of the major influences upon the total life of the church in this century has been wars—and in dimensions undreamed of before. During World War I, the belief in America's "Manifest Destiny" and President Wilson's insistence that "the world must be made safe for democracy" warranted enthusiastic support from the churches. The most active Christian participation with "the boys" on location came from the YMCA huts and the

Salvation Army. Pacifist groups were held in outright contempt by most Protestant congregations amid the revivalism of the Sunday-Rodeheaver campaigns. Patriotism invaded every congregation without the aid of radio, and all America was playing and singing "Over There."

World War II necessitated a total mobilization of forces, including women's volunteer forces. Conscientious objectors were somewhat vocal, but many were drafted by local boards for non-combat duty, with some serving as medical corpsmen. Some of these objectors were sincere enough to jeopardize their professional careers, but found fulfilling the needs of others to be a more rewarding compensation.

> In fact, my whole wartime experience has become one of my most valued treasures, . . . it taught me more about life, mankind in general, men in particular, human relationships, far-away-places, and above all, myself, than anything else I've ever read or done.[1]

The most immediate effect of the war upon the churches was a constant shifting of the population into the military training areas and to the war plants which were producing the arms and war materials.

The churches gave an unusually empathetic support to the military visitor. Soldiers and sailors were special guests in the worship services—and often guests for "Sunday dinner." The war itself was never marked by the idealistic patriotism of World War I, but by a "must-do" spirit that refused to be motivated by the trite enthusiasm of the commercial pep songs of Tin Pan Alley. If the spirit could be caught in one song, it would have to be Kate Smith's performance of Irving Berlin's "God Bless America." A most striking personal, musical experience for me occurred among the military personnel in Korea, during the postwar occupation. The soldiers all over Korea were singing "Ari Dong," a Korean folk song—in Korean. This simple pentatonic tune became a theme for the forces, rather than any of the songs heard at the Red Cross stations or on the Army's radio station.

The war period was difficult for the churches. Stability in any of its ministries was impossible. The music was relegated to small choirs with few men, and music printing came to a halt. The postwar harvest for the churches, however, was enormous. The churches realized unprecedented growth, and the formation of many new families became strongly church oriented. By 1950, Protestants had reached nearly fifty million members,[2] and the ex-GIs constituted the largest body of new ministers and missionaries that the churches had ever known.

The war in Korea was a quick leftover from World War II and a token reaction of the United Nations to the invasion of South Korea. America was tired of war, and the churches became almost indifferent to the prolonged "police action." Unfortunately, Korea became a pattern for limited warfare and military action which America had to bear again in Vietnam. Here the television cameras brought the sights of war into America's living rooms daily. The churches, both institutional and independent, began to assume a strong political stance and, in many cases, an antiwar policy. This position isolated the military personnel from civilian and church relationships, and the sense of "Manifest Destiny" for Christianity and democracy was forgotten. Another major social division occurred when young men who were able to go to college were granted deferments while the less fortunate were drafted for combat duty. The institutional churches were maintaining their antinuclear and antiwar policies and minimizing their ministries to "the boys."

A second influential force in American church life was the Great Depression. It was a dominant and common element in the life of every family and church in America. The causes and dimensions of this economic crisis are still the subject of intense study and analysis, but its effects upon the family and the churches were drastic. The immediate effect was a migratory society—moving a family by any means possible in search of subsistence; combining families in a paternal or maternal home for survival; and trainloads of men in empty freight cars, moving anywhere to find work, hoping to send for the family later— many never to be heard from again.

The family unit became smaller, with the birth rate going from 24 in 1920 to 16.6 per thousand population in 1933. During World War II the rate plummeted to 10.6 in 1944, then shot up to 20.8 in 1947.[3] Divorce rates declined during the depression years, perhaps because common-law unions were never recorded and many marriages were dissolved without due legal process. Divorce has been climbing at disturbing rates since World War II, and the single-parent family has become a major element of outreach ministry in contemporary Protestantism.

The reality of disease and death were ever present during the first half of the century and probably found more expression in the gospel songs and spirituals than in any other form of religious music. The Lorenz music magazines regularly published special funeral music. Since no specific antibiotics were available until the early 1940s, any type of infection could be deadly. During World War I, more United States troops died of disease —55,000—than were killed in battle—48,000.[4] Influenza took a heavy toll, but the scourge of the nation—and the world—was tuberculosis, which increased dramatically after the war. This was another significant factor in the migration of many families to the higher and drier climates of the West as a last hope for a recovery from the disease. Heart disease and cancer were present; but with an already low life expectancy, they did not receive the medical or public concern which dominates medical research now. This might be seen more clearly in the fact that the city of El Paso, Texas, had five large tuberculosis sanitariums and only one small general hospital for a city of about one hundred thousand.

Probably the most direct and far-reaching influence upon church music in the twentieth century has been the fringe effect of our scientific developments in the fields of communications—radio, printing, electric organs, sound systems, television, and recordings of religious music in popular musical idioms. Only within the context of these multiple external influences can we hope to understand twentieth-century developments in the hymnody, choral, and instrumental music of our public worship.

7

Folk Developments

One of the church-related influences, already mentioned, was the Negro spiritual. A primary factor in its early influence was the concert tours of the Fisk Jubilee Singers. One of their early triumphs was an appearance on Patrick Gilmore's second World Peace Jubilee (1872), singing "The Battle Hymn of the Republic" to the tune "John Brown's Body." As they sang the refrain "Glory, Glory, Hallelujah,"

> the huge audience (40,000) was on its feet. Ladies were waving their handkerchiefs, and hats were flung into the air by men. On the final chorus, the singers sang to the accompaniment of the orchestra and thunderous roars of artillery. The audience became ecstatic.[5]

Their tour concerts usually included only one or two of their "slave songs," but their audiences were so generous that these "Jubilee Songs" soon constituted the major portion of their programs.[6]

The inherent beauty and potential value of these spirituals— so well preserved in the segregated communities, churches, and Negro colleges of the South—remained dormant until distinguished black musicians and educators began to collect, arrange, publish, and thrust them into the mainstreams of American church music. Through the teaching and writings of John W. Work II, the Fisk University students began learning about their musical heritage, and America became aware of this great treasure of folk music. He and his brother, Frederic Jerome, "collected, harmonized, and published several collections of slave songs and spirituals. The earliest of these collections, *New Jubilee Songs as Sung by the Fisk Jubilee Singers,* was published in 1901."[7] John W. Work II trained and performed with both professional and student groups of Jubilee Singers for eighteen years. In 1909, with a professional Jubilee Quartet, they recorded twenty records of spirituals for the Victor Talking Machine Company.

John Wesley Work III (1901-1967) inherited a rare musicality from his parents and assumed their devotion to Fisk University and the religious music of black Americans. A precocious child, he took his preparatory and college work at Fisk. Although he did not major in music, he studied piano and began composing in his teens. He also participated in the choral ensembles directed by his father and gave a senior voice recital in 1923. The literature was impressive—Handel oratorios, German lieder, Italian opera, English art songs, and two spirituals which he had arranged. His accompanist was C. Warner Lawson, who later earned degrees from Yale and Harvard, served on the faculty at Fisk, and became Dean of Fine Arts at Howard University. Lawson was also a highly esteemed leader in the academic affairs of the National Association of Schools of Music.

After his graduation, John W. Work III went to New York to prepare for a singing career and entered the Institute of Musical Art (now the Juilliard School). He returned to Fisk in 1927 to complete the contract of his mother, who had suffered a stroke and died on February 12, 1927. This was the beginning of his thirty-nine years as a teacher at his alma mater. He was appointed director of Jubilee Music and directed the Mozart Choral Society. He also continued arranging and programming spirituals.

These spirituals were not received without some adverse comments from some critics who considered this music unfit for the concert stage. Work's strongest support came from George Pullen Jackson, professor at Vanderbilt University, who wrote in the *Nashville Banner* for April 5, 1930, about the "Negroid compositions" arranged by Work III:

> The charming thing about those arrangements is that they never dim the original musical line. On the contrary, they seem to

bring that idea out into greater clarity, to set off its beauty as the setting does the beauty of the diamond.[8]

In order to further his research and study of the spirituals, work songs, blues, and secular music of the Negro, Work III was granted a Rosenwald fellowship to study at Yale in 1931-32. He stayed two years at Yale, and the focus of his work was on composition. His purpose was to extend the serious development of Negro music into the larger forms. He also worked toward the acceptance of the spiritual in public worship. In the latter effort, he promoted the works of other Negro composers —Nathaniel Dett, Edward Margetson, Hall Johnson, Henry T. Burleigh (soloist at St. George's Episcopal Church in New York), William L. Dawson, and Jester Hairston. The Westminster Choir would soon add credence to Work's efforts by featuring spirituals in all of their concerts.

In his evaluation of another folk movement in the South—the seven-shape-note singing school—Work III revealed his own understanding of the deep spiritual and esthetic values inherent in the Negro spiritual:

> Shape-note singing in southeast Alabama has stifled all other folk expressions. No spirituals or other social folk songs are sung. . . . Then, too, the musical tastes of the people have developed an appreciation for the intellectual aspects of musicianship rather than an appreciation—which is necessary for the pleasure in singing spirituals—for the sensuousness of a single strand of melody.[9]

The validity of this judgment was already being confirmed in the unaccompanied solo concert performances of "Were You There," "He's Got the Whole World in His Hands," and other spirituals by the great contralto Marian Anderson.

The desire of Work III to "promote the serious development of Negro music into larger musical forms" was not neglected. In 1946 he entered his cantata *The Singers* in a composer's competition sponsored by the Fellowship of American Composers, of which Roy Harris was president. *The Singers* won first prize against many of the nation's distinguished composers. In his late and larger works, his style became more assertive, chromatic, and dissonant.

After *The Singers*, he wrote *Golgotha Is a Mountain* (1949), *Danse Africaine* (1951), *I've Known Rivers* (1955), and the choral cycle for Broadman Press, *Isaac Watts Contemplates the Cross* (1962). The diversity of his texts included well-known Scripture and hymn texts such as "How Beautiful Upon the Mountains," "For All the Saints," "Now for a Tune of Lofty Praise," "Lord of All Being," and "Jesus, Thou Hast Called Us to Thee." He utilized frequent changes of texture from unison (or solo) to as many as five or seven voice parts, reminiscent of the "call and response" structure. In all of his music, and especially the spirituals, he maintained a fidelity to the spirit of the text, while others were sacrificing the spiritual to the commercial value of its musical caricature.

John W. Work III lived to hear the Negro spiritual as a well-established component of almost every high school and college choir concert. The inherent spiritual quality of these songs has earned for them a prominent place in Protestant worship, both as solos and congregational song.

Garcia evaluated the work of John Work III as the prophetic fulfillment of his father's hope expressed in his *Folk Song of the American Negro* (1915) for "some Negro composer, possessed of the same spirit that vitalizes Negro folk song, to give to the world productions throbbing with our own life forces and worthy to be bound in gold."[10]

The Twentieth-Century Gospel Song

The concerns of Work III for the continuing stylistic purity of the Negro spiritual were valid. The seven-shape-note singing schools were not the only threat in the South, Southwest, and Midwest. Other social and economic forces were already interacting to bring about a convergence of the gospel song, the spiritual, and jazz into a commercialized "Gospel," disseminated through radio and recordings. This new genre was created by both blacks and whites. One of the more prominent early writers to combine elements of the spiritual with the traditional gospel song was Charles A. Tindley, a Negro Methodist minister in Philadelphia. His "We Will Understand It Better By and By," "Nothing Between," and "Stand by Me" were popularized as solos, but his "I'll Overcome Some Day" became the basis for the theme song of the civil-rights movement—"We Shall Overcome."[11]

Writers and publishers, especially in the South, were combining elements of syncopation from the spiritual with the simple tunes and texts of country and western music to create this new genre of the "Gospel Song." The seven-shape-note singing schools provided the thrust and musicianship necessary to support an enormous output of shaped-note songbooks filled with the challenge of "new songs."

The major publishers of these books during the first half of the century were A. J. Showalter of Dalton, Georgia; James D. Vaughan of Lawrenceburg, Tennessee; Eugene M. Bartlett's Hartford Music Company of Hartford, Arkansas; and the Stamps-Baxter Music Company of Dallas, Texas (Virgil O. Stamps was associated earlier with Vaughan, and J. R. Baxter was with Showalter).

The market for their books was mostly rural and was promoted by the two- and four-week singing schools held in the small rural churches. For larger "conventions" with "dinner on the ground," all denominations would cooperate in a "fifth Sunday singing" in a larger church, school auditorium, or county courthouse. Since many small rural churches only had "preaching" on one or two Sundays each month, this left the fifth Sundays free for all to participate in these religious, musical, and social events.

The consideration of this music in a serious study of church music can be justified on both musical and religious grounds. It could reasonably be termed folk music, in spite of their extensive publications. The composers' training was limited to the group instruction in the annual singing school and a do-it-yourself theory book devoted entirely to understanding and writing their own self-styled gospel songs. Their formidable talents were limited only by an absence of any formal music instruction. The music is also a valid grass-roots expression, written according to the rigid "rudiments" of their own textbooks. These separate textbooks were a departure from the short chapter on "rudiments" printed as a preface to the oblong tune books of the nineteenth century. One of the early theory books was commissioned by James D. Vaughan in 1912 and written by B. C. Unseld—earlier associated with Lowell Mason and a contributing composer and author of the monthly "Question Box" on theory in the Lorenz music magazines. Unseld became the music editor for Vaughan from 1913 until his death in 1923. These theory texts hastened the demise of the older alto-TENOR-bass three-part tune books, since all of these publishers had gone to the standard four-part SOPRANO-alto-tenor-bass format of the English hymn. The part writing now conformed to the strict German rules of voicing and chord progression. The musicianship demonstrated in these singing school classes was amazing. With no accompaniment, they could read at sight almost any new song printed in shaped notes. Many pianists could also read the shaped notes and play the songs in any key which they knew on the keyboard.

Another musical justification for their consideration is the survival of so many of these songbooks in many rural and small-town congregations. Granted that many of these congregations now consist largely of older people who have had no other music instruction, yet the shaped notes still provide the musicianship necessary for effective congregational singing in four parts. Another factor is that the standard hymns normally used in these morning worship services often vary little from those used by their urban brethren. Donald Hustad has judged that the "typical" morning worship hymns "listed roughly in the order of broad preference" were:

1. "All Hail the Power of Jesus' Name"
2. "Come, Thou Almighty King"
3. "Holy, Holy, Holy"
4. "O for a Thousand Tongues to Sing"
5. "Love Divine, All Loves Excelling"
6. "O Worship the King"
7. "Crown Him with Many Crowns"

8. "Faith of Our Fathers"
9. "O God, Our Help in Ages Past"
10. "Come, Thou Fount of Every Blessing"[12]

Hustad also observed that "many congregations repeat the same ten, fifteen, or twenty hymns over and over, Sunday after Sunday." Practically all of these hymns are included in these shaped-note songbooks as standard hymns—and printed in shaped notes.

A major point of criticism of these songbooks and the singing tradition is the emphasis placed upon the music and musicianship rather than the words. Another point is the quantity of the publications, with their constant increase in the number of "new songs." The Vaughan Company published 105 songbooks. Of these (to quote the preface of one), 102 were considered "pure sweet gospel songs . . . prepared with great care and much prayer, and is, in our humble judgment, a book of highest excellence."[13] The religious intentions, in this instance, were honest enough. Vaughan's publications became so popular that by 1925 they had printed a total of three million songbooks. The Stamps-Baxter Company published 157 songbooks (1926-1971) and eleven theory books. A feature story in *Time* magazine dated November 7, 1949, emphasizes the durability of the shaped-note literature and singing traditions. The occasion was a meeting in

> Nacogdoches, Texas (Pop. 11,700) [of] more than 4,000 delegates to the interdenominational Tri-State (Texas, Louisiana, Arkansas) Singing Convention. . . . In spite of heavy rains, sticky red clay roads and a football game across the way, they crowded into the white gymnasium at Stephen [F.] Austin State Teachers College.[14]

The meeting consisted of two straight days of singing by quartets, some soloists, group singing of well-known favorites, and sight-reading of many new songs by the entire delegation. The story also focused on the Stamps-Baxter Company and its cumulative sales of "as many as 4,000,000 copies" of their songbooks and the publication of some six hundred new gospel songs each year.

Both Vaughan and Stamps-Baxter published monthly news-magazines which brought news of gospel music and concerts by their professional quartets and provided a forum and advertising medium for their teachers. The weight of such widespread use of these "pure sweet gospel songs" demands some recognition and documentation in any study of twentieth-century Protestant church music.

The characteristic professional performing group representing each of these publishers was the male quartet. Until the advent of television, almost every major radio station had a daily spot which featured a gospel quartet as one of their leading daytime programs. A stylistic stereotype was heard most often in the refrain. The melody was given to the bass as a solo, while the other parts echoed the text in an "afterbeat" syncopation as its accompaniment—a stylized fusion of elements of the spiritual, jazz, and the camp meeting songs, now published in a textbook style. E. M. Bartlett's Hartford Music Company's songs were somewhat less stereotyped. One of his most popular writers was Albert E. Brumley, who was also a music teacher and singer. His "I'll Fly Away" (1931) was one of his best and most recorded. It was featured by D. P. Carter and his Chuck Wagon Gang, a mixed quartet from Fort Worth, Texas. In 1986, I viewed the morning worship service of a major denomination appearing on national television which featured "I'll Fly Away" as the morning anthem, performed by a robed choir of about seventy-five voices. Bartlett's own "Victory in Jesus" (text and music, 1939) has also survived as a current favorite among youth and in revival campaigns and is in many current hymnals.

Southern blacks were also represented in this new gospel by Thomas A. Dorsey. Born in Georgia (1899), he was well grounded in jazz and the blues. He moved to Chicago in 1916, where he became a professional musician, and began writing gospel songs in 1929. He became the successor, if not the protegé, of Charles Tindley. His best-known song is probably "Precious Lord, Take My Hand" (1932), written after the death of his wife and infant son.[15] It has been recorded by Mahalia Jackson, Red Foley, Ernie Ford, and Elvis Presley. His "Peace in the Valley" is almost equally famous.

The continuing popularity and market for the twentieth-century gospel song has ceased to be dependent upon the professional quartets and the singing schools. Radio, television, and the recording industries have become the primary outlets for an increasing demand for many new and varied stylistic expressions of personal religious experience. The combination of a big-name performing artist, a simple country-and-western tune, the beat of soft rock, or the wail of "soul"—all have combined to create a market which has justified its own "chart" of top forty recordings in *Billboard* Magazine. The songs and recordings of Bill and Gloria Gaither have dominated the field for many years, with Andrae and Sandra Crouch close behind.

The 1985 chart of top forty gospel albums had six of the top ten from the Light label and seven of the top forty from the Word label. Of the top forty, nine were on the chart for more than a year, and two were on the chart for more than two years—"Rough Side of the Mountain" (Rev. F. C. Barnes and Rev. Janice Brown) for 121 weeks, and "We Sing Praises" (Sandra Crouch) for 105 weeks. The Walter Hawkins album "Love Alive III" was number 1 for a total of thirteen weeks. The persistence of many old "standards" is noted in two titles—"His Eye Is on the Sparrow" and "Amazing Grace."[16]

A central figure in the writing and marketing of the current style of "Christian Music" since 1970 has been Chris Christian. At this writing, he has been signed to produce "40 albums over the next four years" with Word Records of Waco, Texas.[17] Billed with tongue in cheek as a "Christian" musical influence, his technique is to render the music and "two-way lyrics" similar to their popular counterparts.[18]

The influence of these songs upon contemporary church music is indirect. Through recordings and concert appearances of the artists, the songs enter the popular youth organizations and eventually the various church services as "special music."

8

Twentieth-Century Revivalism

Gipsy Smith

Another strong external influence upon church music was already present at the turn of the century, but no one could have anticipated the impact that revivalism would have upon the music practices in the twentieth century. The Moody-Sankey revivals were a phenomenon that denominational leaders expected to end after Moody's death in 1899. But the response of the English to the gospel songs of Sankey was overlooked. His *Sacred Songs and Solos* "in the first fifty years following its appearance, is reported to have sold more than eighty million copies."[19] It was probably even less expected that at the close of the century, the English would be sending a unique singing evangelist to America—Rodney "Gipsy" Smith (1860-1947).

A true Gypsy, Rodney was the child of illiterate parents, had no formal education, and "grew up as wild as the birds, as frolicsome as the lambs, and as difficult to catch as the rabbits. All the grasses and flowers and trees of the field and all living things were my friends and companions."[20]

Probably the most influential event in his life was the death of his mother when he was five. His recollections of her include the outbreak of smallpox in the Gypsy camp, detailed descriptions of the scenes, and his mother singing a passage from a hymn she had heard as a child, after she followed some other children into a village church:

> I have a father in the promised land.
> My God calls me, I must go
> To meet Him in the promised land.

As a lad of fifteen, he made a public profession of his faith and the commitment of his life to Christ in a little Primitive Methodist Chapel. He recalled that the congregation sang:

> I can but perish if I go,
> I am resolved to try,
> For if I stay away I know
> I must forever die.

> I do believe, I will believe,
> That Jesus died for me,
> That on the cross He shed His blood
> From sin to set me free.[21]

A strong desire to become a preacher prompted him to stand by the roadside on Sundays, as people walked to church, and to sing, pray, and give a testimonial sermon. In the spring of 1877 Smith attended an all-day gathering at one of Reverend William Booth's mission headquarters. After several persons had addressed the group, Booth rose and said, "The next speaker will be the gipsy boy" (he had heard that the boy wanted to preach).[22] When the boy rose to speak, he was shaking and speechless. Booth then said, "Will you sing us a solo?" Gipsy Smith then began his life as an evangelist by singing:

> Jesus died upon the tree,
> That from sin we might be free,
> And forever happy be,
> Happy in His love.
> He has paid the debt we owe;
> If with trusting hearts we go,
> He will wash us white as snow
> In His blood.[23]

His singing would ever after be a focal point in his ministry and was most appealing to his congregations.

Soon after the meeting, Reverend Booth asked him to join his Christian Missions—later to become the Salvation Army. This served to intensify his studies and reading. With his dictionary, Bible, Bible dictionary, and many classics of English literature, the "Gipsy Boy" developed an unusual command of the language and a rare and appealing style of delivery—always punctuated with simple parables drawn from his childhood. He soon became an officer in General Booth's Salvation Army but was dismissed in 1882 for accepting a watch from friends at Hanley, after a particularly successful mission there.

"Gipsy" Smith became even more successful when he proceeded on his own. Armed with a portfolio of letters from distinguished English ministers, he set sail on his first trip to America in 1889. Usually sponsored by Methodist congregations, he held missions (revivals) in New York, Washington, Philadelphia, Boston, Cincinnati, and Denver during his five trips to America before 1900. While in Philadelphia, Smith met with his first Negro congregation—most likely the Methodist church pastored by Charles A. Tindley. He had heard the Fisk Jubilee Singers in England, but

> this congregation excelled even that famous band in the sweetness and grandeur of their performance. I shall never forget how they sang the hymn "Swing Low, Sweet Chariot, coming for to carry me home." It seemed to me at the moment as if the roof of the church must open and the chariot descend into our midst, the singing was so grand and yet so artless—as natural as a dewdrop.[24]

It was during his third trip to America that he and Mrs. Smith went to Denver, Colorado, at the invitation of an English couple who had known him in England. The railway journey of three nights and two days impressed him with the enormous possibilities of the country. He was apparently overwhelmed by the fact that

> forty years ago Denver was inhabited by red indians, and overrun by buffaloes and other wild animals. It has now a population of about two hundred thousand, with magnificent residences, stores, and churches, and is called the Queen City of the West.[25]

He also made a special note of the fact that the city's altitude affected his voice so that he was unable to sing during the services. Also impressive was the scene of his "mission"—a church seating two thousand, "which cost £50,000 to build, and which possessed an organ worth £6,000."[26]

Since revivalism was very much alive in 1900, Smith's missions to America were almost yearly, and the format was rather consistent. Organization of the campaigns was the responsibility of the sponsoring churches or the ministerial alliance. He had no entourage of professional musicians or assistants. He utilized local musicians to organize and direct the chorus and used existing churches or civic auditoriums rather than specially-built tabernacles. However, he soon hired pianists in order to guarantee satisfactory accompaniments for his own solos. The most important of these were William H. Jude, Harold Murray, and E. Edwin Young. Of these, Ensign Edwin Young was "an extremely gifted pianist who has understood Gipsy's requirements better than any other."[27] Smith used Young for over ten years in America, Great Britain, Australia, and New Zealand as accompanist, composer, and compiler of an official hymnbook. Young often gave classical recitals and did hymn improvisations during the services, and Mrs. Young served as Gipsy's secretary. When "Eddie" was no longer available, Murray "had the joy of accompanying hundreds of Gipsy's solos."[28]

One of the first hymnals prepared for the American campaigns was *Hallowed Hymns New and Old* (1907). I. Allan Sankey edited the collection, and the publisher was Biglow & Main Company of New York and Chicago—the same publisher used by his father, Ira D. Sankey. The book had a special supplement by Gipsy which contained several standard English hymn tunes to be used as alternates with many of the familiar gospel-song texts. An interesting case was his use of the tune HYFRYDOL as an alternate for Francis H. Rowley's "I Will Sing the Wondrous Story." The use of this tune with Rowley's text was a favorite solo of Gipsy's and is included in the 1975 *Baptist Hymnal.* In the preface to *Hallowed Hymns,* Sankey explained that the purpose of the hymnal was "the teaching of scriptural truths through the medium of sacred song." The book was divided into four sections: New Songs (105); the best of the famous *Gospel Hymns* (82); Standard Hymns of the Church (75); and responsive readings.

At this point, the "missions" were interrupted by World War I, and Gipsy Smith went to France to minister to "the boys" for three and one-half years in hospitals and YMCA huts. His accounts of the services always spoke of their love for singing, especially the familiar hymns. Their favorites were the

> great standard hymns of the church—"Jesus, Lover of My Soul," "Rock of Ages," "Lead Kindly Light," "My Jesus, I Love Thee," "There Is a Fountain Filled with Blood," "When I Survey the Wondrous Cross," "The King of Love My Shepherd Is," "There Is a Green Hill Far Away," "My Faith Looks up to Thee," and "Abide with Me."[29]

After the war, Gipsy Smith resumed his American travels and conducted one of his longest campaigns in Nashville, Tennessee, from October 1921 to March 1922. A special point of interest was his getting permission for blacks to attend the services and to sit in a reserved section. He also was able to have a special service for blacks, and "nearly 6,000 were present. Two hundred students in the Jubilee Chorus from Fisk University sang Negro folk songs."[30] He mentioned specifically "It's Me, O Lord" and "Study War No More."

One of the early "official" campaign songbooks was *Hosanna in the Highest* (n.d.). Designed as an all-purpose hymnal for Sunday School, church, home, and evangelistic services, it was compiled by William McEwan, with Ensign Edwin Young as music editor. The publisher was Hosanna Publishing Company of Astoria, Long Island, New York. Since the Foreword expresses the appreciation of Smith, McEwan, and Young for the "kindness of the several owners of copyrights who have allowed us to use their songs," it was probably a private-venture publication. Gipsy endorsed it as "a collection of the most beautiful songs of the Gospel in print today. . . . I have always wanted the solos that I have been identified with brought together in one book, and now I am seeing my desire gratified." A large notice was printed on the back page of the index that "The Voices of Gipsy Smith and William McEwan can be heard on Columbia Records Sold Everywhere."

A later book, "Used Exclusively in the Gipsy Smith Campaigns," was *Wonderful Jesus and Other Songs.* Published in 1927 by the Biglow-Main-Excell Company of Chicago, E.

Edwin Young (Bachelor of Music) was music editor, pianist, composer, and arranger of many of the distinctly new songs in the collection. "Wonderful Jesus" (Annie B. Russell and Ernest O. Sellers) was thereafter the official campaign song and a frequent solo by Gipsy in all of his campaigns.

With Young to compose the music, Smith now wrote many of his own solos, a few of which became a part of the standard repertoire of almost every gospel soloists for three decades— "Not Dreaming" and "Jesus Revealed in Me." Since the short congregational "Chorus" had been popularized by Harry Dixon Loes' "Into My Heart," the Smith campaigns adopted an anonymous theme chorus, "Let the Beauty of Jesus Be Seen in Me." *Wonderful Jesus* contained a large section of Special Selections (twenty-two) for chorus choir. Many of these were standard repertoire of the revival choirs, but some were originals (words and music) by Young and his wife Peggy. Another section contained Patriotic Selections (seven) for both the English and the Americans, plus a section of Grand Old Favorites (sixty-eight) of the church. The American authors and composers were markedly contemporary: Charles H. Gabriel, Harry Dixon Loes, E. O. Excell, James Rowe, Ernest O. Sellers, E. Edwin Young, Gipsy Smith, Fanny J. Crosby, and George Schuler.

Young later retired to do graduate study at the Eastman School of Music and to pursue a teaching career at Hardin-Simmons University in 1934, but he continued in church music, concert performances, and piano teaching until shortly before his death in 1980. He had firmly established himself as a composer of church music and concert music for the piano and the symphony. He joined Gipsy again for a campaign in Abilene, Texas, in October 1936, where a local minister wrote of Gipsy: "You would say he is in his prime," and "little past middle years." His itinerary for that winter included open-air meetings at the Texas Centennial Fair Grounds in Dallas; Abilene, Texas; Elizabeth, New Jersey; Honolulu, Hawaii and back to El Paso, Texas, where I was privileged to serve as his pianist. This was his thirty-third trip to America at age seventy-six.

Gipsy Smith continued his American campaigns with unusual vigor. His singing continued to have great popular appeal. His

personal warmth, sense of humor, and poetic spirit were as alive
as the day he sang his first solo for General William Booth. A
frequent guest at Number Ten Downing Street, he still retained
the fervor of his early missions for the Salvation Army. His
gentleness of spirit also brought a freshness and credibility to
revivalism in America that was not known again until the middle and later years of the Billy Graham crusades.

Billy Sunday and Homer A. Rodeheaver

In the meantime, the expected decline in American-style
mass evangelism had not yet occurred. "No fewer than six hundred fifty [evangelists] were roaming the land by 1911."[31]
Moody's mantle had fallen briefly upon J. Wilbur Chapman and
Reuben A. Torrey, both of whom had received extensive education. Chapman was a graduate of Lake Forest College and Lane
Seminary and a veteran of regular pastorates when he began to
hold revivals. Torrey studied at Yale Divinity School and in
Germany. Both made evangelistic speaking trips around the
world, and both were basically conservative. Torrey became
the first "Superintendent" of the Moody Bible Institute (1886)
in Chicago.

For the purposes of this study, their importance lies in the
fact that both used the affable Charles M. Alexander as their
music director. In sharp contrast to Ira D. Sankey, the famed
soloist, "Charlie" Alexander became the model for all evangelistic song leaders thereafter. Born in Tennessee and trained at
Moody Bible Institute, Charlie "warmed up" his audiences and
developed the massed choir with his winning ways and simple,
singable tunes. The congregational singing was enthusiastic—
"every man and woman, every silk hat and busted shoe, has got
to sing tonight."[32]

An early compilation by Alexander was entitled *Alexander's
Hymns,* "as used in the Chapman-Alexander Missions" and published by Marshall, Morgan & Scott, Ltd., London and Edin-
burgh. Daniel B. Towner, director of the music department of
Moody Bible Institute, assisted Alexander with another compilation of *Revival Hymns,* "A Collection of New and Standard

Hymns for Gospel & Social Meetings, Sunday Schools and Young Peoples Societies," and published by the Bible Institute Colportage Association, Chicago, 1905. The appearance of the special choruses "All Hail, Immanuel!" and "Hallelujah for the Cross" for the massed choirs is particularly noteworthy, since the massed choirs, as well as solos and duets, were to become the standard musical fare of twentieth-century American revivalism.

Given a projected decline in American revivalism, no one could have anticipated the popular appeal and religious impact of William A. Sunday (1862-1935) and Homer A. Rodeheaver (1880-1955). "Billy" Sunday was born in Iowa, the son of a Union soldier. "He was sent to an orphanage, worked on his grandfather's farm, and then ran off to Nevada, Iowa, where he worked his way through high school."[33] He played amateur baseball in Marshalltown, Iowa, where he was scouted and signed by the Chicago "White Stockings" as an outfielder and lead-off batter.

One day in 1886, while Homer was drinking with his teammates, a street band from the Pacific Garden Rescue Mission lured him inside, where he heard the familiar hymns of his childhood. He was converted. He continued to play baseball (but never on Sundays), but gave up drinking, smoking, cards, and the theater. On road trips he gave talks at the local YMCA, billed as a baseball star. In 1891 he gave up baseball and went into full-time "Christian work" at the Chicago YMCA.[34] Two years later he began work as an assistant in the Chapman-Alexander evangelistic team, taking care of the advance arrangements and organization of the campaigns. He also busied himself studying the sermons of D. L. Moody and the colorful Southern evangelist, Sam Jones.

After Chapman returned to the pastorate in 1895, Sunday was on his own. However, after his first revival in Garner, Iowa, other invitations followed. He worked the small cities of Iowa until 1900, when he was able to hire a singer, Fred Fischer. By 1904 he added an advance man and required a tabernacle with a 300-voice choir in the style of his former colleague, Charles Alexander. His most fortuitous move came in 1909 when he began a twenty-year ministry with the inimitable Homer A. Rodeheaver. Their gradual move was to the major cities of the West, Midwest, and the Eastern seaboard, including Detroit, Dallas, Washington, Philadelphia, Baltimore, Boston, and New York.

As the advance man for the Chapman-Alexander team, Sunday had learned the techniques of planning and organization. Weeks before a campaign was to begin, his workers arranged luncheons, dinners, and prayer meetings and marshaled the forces of the cooperating ministers of the city. Meetings were held in factories, offices, and places of business for weeks prior to the regular tabernacle services.

His sermons were in a familiar style of discourse, presented in shirt sleeves and with continuous movement for accentuation or pantomime. The delivery came in torrents of words and in a coordinated rhythm of walking, leaping, or pounding on the platform. He attacked the deadly social vices of the saloon, dancing, cards, divorce, the theater, tobacco, and fictional literature. All were the enemies of God, womanhood, motherhood, cleanliness, hard work, and patriotism.

The New York City campaign (April 15–June 17, 1917) is generally regarded as the climactic revival of Sunday's career. America had entered World War I, and New York City was different—at least in the minds of the press and its sophisticated citizenry. The feature story in the "Religion and Social Service" section of *The Literary Digest* for April 21, 1917 was titled "Billy's Rubicon." "Can Billy Sunday win in New York?" was the lead sentence. The charges against him were familiar: commercialism, use of slang, insincerity, and being out-of-date among the more liberal and socially oriented clergy of New York City. A large feature article in the magazine section of *The New York Times* by Charles H. Grasty appeared April 22, 1917 on "Billy Sunday as Preacher and Artist" and dealt with Sunday's style of delivery.

Of course any man who speaks movingly gets the help of some kind of emotional lift from within. He does better than he knows. Sunday is carried along by an intense excitement. . . . He never leaves his audience in doubt as to what he is driving at. That is the justification, if any there be for his slang. He brings the gospel right home to "the folks." He makes it concrete and personal. The "Religion and Social Service" section of *The Literary Digest* for June 2, 1917 featured a print of a George Bellows painting entitled "A Realistic Study of a Billy Sunday Meeting" —a typical Bellows work portraying intense (almost frenzied) and powerful activity among the huge crowd inside the tabernacle. The feature story on the same page was an appraisal of Sunday, written by Dr. Lyman Abbott, "one long schooled in the practises [sic] of liberal Christianity," and author of *The Theology of an Evolutionist.*

> Slang, but in no such wholesale quantities as I had been led to expect. . . . Furthermore, there was not even a remote suggestion of vulgarity or coarseness in his address. Whatever was objectionable in Billy Sunday's use of the language of the street was more than compensated for by the entire absence of the pietistic phrases which we are accustomed to expect from professional evangelists. . . . Billy Sunday speaks both of and to Jesus Christ as tho [sic] Jesus Christ were on the platform at his side. His familiarity with God is that of a boy whose father is his constant companion.

The June 18, 1917 issue of *The New York Times* (the day after the final services) carried a front-page headline, "98,264 Persons Hit the Trail in the Ten Weeks of the Campaign." It also featured an interview with John D. Rockefeller, Jr., who had been one of the many prominent supporters of the campaign:

> Billy Sunday did New York a lot of good. He brought the gospel home to men not reached by ordinary ministers. He made religion a subject of conversation among people who never talked of it before.

The point of greatest interest in this review of the total New York City campaign was the complete absence of any comments on the music—the one aspect of the Sunday revivals which has lived on over and over and over again. The Rockefeller interview mentioned Mr. Rodeheaver's volunteer choir, but only to recognize them as a part of the eight thousand volunteer workers in the campaign. The *Times* for the day before (Sunday) mentioned in passing that "Mr. and Mrs. Sunday had as guests at luncheon yesterday, at their temporary home, 184 Northern Avenue, William B. Miller, who is secretary of the campaign here, Mrs. Miller, and Mr. and Mrs. Charles M. Alexander"—the man who had worked with Sunday in the Chapman-Alexander revivals and who had established massed choirs and the techniques of directing congregational singing.

The role of music in the Billy Sunday revivals, nevertheless, was central. Since Homer Rodeheaver joined the team in 1909, the Billy Sunday team had mastered, through music, the most dynamic control of group psychology, emotional inspiration, and a lasting instruction in the basic elements of evangelical theology. This work of the Billy Sunday revivals cannot be understood in terms other than the musicianship, personality, and leadership of Homer A. Rodeheaver.

Although Homer was born in a log cabin near Union Furnace, Ohio, his father brought his family to East Tennessee when Homer was only one year old. The family settled in Newcomb, Campbell County, about three miles southwest of Jellico, Tennessee. Here his father operated a sawmill and lumber business. Homer's early years were spent in and out of the coal mines prevalent in Northeastern Tennessee, logging camps and sawmills; and he attended camp meetings. He also enlisted in the Fourth Tennessee Regimental Band. He attended Ohio Wesleyan University for a year in 1902, where he was elected cheerleader "because of his ability to lead a crowd."[35]

The next year Homer returned to Jellico to enter the lumber business, but evangelist William E. Biederwolf (another former assistant to J. Wilbur Chapman) offered him a job leading the music in his campaigns. Rodeheaver worked with Biederwolf until 1909, when Billy Sunday sought him because he "knew how to direct a large choir, and, above all, had developed the smiling, affable sociability of the professional chorister as Charles Alexander had established the role."[36]

Without modern sound systems, Rodeheaver learned to use his trombone to direct the huge tabernacle congregations, and his solos became a popular feature of the music service. "One of the most popular of all trombone solos was the old hymn 'Safe in the Arms of Jesus,' because of a chime accompaniment [on the piano] that was put in by our accompanist."[37] His twenty years with Billy Sunday provided him "the opportunity to sing before more people and lead more people in song than any other man who ever lived. . . . Because through a period of twenty years, ten months of the year, six day of every week we averaged two meetings a day."[38]

The seating capacity of the tabernacles "ranged from five to six thousand in the smaller cities to between sixteen and twenty thousand in Philadelphia, Boston, New York, and Chicago. Platforms were built to seat as many as two thousand singers."[39] Working through the cooperating churches, the advance team was able to fill the platform with good singers.

> The choir in Philadelphia, organized by Mr. H. C. Lincoln, that veteran organizer, had a membership of considerably over five thousand. We divided them into three groups, No.1, No.2, and a male chorus, each of about two thousand.[40]

The choruses sang on alternate nights during the week, and each would sing in one of the three services on Sunday. The men sang on Thursdays and for the special service for men only. The favorites of the mixed choruses were "Sail On," "Master, the Tempest Is Raging," "Hallelujah, What a Savior," "He Lifted Me," and well-known classics such as Handel's "Hallelujah Chorus," Gounod's "Unfold Ye Portals," and Mozart's "Gloria" from the Twelfth Mass. "Sail On" (Gabriel) "was the first great chorus song to be recorded at the Victor Company for the phonograph."[41]

The men's chorus was particularly appealing to the audiences, and they featured "Onward Christian Soldiers," "Stand Up for Jesus," "My Anchor Holds," and that universal favorite for men, "The Church in the Wildwood."

A definite factor in the recruiting of choir members was an assigned seat on the platform within easy hearing distance. Another element, according to Rodeheaver, "lay in the use of marvellous old hymns of the Church and the beautiful, melodious gospel songs."[42]

Vocal solos and duets were a prominent part of the music service. Mrs. Virginia Asher, who worked among business women during the campaigns, joined Rodeheaver in performing the most popular duet in the history of gospel music—"The Old Rugged Cross." Written in 1913 by Reverend George Bennard, it was an immediate success when first presented in one of the big tabernacles. The Asher-Rodeheaver recordings of the song, for both Victor and Columbia, had sold more than a million records at the writing of *Twenty Years with Billy Sunday* (1936), and the popularity of the song has hardly diminished to this day. "We could scarcely get through an evening service without singing 'The Old Rugged Cross.' 'In the Garden,' by C. Austin Miles, was next in popularity."[43]

The appeal of participation in the congregational singing was undoubtedly uppermost in the minds of the people. It was also at this point that Rodeheaver has received the most criticism for featuring the songs "Brighten the Corner Where You Are," "Since Jesus Came into My Heart," and "If Your Heart Keeps Right." The melody and text of the refrain to the latter became the logo for Rodeheaver's publishing firm, for Rainbow Records, and even for the decor of his home on Rainbow Point at Winona Lake, Indiana.

"Brighten the Corner" (Ina Duley Ogdon and Charles H. Gabriel) was by far the most popular of all the congregational songs. It was also a major point of attack among later theologians and musicians. It was criticized for its "jazzy" rhythm—largely by people of the "microphone" generations who sing their hymns in acoustically deadened auditoriums. Such judgments are in proper perspective only when the song is sung (or heard) in a "live" wooden tabernacle by a congregation of five to twenty thousand people. In this sound environment, the element of jazz is lost in the inevitably slower tempo. My own childhood recollection (and it is vivid) is that the tempo was at least *andante* by modern standards. Justifiably criticized for its theological content, the song's original function, its social environment, and the intentions of its author, composer, and publisher must be remembered. Rodeheaver gave his own explanation for the use and popularity of the song:

> The reason we have used "Brighten the Corner" so much is because it is a song of optimism and good cheer,—there are so many sad hearts these days that we need songs of this kind.[44]

It was not surprising to Rodeheaver, when he went to France in July 1918 to work with the YMCA, to find the doughboys singing "Brighten the Corner" in the trenches. On a later evangelistic tour of the Orient, little children in the outlying areas of Siam were singing it.

But Homer Rodeheaver could never envision the scene on the Tarawa Atoll, November 25, 1943. The United States Marines had suffered the loss of 980 comrades and 2,101 wounded. The Japanese defenders had been destroyed, and Tarawa had fallen. The natives were emerging from their hiding places and were returning to their thatched huts to light cooking fires. As they were confronted by some battle-exhausted Marines, "Shyly and sweetly, some of the girls began to sing 'Brighten the Corner Where You Are,' " confident that this song would assure their goodwill and safety. As Robert Leckie described the scene, the Marines "felt heavy with themselves and their world, as though they had blundered into some Eden which had not known the serpent."[45] Surely "Brighten the Corner" deserves some extratheological and musical considerations.

Rodeheaver's musical influence was expanded when he began the Rodeheaver-[B.D.]Ackley publishing company in Chicago, with *Great Revival Hymns* (1910). It was compiled and edited by Rodeheaver, Ackley (Sunday's secretary), and J. B. Herbert. Herbert also did a *Collection for Male Voices.* Charles H. Gabriel joined the company in 1912 as music editor and composer ("Brighten the Corner" and "Sail On"). In 1936 the company purchased a principal competitor, the Hall-Mack Company of Philadelphia. In 1941 the newly consolidated firm moved its headquarters to Winona Lake, Indiana. According to Parker, their total publications included 49 books, 23 compilations by Rodeheaver and 57 in conjunction with others, 149 collections, and 4 periodicals. These books and music collections made the Rodeheaver Hall-Mack Company the largest publisher of gospel music literature in the world by 1945.

In 35 years it has sold more than $7,000,000 worth of song books and other printed material and its annual income is now close to $400,000, having gone up every year since 1930 in spite of depression and war.[46]

A more detailed study of a Rodeheaver publication will appear later in a survey of hymnals published by independent publishers in the twentieth century. As of this writing, the Rodeheaver Hall-Mack Company has been acquired by Word, Incorporated, of Waco, Texas.

Billy Graham and Cliff Barrows

Although revivalism remained active during the depression years, no Moody or Sunday appeared to maintain the fires of mass evangelism. The radio revivalists were a reasonable and, hopefully, more successful gospel medium. Revivals continued to be sponsored by local churches, using guest preachers and musicians. However, one revival team deserves mentioning in this account, if for no other reason than it was in one of their services that William F. (Billy) Graham made a public profession of his faith, and a musical influence upon Graham became permanent. The evangelist was Mordecai F. Ham, a former pastor of the First Baptist Church of Oklahoma City, who became a full-time evangelist after World War I and the great epidemic of influenza.

His music director was William J. Ramsay, a gospel song composer and compiler of *The Ham-Ramsey Revival Hymns* (Chattanooga, Tennessee, n.d.), "a collection of high class Gospel Music for use in Evangelistic Meetings, Church Services, Sunday Schools, and Young People's Societies." The editors' foreward reads in part, "The editors of this book have endeavored to select such songs as contain a message, exalt the Christ, 'preach the word,' and to emphasize such doctrines as are assailed by the 'false Teachers of this present evil age.' " The categories listed in the hymnal were: Congregational Songs; Special Service Songs; Great Standard Songs and Hymns; Children's Songs; Solos, Duets and Quartets; Chorus Choir Selections; Invitation Hymns; and Devotional Hymns.

The Ramsay musical format utilized the chorus choir performing many of the standard choral selections well known from the Rodeheaver years. Soloists were not a prominent feature, but the short choruses were used frequently. During the thirties, the meetings were held in large wooden tabernacles built on the Billy Sunday pattern and without any sound systems. Sawdust was used for the floor to minimize the reverberation and to keep down the dust, but the live auditoriums enhanced both the choral and congregational singing.

It was during a 1934 campaign in Charlotte, North Carolina, that Billy Graham responded to the invitation songs "Just As I Am," and "Almost Persuaded." These would soon become the only songs of invitation used by the Billy Graham crusades.[47]

The resurgence of religious fervor after World War II found expression at almost every level of denominational and personal religious experience. Although the radio ministries had already reached undreamed-of dimensions in "Bringing Christ to the Nations," "The Old-Fashioned Revival," and the Mormon Tabernacle Choir's "Music and the Spoken Word," this was not unexpected. However, the return of mass evangelism in the Billy Sunday tradition was not anticipated among religious leaders—and certainly not the worldwide impact of the Billy Graham crusades.

The crusades grew out of the mid-century organization called Youth for Christ, International. All of the longtime members of the Graham team served in the organization in the 1940s. Graham served (1945-1947) as a field representative and worked with teams throughout the United States, Canada, and the British Isles. In this capacity he met and worked with a young music director, Cliff Barrows. In 1947 the Graham-Barrows team began to operate out of Minneapolis, holding city-wide revivals. Mrs. Barrows was accompanist and Grady Wilson joined the team as an "associate evangelist." Graham had met George Beverly Shea much earlier in Chicago, when Shea was working as staff soloist and announcer at radio station WMBI (Moody Bible Institute), where Donald Hustad was often his accompanist. Graham and Shea had also worked together (1944) on a radio program "Songs in the Night." In November 1947 the Graham-Barrows-Wilson team went to Billy Graham's hometown of Charlotte, North Carolina, for a city-wide revival and asked Shea to be guest soloist. This was the beginning of the long working relationship of the "Team."

It was the 1949 Hollywood tent revival that catapulted the young evangelistic team into national recognition. The conversion of many celebrities and the ensuing publicity extended the revival from four to eight weeks. Designation of the meeting as being "in the Billy Sunday tradition" by *Time* magazine was followed by the statement that Graham "dominates his huge audiences [more than 6,000 nightly] from the moment he strides onstage to the strains of 'Send a Great Revival in My Soul.' "[48] In addition to the gospel solos of George Beverly Shea, the team utilized local celebrity groups such as the "Haven of Rest" quartet and the "Old-Fashioned Revival" quartet. They also used an electric organ. Lorin Whitney, organist for the "Haven of Rest" radio program since 1934, served as organist. One of the "celebrity" converts was Stuart Hamblen, a native of Abilene, Texas, and the son of a Methodist minister. Hamblen was already a media personality with his own show, "Stuart Hamblen and His Lucky Stars," and a composer of religious songs. His "It Is No Secret What God Can Do" became an immediate hit song of the crusades—and was used by Shea in a 1985 crusade in Florida. Hamblen's "This Ol' House," another religious song, was one of the top ten songs on TV's Saturday Night "Hit Parade" for many weeks during the early fifties. Another big hit of the early crusades was Shea's own setting of "I'd Rather Have Jesus."

The Hollywood revival quickly developed into a multifaceted ministry. A documentary film was made of the Portland, Oregon, crusade and planned as promotional material, but became the format for a television ministry. It also led quickly to a movie ministry which was incorporated as World Wide Pictures. The radio ministry, "The Hour of Decision," began in 1950 and grew to a nine-hundred-station network in several countries. In the same year, George Wilson began the formation of the nonprofit organization "The Billy Graham Evangelistic Association, Inc.," which thereafter paid a fixed salary to each member of the team. This eliminated special offerings or gifts from crusade funds. In 1950 Tedd Smith also joined as a member of the musical team.[49] According to an RNS news release to the *Baptist Standard* (Texas Baptist paper) in 1983, the Association and its affiliated organizations received a total income of $64.8 million dollars, with offices in Minneapolis, Atlanta, London, Paris, Frankfurt, Winnipeg, Honolulu, Auckland, Sydney, Buenos Aires, Mexico City, and Tokyo.[50]

After the Hollywood revival, the organ became a permanent addition to the music program. Lorin Whitney continued to play for occasional crusades, but Paul Mickelson joined the team (1950-1957) as official organist. He resigned after the 1957 New York crusade to become the director of religious recordings for RCA. One year later he left RCA to become vice-president of Word Records in Waco, Texas.[51] The next full-time organist was Donald P. Hustad (1961-1963). An organist, arranger, compiler, music educator, composer, and author (*Jubilate!*), he has written music that has permeated the instrumental, choral, and ideological values in our contemporary Protestant church music.

The musical content of the early crusades is reflected in the first songbook, *Singing Evangelism* (1950). The guideline for the collection was the use of the familiar. Unlike Alexander and Rodeheaver who used so many "new" songs in their services, Cliff Barrows left the new music to the soloists and guest musicians who were featured regularly. Some of the favorite solos often moved to the congregation. The early formats also reflected the Youth-for-Christ influence, with many short choruses, totally familiar hymns, and borrowed regulars from the "Old-Fashioned Revival" ("Heavenly Sunshine" and "Jesus Saves") and Homer Rodeheaver ("The Old Rugged Cross," "In the Garden," and "Since Jesus Came into My Heart"). With Southern California filled with many wartime immigrants from Texas and Oklahoma, the theme song was, appropriately, B. B. McKinney's "Send a Great Revival in My Soul" and was printed on page 1-A of the *Singing Evangelism*.[52]

The selections for the chorus choir were the familiar titles from the Rodeheaver campaigns—"Sail On," "Hallelujah! What a Saviour," "Ivory Palaces," "Make Me a Blessing," "Saved, Saved," and "He Lives." Two spirituals were listed—"Jesus Will Walk with Me" and one which became a choral theme for many years, "Ev'ry Time I Feel the Spirit." Two favorite solos of the period were included—"The Love of God" and "The Great Judgement Morning."

The Southern background and experience of both Graham and Barrows probably accounts for the inclusion of such regional favorites as "Amazing Grace," "Sweet By and By," and "There Is Power in the Blood." According to many sources, the all-time favorite with the crusade audiences has been Fanny J. Crosby's "Blessed Assurance" with Phoebe Palmer Knapp's tune. Another universal favorite has been Bennard's "The Old Rugged Cross"—not only rated as the best "all-time gospel song, but also the most popular of all Protestant hymns, of whatever type," in a poll taken by chaplains in World War II, according to Robert Stevenson.[53] The hymn continues to be a favorite in the polls of *The Christian Herald*, but their 1960 poll showed that "How Great Thou Art" had already risen to fourth place after only five years of performance in the crusades as a solo with the choir joining on the refrain. In 1968 "How Great Thou Art" was in second place behind "What a Friend We Have in Jesus." Among current favorites, "Amazing Grace" is probably the best known and most performed, but "How Great Thou Art" has moved from the solo category to a congregational praise hymn, and it is included in almost all of the more recent denominational and independent hymnals. The Hope Company's *The Singing Church* (1985) has placed it on page 1.

From the first *Singing Evangelism* to the *Billy Graham Crusade Songs* (1969), there were many interesting changes in contents. In the midst of the Vietnam War, probably the most prominent was the inclusion of many patriotic and militant Christian hymns—"A Flag to Follow," "A Mighty Fortress," "Am I a Soldier of the Cross," "Faith of Our Fathers," "My Country 'Tis of Thee," and "Onward Christian Soldiers." Although the number of titles was reduced from 108 to 67, at least

12 standard hymns of worship and praise were added, including "Praise to the Lord, the Almighty" (LOBE DEN HERREN), "O God, Our Help in Ages Past" (ST. AGNES), and "Jesus Shall Reign" (DUKE STREET).

Worship-oriented hymns, as well as some contemporary songs, have become more plentiful in more recent editions. This trend toward the objective hymns of worship and praise, according to Stansbury, is unique in the history of American mass evangelism.[54] A further striking characteristic of the 1969 edition is the deletion of the short choruses. Only the African folk tune "Kum Ba Ya," then popular among the young people, is included. "Just As I Am" and "Almost Persuaded" are still the only titles listed in 1969 which could be classified as songs of invitation. Another European tune, LANDAS, arranged by William J. Kirkpatrick for the Lidie H. Edmunds hymn "My Faith Has Found a Resting Place," has also become a great favorite in America.

According to Stansbury, the hymns used most often through all of the crusades would be "Blessed Assurance," "To God Be the Glory," "All Hail the Power of Jesus' Name," "Trust and Obey," and "Revive Us Again."[55]

The influence of the crusades upon church music has not been limited to hymn and solo literature. Beginning with the 1954 London crusade, special songbooks were printed for the choir. This first book contained eighteen gospel songs, two worship hymns, two Negro spirituals, three choruses, and one English motet.[56] In 1957 *The Chancel Choir* was issued by the Walfred Publishing Company, *The Chancel Choir, No. 2* in 1961, and *The Chancel Choir, No. 3* in 1966. Another collection compiled by John W. Peterson, *The Cliff Barrows Choir*, was published by Singspiration in 1965. This collection contains eight of Peterson's songs and arrangements. Sixteen titles of the total of thirty-three were composed after 1950. These collections have been a source of special choral literature for church choirs throughout the world.

Special guest artists have added charisma to the music of the crusades. In addition to George Beverly Shea, who made regular nightly appearances, soloists Stuart Hamblen, Roy Rogers and Dale Evans, Ethel Waters, Jerome Hines, Anita Bryant, and Norma Zimmer were frequent and very popular guests in the early decades of the crusades. In recent years, the guests have also included the ranking stars in the field of contemporary Christian music. The acceptance of new solo literature has been mixed, but the prestige of the artist often brings a high level of distribution for new songs, or new life for the already familiar.

The Billy Graham crusades have brought universality and a degree of permanence to many gospel songs and great worship hymns, making it difficult to grasp the international impact upon the musical life of the church. It was very interesting to note a recent visit of Pope John Paul II to France, when thousands of French citizens greeted him publicly by singing the short chorus, "Alleluia." It is certain that many of the songs used most often in the crusades are now being sung by more people than any others in the entire history of Christianity. Almost equally universal is the music in *The Chancel Choir* series and the organ and piano arrangements of Donald Hustad and Tedd Smith.

Notes

1. Personal letter from Lew Ayres, April 17, 1976.

2. Blake, Manfred Nelson, *A Short History of American Life* (New York: McGraw-Hill Book Co. Inc., 1952), p.636.

3. Ibid., pp.631-632.

4. Carman, Harry J., Kimmel, Wm. G., and Walker, Mabel G., *Historic Currents in Changing America* (Chicago: John C. Winston Co. 1942), p. 634.

5. Garcia, William Burres, *The Life and Choral Music of John Wesley Work* (1901-1967) (Ph.D. Diss., The University of Iowa, 1973), p.19.

6. Ibid., p.15.

7. Ibid., p.31.

8. Ibid., p.55.

9. Ibid. p.75, citing Work III, "Plantation Meistersinger," *Musical Quarterly* XXVII (Jan. 1941), p.106.

10. Ibid., p.246.

11. Reynolds, William J., *Companion to Baptist Hymnal* (Nashville: Broadman Press, 1976) p.445.

12. Hustad, Donald P., *Jubilate! Church Music in the Evangelical Tradition* (Carol Stream, Illinois: Hope Publishing Company, 1981), p.255.

13. Fleming, Joe Lee, *James D. Vaughan, Music Publisher, Lawrenceburg, Tennessee, 1912-1964* (S.M.D. Diss., Union Theological Seminary, 1972), p.62.

14. *Time*, Vol. LIV, No. 19, p.44.

15. Malone, Bill C., *Southern Music, American Music* (Lexington, KY: The University Press of Kentucky, 1979), p.75.

16. Darden, Bob, "Gospel Lectern," *Billboard Magazine*, October 5, 1985. p.56.

17. Ibid.

18. Ennis, Michael, "Onward Chris Christian—rock soldier," *Texas Monthly,* December 1985, p.14.

19. Reynolds, William J., *Hymns of Our Faith* (Nashville: Broadman Press, 1964), p.398.

20. Smith, Gipsy, *Gipsy Smith, His Life and Work* (New York: Fleming H. Revell Company, 1906), p.25.

21. Fant, Clyde E. and Pinson, William M., *Twenty Centuries of Great Preaching*, Vol.VIII (Waco, Tex.: Word Books, Inc., 1971), p.91.

22. Smith, p.93.

23. Ibid., p.94.

24. Ibid., p.172.

25. Ibid., p.244.

26. Ibid.

27. Murray, Harold, *Sixty Years an Evangelist* (London: Marshall, Morgan & Scott, Ltd., 1937), p.92.

28. Ibid.

29. Smith, Gipsy, *Forty Years an Evangelist* (New York: George H. Doran Company, 1923), pp.143-144.

30. Ibid., p.192.

31. Weisberger, Bernard A., *They Gathered at the River* (Boston: Little, Brown and Company, 1958), p.236.

32. Ibid., p.237.

33. Ibid., p.243.

34. Ibid., p.244.

35. Parker, Thomas Henry, *Homer Alvan Rodeheaver (1880-1955), Evangelistic Musician and Publisher* (Ed.D. Diss., New Orleans Baptist Theological Seminary, 1981), p.32.

36. Ibid., p.33.

37. Rodeheaver, Homer, *Twenty Years with Billy Sunday* (Nashville: Cokesbury Press, 1936), p.73.

38. Ibid., p.74.

39. Ibid., p.75.

40. Ibid.

41. Ibid., p.77.

42. Ibid., p.76.

43. Ibid., p.78.

44. Rodeheaver, Homer, "Wrecking the Service with the Wrong Song," *The Choir Leader*, E. S. Lorenz, ed., Vol. XXXVIII, No. 8, p.216.

45. Leckie, Robert, "Tarawa: Conquest of the Unconquerable," *Illustrated Story of World War II* (Pleasantville, NY: The Reader's Digest Association, Inc., 1969), p.257.

46. Butterfield, Roger, "Homer Rodeheaver," *Life*, Sept. 3, 1945, p.65.

47. Pollock, John, *Billy Graham* (New York: McGraw-Hill Book Company, 1966), pp.7-8.

48. *Time*, Vol. LIV, No. 20, p. 64.

49. Stansbury, George William, Jr., *The Music of the Billy Graham Crusades, 1947-1970* (D.M.A. Diss., The Southern Baptist Theological Seminary, 1971), p.24.

50. *Baptist Standard*, Vol. 96, No. 21, p.10.

51. Stansbury, p.51.

52. Ibid., p.120.

53. Stevenson, PCMA, p.110.

54. Stansbury, p.144.

55. Ibid., p.139.

56. Ibid., p.162.

Part III:

Twentieth-Century Hymnody

9

The Merging of Traditions

Any consideration of church music in the twentieth century always leads to the major catalysts which have made possible the explosive development of Christian ministries through music. The first of these would be a unity of our worldwide community through the elimination of distance. This became a reality through an incomprehensible technology of travel and communications; the printing and distribution of information; the general music instruction; and the electronic aids to the visual and aural delivery of the gospel message through the medium of music.

All of these forces, at the same time, have brought Protestants to rethink their theology; their spiritual values; their communal spirit; the bases for their existence; and the techniques for expediting their biblical commission. The approaches to the best use of these technical resources have been varied in both denominational and independent responses. Since it represents the basic theology and democratic expression of worship and outreach, one of the best indicators of our Christian reactions to life in the twentieth century is found in the structure and contents of our hymnody. An examination of the denominational hymnals will reveal the expressions of each major American denomination.

At the dawn of the new century, there were strong commitments by all of the established denominations to publish new hymnals. All of these were now laid out as hymnal and tune book. Two strong motivations were an effort to heal many of the wounds of the Civil War and a sincere evangelical commitment to world missions. The various synods of Lutherans were attempting mergers and reorganization and, after World War I, the adoption of English as the official language of their liturgy and hymnody.

The official hymnals of the mainline denominations were designed by committees, with a mandate to find expression of the theological ideals of their particular denomination and, in some instances, to determine the form and order of their public worship. The ideals set forth in each preface by the committees were varying expressions of the theme of worship and praise; a deeper understanding of God's nature; the coming of the kingdom of God; an attempt to relate Christianity to the growing urban life; and the hope for a Christian social order.

The poetic heritage of twentieth-century American hymnody was distinctly English, but the contents were increasingly marked by a theological optimism in America. Some of our hymnists were still translating Latin hymns, but more were writing original texts. The quality of this new American verse prompted Canon Percy Dearmer (1867-1936) to write that "it was just in America that the best hymns, and those most in accord with the convictions of the present age, were being written."[1]

Denominational hymnals usually drew heavily from their own writers and composers. There was evolving, however, such an ecumenical quality in the texts that many later hymnals contain texts from a large number of other denominational hymnals. There were many contributing factors, but one of the important ones was the establishment of hymnology as a valid academic discipline. This was inevitable because of the volumes of serious religious poetry which had accrued in Latin, German, and especially in nineteenth-century English. Also, because of the growing interest in church music as a profession, hymnology became a basic element of the college and seminary curricula. Currently, research in the field of hymnology accounts for a large segment of the theses and dissertations in our major universities and seminaries.

Another very important factor was the organization of the Hymn Society of America, founded in New York City in 1922, and its effective work in the development of American hymnody through research and creative writing. The early years of the Hymn Society were largely regional in organization and influence. But through their patronage of research and hymn-writing competitions, the Society has a current membership of more than thirty-five hundred ministers, organists, choir directors, poets, hymn writers, and composers, with the national headquarters now located in Fort Worth, Texas.

The published papers of the Society and the quarterly magazine, *The Hymn*, have made the most significant contributions to the literature of Hymnology. The topics for the hymn-writing contests have included hymns on the city, ecumenical hymns, hymns for youth by youth, rural hymns, hymns on the home, hymns on a new world order, hymns on Christian education, stewardship hymns, marriage and the family, social welfare, hymns for children, hymns on the ministry, Bible hymns, Lord's Day hymns, ecology, hymns of hope, the mission of the church, time and space, hymns for America, hymns on aging and the latter years, and hymns for human relations.

The most far-reaching project of the Hymn Society has been the *Bibliography of American Hymnals*, edited by Leonard Ellinwood and Elizabeth Lockwood. Recently published in microfiche by University Music Editions of New York, the Bibliography lists seventy-five hundred hymnals published in North and South America from 1640 to 1978, and in all languages which use the Roman alphabet.

Early twentieth-century Protestantism also provided a sharp contrast to the denominational hymnals. The nonliturguical churches of the South, Midwest, and the West Coast were enthusiastic patrons of the American composers and the gospel hymn writers. The independent publishers provided these churches with new texts, new tunes, and new hymnbooks almost annually—and without the consensus of an appointed, authoritative hymnal committee. The format of the hymnals was all-purpose (with standard hymns, gospel songs, large choir choruses, short congregational choruses, children's songs, and favorite gospel solos). Most of the publishers advertised orchestrations available for the entire hymnal, and many published their major collections in shaped notes. They were thus accommodating the urban churches with instrumentalists and the skilled musicianship of the rural shaped-note singers who devoured their new songs and new music. These Midwestern and Southern publishers embodied the evangelistic spirit of the frontier, and their new songs were an accurate reflection of the religious life of this new land.

In general, the musicians and theologians joined forces to keep the gospel songs out of the denominational hymnals, and sharp controversies arose in their attempts to define and categorize "hymns" and "gospel songs." These attempts were based upon their literary value, theological content, and musical style characteristics. The gospel song was derided by many as being no more than doggerel verse, written by amateurs with little poetic skill. The texts were also attacked as being sentimental, egocentric, having crude poetic imagery, and little foundation in biblical theology. Further, they argued, the gospel song was not addressed to God, but was an interpersonal message of testimony. A basic element of worship was thus bypassed, making such songs unfit for corporate worship. So the majority of the denominational hymnals retained their European traditions and, in many cases, were ignoring a large body of excellent literary hymnody already being written in America.

Advocates of the gospel song countered with the premise that being "fishers" of persons was a basic mission of the church. They also insisted that the music should be consistent with the knowledge and musical experience of the persons singing or listening, in order to convey the truth of the texts effectively. The songs of personal testimony were compared with the woman at the well, who went into the city saying "Come, see a man, which told me all things that ever I did: is not this the Christ?" (John 4:9); and the man who was born blind who said, "Will ye also be his disciples?" (John 9:27). Donald Hustad, in his book on evangelical worship (*Jubilate!*), countered the criticism of all gospel songs as being subjective, with the fact that many of the psalms are in first person and entirely subjective, including the most beloved of all, the twenty-third.

The music of the gospel songs has also been an interesting

subject of the continuing controversy. The urban organists and quartet choirs used hymns and chorales written in the traditional four-part harmonic style of the English hymn or the Lutheran chorale. The quartets could read the separate parts, and the congregations could either sing the tune, read a part, or listen. The thorough bass style of the harmony created rapid harmonic changes, which made the parts more difficult to follow. In contrast, the music of the gospel song was attacked as being trivial, using only the basic chords of the tonic, subdominant, and dominant. The harmonic changes were slow, and the roots of the triads were usually in the bass part. This made an easy bass line, and the other singers could better read and sing their parts in tune. The rhythmic vitality of the gospel songs was an object of ridicule among musicians and theologians alike, and they were declared unfit for the setting of a sacred text—perhaps reminiscent of the sixteenth-century church's scorn for the "Geneva Jigs" of the early metrical psalmody.

It was Charles Ives who first gave an academic endorsement of the "Gospel Hymns of the New England camp meetin' of a generation or so ago," when he declared they had a

> vigor, a depth of feeling, a natural soil rhythm, a sincerity, empathetic but inartistic, which, in spite of a vociferous sentimentality, carries him [the man born down to Babbitt's Corners] nearer to the "Christ of the people" than does the *Te Deum* of the greatest cathedral. These tunes have a truer ring than many of those groove-made, even measured, monotonous, non-rhymed, indoor-smelling, priest-taught, academic, English or neo-English hymns (and anthems).[2]

A further endorsement by Ives was his use of many of these "Gospel Hymn" tunes as thematic material in some of his large compositions. Citing Robert Mays' Indiana University thesis (1961), Stevenson adds:

> whereas only a scattered few [gospel hymn tunes] enter the usual denominational hymnal, no less than ten of the thirteen tunes quoted by Ives [in his second, third, and fourth symphonies and his third violin and piano sonata] are in the *Baptist Hymnal*, 1956.[3]

Stevenson also notes that the same *Baptist Hymnal* allots seven native-born American composers ten or more tunes each: P. P. Bliss (12), W. B. Bradbury (11), W. H. Doane (14), C. H. Gabriel (12), L. Mason (15, of which five are arrangements), B. B. McKinney (16), G. C. Stebbins (11). J. B. Dykes and Joseph Barnby, the top-ranking foreigners, garner only seven and nine tunes each, respectively.[4]

Ives' endorsement of the "Gospel Hymn" in his complex scores alerted other serious composers to the distinctly American qualities inherent in the tunes—especially Aaron Copland and Virgil Thomson. But their sophisticated treatments of the tunes in no way contributed to their longevity or their later inclusion in many denominational hymnals. The bases for their survival are similar to those of the more "literary" hymns and tunes of the skilled poets and tunesmiths.

It is very difficult to determine whether a text or its tune is the more important factor in the twentieth-century survival of any particular hymn or tune. In some instances, a grand new hymn like "God of Grace and God of Glory" (Fosdick), which was introduced with the tune REGENT SQUARE, became more widely used when associated with CWM RHONDDA. In other cases, the hymn and its tune become so permanently linked, that it is impossible for the listener to hear the melody without a simultaneous response to the text, for example, STILLE NACHT ("Silent Night"), MELITA ("Eternal Father, Strong to Save"), or ST. CHRISTOPHER ("Beneath the Cross of Jesus").

A dramatic case in point was the 1983 movie *The Day After,* produced by ABC Motion Pictures and directed by Nicholas Meyer. The setting was Lawrence, Kansas, and the movie was designed to portray the horrors of nuclear warfare. The original music was by David Raksin, but the themes were based upon an orchestral suite, *The River,* by Virgil Thomson (a native of nearby Kansas City). The suite, in turn, was based upon Thomson's score for the 1948 Pare Lorentz movie by the same name. The two main themes taken from *The River* by Raksin were the early folk hymn tunes, FOUNDATION and RESIGNATION. The movie did not use music at any point to heighten the dramatic or scenic effects. FOUNDATION was used for the background music during the introduction of the principal members of the cast. RESIGNATION was used in the same manner for the supporting cast. Music was not used again until the end of the movie when the screen went blank for the long list of credits. Then a line from the movie was repeated against the background of the empty screen—"Hello! Is anybody there? Anybody at all?" During the credits, FOUNDATION was restated in a simple two-voice canon, then created the climax with a very dissonant harmonization for the powerful ending.

If the producers did not know the origin of the themes, they were inadvertently conveying a powerful message to their Christian viewers almost everywhere. The FOUNDATION tune is used most often in twentieth-century hymnals for the second-most-published hymn text, "How Firm a Foundation." One of the stanzas goes:

> When through fiery trials thy pathway shall lie,
> My grace, all sufficient, shall be thy supply;
> The flame shall not hurt thee; I only design
> Thy dross to consume, and thy gold to refine.

The RESIGNATION tune is used almost exclusively with the paraphrase of Psalm 23, "My Shepherd Will Supply My Needs," and a choral arrangement of this setting was published by Thomson. It is of great interest to note here that the most-published hymn text in all of the twentieth-century denominational hymnals is "God Moves in a Mysterious Way His Wonders to Perform."

Noted performers have made many hymns so well known that a short-term survival is guaranteed as "special music," then the song becomes a congregational expression—as Gipsy Smith's "Count Your Blessings" and "Wonderful Jesus"; Homer Rodeheaver and Virginia Asher's "The Old Rugged Cross" and "In the Garden"; Beverly Shea's "I'd Rather Have Jesus" and "How Great Thou Art"; and even John Charles Thomas singing Albert Hay Malotte's "The Lord's Prayer." After Thomas introduced this solo art song in 1935, it first was arranged for choir, then sung in unison by large congregations, and now is in a hymnal (*The Singing Church*) with a simplified accompaniment.

Survival and trends are well documented in an exhaustive study by Katherine S. Diehl of twentieth-century denominational hymnals, which includes:

> the full music editions of hymnals published by religious bodies in the Judeo-Christian tradition, and approved for use at the chief services of worship by these bodies since 1900 and through December 31, 1965.[5]

This Index of hymnals includes the *Army and Navy Hymnal* and a 1964 report on the contents of the latest *Methodist Hymnal* by editor Carlton R. Young. Also included are four "unaffiliated" hymnals for youth and evangelical worship, two Canadian, one Scottish, one British Baptist, three Anglican, one Jewish, and the *Oxford Book of Carols.* The writer has excluded the Jewish hymnal, the Catholic plainsongs, and the entries from the Scottish psalter. However, the entries from the Canadian and Anglican hymnals will be represented in the statistical analyses. All hymns are indexed by: I. First Lines and Variants; II. Authors and First Lines; III. Tune names and Variants; IV. Composers and Tune Names; and V. Melodies.

The "first-line" index of hymn texts indicates every hymnal in which the hymn occurs with its page number. No evaluations are made at any point. However, the inclusion of any hymn or gospel song in a denominational hymnal indicates its survival through its very acceptance by the editorial committee as well as the general church conference or convention. This approval and publication does not assure its continuing use by the separate congregations; but it is, at the same time, a good objective indicator of the official guidelines for congregational participation in that church's corporate worship.

It is of great interest to note that Isaac Watts heads the list of composers of titles contained in the various hymnals with 246. Next in order with 242 is Charles Wesley. James Montgomery is a distant third with 97. Of particular interest is Canon Pearcy Dearmer, a twentieth-century author and translator, with 82. Then Fanny J. Crosby has 65 and John Newton 59. William

Cowper is eighth with 18 and ninth is a tie between Louis F. Benson and John H. Holmes with 13 each. The inclusion of 24 spirituals is especially significant, with many appearing in three to five hymnals. "Were You There?" is in eleven.

The prolific hymnists of the eighteenth and nineteenth centuries are still dominating our denominational hymnals through their quantities in print, but another interesting fact is the catholicity of so many of these hymns. Granted that many of the early writers have been edited in order to maintain the purity of sectarian doctrines, but an amazing number of titles have struck universal themes, and are included in as many as twenty to sixty-nine hymnals. William Cowper had only eighteen titles listed, but his "God Moves in a Mysterious Way" was the most universal, being included in sixty-one hymnals. The second-most-published is "How Firm a Foundation" (fifty-three hymnals), from John Rippon's *Selection of Hymns* (1787). John Newton's "How Sweet the Name of Jesus Sounds" is listed in forty-nine hymnals. G. W. Doane's "Fling Out the Banner" appears in thirty-seven, and William Whiting's "Eternal Father, Strong to Save" in thirty-six.

Universal themes began to appear more often in the writings of the late nineteenth- and early twentieth-century hymnists and effectively indicate the trends in American hymnody. The American authors and their titles which appear in more than thirty hymnals are: Washington Gladden's (1836-1918) "O Master, Let Me Walk with Thee," forty-five hymnals; Frank Mason North's (1850-1935) "Where Cross the Crowded Ways of Life," forty-one; Joseph H. Gilmore's (1834-1918) "He Leadeth Me," forty-one; Daniel C. Roberts' (1841-1907) "God of Our Fathers, Whose Almighty Hand," forty; William F. Merrill's (1867-1954) "Rise Up, O Men of God," thirty-nine; Mary Ann Thomson's (1834-1923) "O Zion Haste," thirty-eight; and Ernest W. Shurtleff's (1862-1917) "Lead on, O King Eternal," thirty-six.

Other American hymns of the late nineteenth and early twentieth centuries which were widely accepted in denominational hymnals, but which are not presented here in any order, would include Louis F. Benson's "O Thou Whose Feet Have

Climbed Life's Hill"; Laura S. Copenhaver's "Heralds of Christ"; Harry W. Farrington's "I Know Not How That Bethlehem's Babe"; Harry Emerson Fosdick's "God of Grace and God of Glory"; Eliza E. Hewett's "More about Jesus"; Josiah G. Holland's "Judge Eternal, Throned in Splendor"; J. Edgar Park's "We Would See Jesus"; Adelaide A. Pollard's "Have Thine Own Way, Lord"; John Sammis' "Trust and Obey"; Jay T. Stocking's "O Master Workman of the Race"; and Howard A. Walter's "I Would Be True." The literary hymns continued to dominate the denominational hymnals, while the gospel songs remained the mainstay of the independent publishers.

The universality of hymn tunes has been more pronounced in the twentieth century. One determining factor was an oral as well as a published heritage of standard psalm and hymn tunes used by many congregations, but with their own acceptable texts. Within any denominational hymnal, for example, John Hatton's DUKE STREET can be found, and many times with multiple texts which might be completely unrelated in their poetic content. However, this practice was diminishing in the twentieth century for two major reasons: (1) The romantic concepts of the nineteenth century linked text and music in an interpretive and emotional relationship, rather than the disinvolved carrier of texts so characteristic of the earlier classical hymn tunes. The gospel songs, with their custom settings of each text, probably exerted additional influence toward this ideal. (2) The modern practice of engraving all of the text of the hymn between the two staves of the music made it possible to print the words and music from a permanent plate. Once this plate was made (and copyrighted), the publication of a hymnal became a simple matter of selecting and arranging those hymn plates in the desired numerical order.

Again, based upon Diehl's study of seventy-eight denominational hymnals, our familiar Christmas carols were the most universal tunes, with *Adeste Fideles* appearing in seventy-six. Among the top-ranking hymn tunes, Louis Bourgeois' OLD HUNDREDTH appeared in sixty-nine hymnals; Arthur S. Sullivan's ST. GERTRUDE was second in sixty-eight; and William Croft's ST. ANNE was third in sixty-seven. The influence of the

German chorale is especially strong, in that the PASSION CHO-
RALE, EIN FESTE BURG, and NUN DANKET were included in
sixty-six hymnals. Though not composed as hymn tunes, Franz
J. Haydn's AUSTRIA, Robert Schumann's CANONBURY, and Carl
M. von Weber's SEYMOUR were included in more than fifty
hymnals.

Nineteenth-century English composers were led by John B.
Dykes' tune NICAEA (sixty-six), ST. AGNES (sixty), LUX BENIGNA
(fifty-five), and his BEATITUDO (fifty). Felice de Giardini might
be included as English, since his ITALIAN HYMN (MOSCOW) was
written while he was in England through the influence of Lady
Huntingdon, and it appeared in sixty-six hymnals. Other
English composers whose tunes were used in more than fifty
hymnals were George Elvey (DIADEMATA and ST. GEORGE'S
WINDSOR); Henry Smart (REGENT SQUARE and LANCASHIRE);
William H. Monk (EVENTIDE); Samuel S. Wesley (AURELIA);
Edward J. Hopkins (ELLERS); Aaron Williams (ST. THOMAS);
Alexander Reinagle (ST. PETER); Alexander Ewing (EWING);
Thomas Tallis (TALLIS' CANON); Henry F. Hemy (ST. CATHER-
INE); and Ithamar Conkey (RATHBUN).

The universality of the hymn tunes is further emphasized by
153 tunes which appeared in thirty to forty-nine hymnals. The
English composers accounted for 41 percent of these, with
Dykes, Barnby, and Sullivan combining for thirty-one tunes.
The American composers contributed 17 percent with twenty-
six tunes. Mason and Bradbury had three each, but very significant is the entry of many of the gospel song composers into this
group—George C. Stebbins, I. B. Woodbury, W. H. Doane,
Thomas Hastings, William G. Fischer, Henry K. Oliver, William
F. Sherwin, Robert Lowry, Arthur H. Messiter, William G. Tom-
er, and C. Harold Lowden. The German influence was even
stronger, with 32 chorale tunes used in thirty to forty-nine
hymnals.

This increasing use of chorale tunes, plus the acceptance of
traditional American folk tunes and Negro spirituals, indicates
a convergence of musical style idioms in our congregational
worship. The folk tunes and chorales are, from their inception,
adaptable to congregational use. The spirituals, even though

equally adaptable, had to live down two generations of entertaining arrangements for high school, college, and even church choirs, before joining the congregation. The new interest in folk music during the 1950s and 1960s brought about serious compositions of religious folk-like hymns, musicals, and solo literature. It also brought the guitar into the sanctuary.

Since most of this convergence of musical styles came after 1950, some of this broadening of musical tastes might well be attributed to the *Army and Navy Hymnal.* Designed specifically as an ecumenical and all-purpose hymnal, it contained a balanced mixture of the traditional worship hymns, gospel songs, and choral music. It was also used in all divine services, which were attended by millions of American men and women during World War II. Other elements especially favoring the German chorale were its widespread exposure through radio's "Lutheran Hour" and hundreds of concert performances by the a cappella choirs of church-related colleges from all over America.

Major trends in denominational hymnals during the twentieth century are most apparent when surveying specific hymnals representative of the period. This is particularly obvious in two Methodist publications. *The Methodist Hymnal* (1932) was issued as a joint publication in the midst of the depression. A joint commission was appointed by the Methodist Episcopal Church, South, and the Methodist Protestant Church. The distinguished hymnologist Robert G. McCutchan was chosen as editor.

The division of the hymnal's contents were Worship (58 hymns); God (23); Jesus Christ (89); Holy Spirit (14); The Gospel (72); The Christian Life (123); The Living Church (47); The Christian Home and Family (8); Hymns for Children (20); Kingdom of God (59); The Eternal Life (20); and Special Seasons and Services (32). Other musical sections included Ritual Music and Holy Communion, Responses, and Ancient Hymns and Canticles.

The texts were predominantly English or literary in origin. Charles Wesley contributed fifty-one hymns and John Wesley seven. Isaac Watts was next with seventeen. Then came a large group, mostly from the great Anglican hymnists, who averaged from six to ten hymns each: William Cowper, Percy Dearmer, Philip Doddridge, John Ellerton, Frederick Faber, Reginald Heber, John Keble, Henry F. Lyte, James Montgomery, John M. Neale, and John Newton.

American hymn texts represented thirty-eight authors, thirteen of whom lived into the twentieth century. Of the Americans, only eleven had more than three hymns. The poetry of John G. Whittier accounted for nine texts. Fanny J. Crosby and Samuel Longfellow each had seven, and the remainder had only three, four, or five. However, all came from strong literary backgrounds. They included Katherine Lee Bates, Louis F. Benson, G. W. Doane, Oliver W. Holmes, Frederick L. Hosmer, Frank M. North, Ray Palmer, and Samuel F. Smith. Except for Fanny J. Crosby, the gospel-song literature, so popular in the South, was practically omitted. It is interesting to note, however, that her songs were: "Pass Me Not"; "Near the Cross"; "Blessed Assurance"; "I Am Thine, O Lord"; "Rescue the Perishing"; "Close to Thee"; and "Saviour, More Than Life to Me."

The hymn tunes were also predominantly English. John B. Dykes had twenty-eight settings, Joseph Barnby had thirteen, and Sir Arthur Sullivan eleven. The multiple use of these tunes was almost the norm. American tunes were from more than fifty composers. Twenty-one of these lived into the twentieth century, and twelve had more than three text settings. These twelve were led by Lowell Mason (32) and William Bradbury (10). The other ten composers were W. H. Doane, William G. Fischer, Karl F. Harrington, Thomas Hastings, Peter Lutkin, Robert G. McCutchan, George F. Root, George C. Stebbins, and I. B. Woodbury. Although dominated by the Lowell Mason group, some important concessions were apparent in the inclusion of seven early American tunes—CAMPMEETING, FOUNDATION, ALIDA, CONTRAST, LUCAS, AMAZING GRACE, and CLEANSING FOUNTAIN. The "Amazing Grace" setting gives SPOHR as an alternate tune, and the four stanzas of text are all from John Newton's original poem—the anonymous stanza "When we've been there ten thousand years" was not added.

The Methodist Hymnal (1966), edited by Carlton R. Young,

another distinguished hymnologist and composer, appeared during the Vietnam crisis and the social upheaval of the 1960s. The expressed concerns of the hymnal committee were: (1) the rich heritage of ecumenical hymnody, (2) a hymnal of sufficient diversity to allow for the variety of religious experiences, and (3) to serve the religious needs of the next generation by providing a "hymnal that makes it possible for us to sing our common faith in Christ as Lord and Savior."[6] Austin C. Lovelace served as chairman of the subcommittee on tunes, and Nolan B. Harmon chaired the subcommittee on texts.

The contents were organized simply as: The Gospel and Christian Experience (292 hymns); The Church (61); The Christian Year (134); Times, Seasons, Occasions (65); and Canticles with Music (11). The hymnal also contains the Psalter, Canticles and Other Acts of Praise, and detailed instructions for chanting. There are nine chants in accompanied plainsong, as well as traditional English chants in four-part harmony.

The committee's serious concern for ecumenical heritage is apparent in the sources of anonymous texts. From a total of twenty-four such texts, ten are early Latin hymns, two are early English, and three are Greek. The Lutheran content is most interesting. There are fourteen chorale translations by Catherine Winkworth and forty texts or tunes from German or Scandinavian *Gesangbuch* collections. There are also more than eighty tunes which have German authors or arrangers.

A significant emphasis upon the American heritage is the inclusion of eight American folk hymns—seven Negro spirituals and one Indian, with some of the spirituals arranged by John Work III. Another emphasis is the inclusion of eight traditional American melodies, most of which have been taken from the *Kentucky Harmony, Southern Harmony,* and *Sacred Harp.* Most of these tunes have been reharmonized by the editor (C.R.Y.), Austin C. Lovelace, or V. Earl Copes. Other traditional melodies are Welsh (7), Irish (4), English (7), and French.

Work toward a new *Methodist Hymnal* was begun in 1980-84 with a survey of hymns used most often in United Methodist Churches. The results of this survey furnish an important guideline for the work of the Hymnal Revision Committee's plan to present a recommended list of texts and tunes to the General Conference in 1988. If it is approved, a new *Methodist Hymnal* will probably be issued in 1989.

The Hymnal Revision Committee is chaired by Bishop Reuben P. Job, with Raquel Achon as vice-chairperson and Roger N. Deschner as secretary. The Hymns Committee is chaired by Bonnie S. Jones, and the subcommittees are chaired by Marjorie Tuell, *Texts;* Robert C. Bennett, *Tunes;* Charles M. Smith, *Psalter;* and Charles H. Webb, *Service Music.* Carlton R. Young is serving again as editor.

Some of the primary sources for the hymns appear to be *The Book of Hymns* (United Methodist), *The Methodist Hymnal* (1935), and *The Hymnal* (Evangelical United Brethren). Especially significant are recent publications, *The Hymnal, 1982* (Episcopal); *Lutheran Book of Worship* (1978); *Word Hymnal; Hymns for the Family of God;* and notable hymn texts of Timothy Dudley-Smith, Fred Pratt Green, and Brian Wren.

At this writing, the Committee's list of service music and hymns includes 753 items and must be trimmed by more than a hundred before reporting to the General Conference.[7]

The survey has revealed a marked ecumenicity among denominational hymnals, especially among the top 25 percent of hymns utilized by Methodist congregations. If the committee is committed to this guideline, nearly a hundred titles in the new hymnal would be familiar to almost all Protestant congregations. Another special effort is being made to include foreign hymnody from China, Japan, Korea, Taiwan, and much Hispanic—where Methodist mission activities are strong. The early American heritage continues, the Native American is also recognized, and even more Black American spirituals will be introduced and arranged by William Farley Smith. The Methodist heritage is to be increased through the inclusion of Wesley poems and hymns to almost seventy-five texts. About one hundred selected gospel songs, rounds, and choruses will be suggested, with most being time-honored favorites from the nineteenth century. It is also interesting to note that a few youth-type choruses of a generation past are now being included in many major denominational hymnals.

The Hymns Committee has been the focus of considerable media attention, at this writing, over the desire by many to eliminate hymns based upon a militaristic imagery such as "Onward Christian Soldiers," "Battle Hymn of the Republic," and so forth. Although such elimination would run counter to the "church militant" spirit of missions and evangelism at the turn of this century, final action on the matter will probably be left to the General Conference of 1988. Garnering less media attention is a strong desire by many committee members for more inclusive and nongender language in the hymn texts, which will probably be resolved in a less controversial manner and in good poetic form.

The tunes are more numerous, and their sources so diverse, that no single composer will have any significant number. Many tunes of monophonic origin will be published as single melodic lines, and others will probably be harmonized by Carlton Young or Charles Webb. With an increase in Wesley texts, however, many of the standard favorites will be used or recommended as alternate tunes. The most frequent tunes used with multiple texts will continue to be CANTERBURY, DIADEMATA, DUKE STREET, HYFRYDOL, HYMN TO JOY, ST. AGNES, and ST. CATHERINE. The German Chorale remains a large component, through its music and translated texts, with about forty due to be suggested to the General Conference.

The new *Methodist Hymnal* appears to be moving strongly toward the historical heritage, traditional practices, and contemporary theological positions of the United Methodist Churches in America.

Two Presbyterian hymnals show interesting trends during this century. *The Hymnal,* another publication of the depression era, was issued in 1933 by the Presbyterian Board of Christian Education. It was edited by Clarence Dickinson, a prominent teacher and writer on the history and practice of church music. *The Hymnal* had its nineteenth printing in 1945. In the Preface the hymnal committee set forth some of their guidelines. In the interest of compactness,

Those hymns have been omitted, therefore, which, upon careful investigation, have been found to be seldom, if ever, used. On the other hand, old hymns which through the years of association have become fixed in the affections of many people have been retained, even though they may, in many cases, fall below the general standard set for the Hymnal. The rich treasure of the heritage hymns of the church has been carefully preserved and their representation considerably enlarged.[8]

The most obvious preservation of the "heritage hymns" was a large section devoted to Chants, Ancient Hymns, and Canticles. Although the majority were in English-style chant, and as early as John Merbecke, some plainsong chants were included. Many of the hymn texts were from anonymous Latin (9) and English (5) sources. Many texts and tunes were drawn from the early Scottish and Genevan Psalters. In addition to the Psalter tunes, many traditional English (16), Welsh (14), and Irish (4) tunes were used. No such American tunes appeared, and only one anonymous American text was found—"I Sought the Lord." The German heritage was treated heavily, with ten of Winkworth's translations and thirty-two German authors listed. The influence of the chorale was even stronger, with ninety-six German composers or *Gesangbuch* tunes.

The texts were mainly from the nineteenth-century English hymnists, written, for the most part, by the clergy. One hundred eighty-three of the authors were identified as "Bishop," "Canon," or "Reverend." All of the major contributors were English except for nine texts by Louis F. Benson, the distinguished American hymnologist who had edited *The Hymnal* (1911) and six texts from the poetry of John G. Whittier. Isaac Watts led all contributors with twenty hymn texts. Charles Wesley was second (15) and John M. Neale's translations (14) were third. The complete English domination is emphasized by the list of authors who contributed four texts or more: Cecil F. Alexander, Horatio Bonar, John Bowring, William Cowper, Philip Doddridge, John Ellerton, Frederick Faber, Frances R. Havergal, Reginald Heber, Frederick Hosmer, William How, Henry F. Lyte, John S. B. Monsell, James Montgomery, Nahum Tate, and Godfrey Thring.

The multiple use of tunes persisted in *The Hymnal* 1933, with eighty-seven tunes used with more than one text. Most were used with only two texts, but the tunes ST. AGNES, QUEBEC, and LANCASHIRE were used with four each. The English composers are the usual major contributors—Dykes, Barnby, Sullivan, Smart, Elvey, Handel, Maker, and Stainer.

American composers were sparse and represented mainly by Lowell Mason with fourteen tunes. William Bradbury, William P. Merrill, and George W. Warren each had three tunes, and Robert Lowry, Thomas Hastings, William F. Sherwin, and I. B. Woodbury had two each. There were twenty-four other American composers with single entries, and the most interesting fact is that eighteen of these were active in the twentieth century—some as late as the 1950s.

The Hymnal (1933) served as a good repository of the best of English hymnody and established our hymnic heritage from our early Christian traditions. However, the committee ignored some of the excellent work being done by their American contemporaries in both texts and tunes.

The second Presbyterian publication which is very indicative of twentieth-century trends is *The Hymnbook* (1955). This was a joint publication of The Presbyterian Church (U.S.); The Presbyterian Church (U.S.A.); The Reformed Church in America; The Associate Reformed Presbyterian Church; and The United Presbyterian Church. Representing three and one-half million people,

> The interweaving of the strands of worship from five denominations, . . . has added immeasurable richness to the book. It has been responsible for the inclusion of many of the psalms in meter, a happy recovery of one of the great sources of strength of both the Geneva and Scottish traditions. . . . This concerted effort of five churches has also secured the admission of a representative body of so-called "gospel songs," which properly have a place in the devotional life of the Church.[9]

The contents of *The Hymnbook* are organized under the headings Worship (80 hymns); God—God the Father (49); Jesus Christ (105); The Holy Spirit (9); The Holy Trinity (3); The Holy

Scriptures (14); Life in Christ (170); The Church (47); The Kingdom of God on Earth (40); and Miscellaneous (10).

The distinct heritage of the Psalter is most obvious, in that 72 of the 150 Psalms of David provide the texts for 107 of the hymns listed. Fifty-five of the texts are taken directly from *The Psalter* 1912. Translations of early Latin hymns contribute 11 texts. Twenty-seven anonymous texts are from England (5), America (4), Negro (3), Germany (4), and various other nationalities, revealing a folk interest as well.

Eighteenth- and nineteenth-century hymnists are the major contributors. Isaac Watts leads with twenty texts, followed by sixteen translations by John M. Neale, then Charles Wesley with fifteen. Other major contributors with six to ten hymns each are: William Cowper, John Ellerton, William W. How, and John Newton. A large group with four or five hymns each includes: Horatio Bonar, Percy Dearmer, Philip Doddridge, Frederick Faber, Frances R. Havergal, Reginald Heber, Henry F. Lyte, and John S. B. Monsell.

The "gospel songs" which "properly have a place in the devotional life of the Church" are Fanny J. Crosby's "Jesus, Keep Me Near the Cross," "All the Way My Savior Leads Me," "I Am Thine, O Lord," "Jesus Is Tenderly Calling Thee Home," and "Blessed Assurance, Jesus Is Mine." Other gospel-song authors and composers are limited to P. P. Bliss' "Wonderful Words of Life"; Annie S. Hawks and Robert Lowry's "I Need Thee Every Hour"; Eliza E. Hewitt's "More About Jesus"; Edward Hopper's "Jesus, Saviour, Pilot Me"; and Adelaide Pollard's "Have Thine Own Way, Lord." The Negro spirituals "Were You There?" "Lord, I Want to Be a Christian," and "Let Us Break Bread Together" were probably placed in the same category by the hymnal committee.

The other American authors comprise a distinguished list of poets, hymnists, and ministers—Oliver W. Holmes, John G. Whittier, James R. Lowell, Henry Van Dyke, William P. Merrill, Louis F. Benson, Samuel Longfellow, Ray Palmer, Harry E. Fosdick, and Washington Gladden.

German texts are still a significant trend, with fourteen of

Winkworth's translations and about thirty-five texts from other German sources.

The tunes in *The Hymnbook* are of special interest. Since so many of the texts are taken from the Psalters and nineteenth-century hymnists and translators, there are eighty-two tunes that are used with multiple texts. Seventeen tunes have three texts and one has four. Despite this older tradition, a wide spectrum of German, English, and American composers are represented. Since thirty-eight anonymous tunes are used, many arrangers were required to adapt tunes and texts appropriately.

The English composers are less prominent in *The Hymnbook*, but are still a significant number. John B. Dykes has thirteen tunes, but Ralph Vaughan Williams has nine harmonizations of folk melodies. Barnby is limited to eight tunes, Sullivan seven, and Thomas Tallis has five. There are five early chants by John Merbecke which are partially arranged by Healy Willan. English composers contributing four tunes are William Croft, George F. Handel, Frederick Maker, George Elvey, and Henry Smart. A major new Welsh element is nine harmonic arrangements of traditional melodies and an excellent unison tune, CHARTERHOUSE, by David Evans, editor of *The Church Hymnary* (1927) for the Presbyterian Church in Britain.

The number of American composers has increased, due to the inclusion of some gospel songs. Lowell Mason still leads with twenty-two tunes, followed by William Bradbury with ten. C. Winfred Douglas has ST. DUNSTAN'S and four arrangements of folk melodies. The gospel songwriters are led by W. H. Doane (6), George C. Stebbins (4), and Robert Lowry (3). Austin C. Lovelace, composer of many significant choral works, has an original tune, HINMAN, for the traditional text "Shepherd of Eager Youth" and a harmonic arrangement of OSLOW.

The Hymnbook presents a careful emphasis upon the church's musical heritage and an acute awareness of the better creative work being done among twentieth-century church musicians.

Another major denominational press and publisher of hymnals in the twentieth century has been Broadman Press of the

Baptist Sunday School Board in Nashville, Tennessee. A comparatively late entry into church music, the Sunday School Board named B. B. McKinney music editor in 1935 and then purchased the rights to Robert H. Coleman's *Modern Hymnal* (1926). In 1940 McKinney published the first "unofficial" hymnal for Southern Baptists, *The Broadman Hymnal*. It was published in both round and shaped-note editions, with instrumental parts available for strings and winds. The all-purpose format was made clear in the subtitle—"Great Standard Hymns and Choice Gospel Songs New and Old, for Use in all Religious Services, such as the Worship Hour, Sunday School, Young People's Meetings, Assemblies, and Evangelistic Services."

The topical index indicates eighty-eight solos, forty-seven songs for youth, thirty-nine for quartets, thirty-two invitations, thirty-seven selections for the choir, twenty-three on missions, eighteen on heaven, ten on temperance, and seven short choruses. More than fifty gospel songs by McKinney (music and/or texts) were included, but the standard works of the Moody/Sankey era were still dominant. The choir selections were choral arrangements from folk to Verdi and Gounod, all with sacred texts. As a climax for this all-purpose hymnal, the vocal parts for Handel's "Hallelujah Chorus" were included. Noticeably absent were the "Mother's Day" songs which were in the *Modern Hymnal*.

The successor to *The Broadman Hymnal* was the first *Baptist Hymnal* (1956) published by the new (1941) Church Music Department of the Baptist Sunday School Board and edited by W. Hines Sims. According to the Preface, the new hymnal was "suited to all types of churches, services, and needs of the denomination. Also it was desired that the hymnal be designed especially for congregational singing."[10] The editorial quality of the book is noteworthy, thanks to the work and research of William J. Reynolds. Indexes are complete—Authors and Composers with their dates; a Tune Index with names for each hymn and gospel song; a Metrical Index; and a First-Line and Title Index. Many of the tunes had names assigned for the first time.

The *Baptist Hymnal* quickly replaced *The Broadman Hym-*

nal and many of the independent publications so widely used in Southern Baptist churches, rapidly gaining the greatest distribution of any hymnal in print at that time. The editors made a strong effort to emphasize contemporary texts and tunes. At the date of publication, 137 authors were living or had died in the twentieth century. The authors were led by Fanny J. Crosby (21), Charles Wesley (19), Isaac Watts (17), and B. B. McKinney (15). American composers were well represented by Lowell Mason (22), B. B. McKinney (19), W. H. Doane (14), Charles H. Gabriel (12), William Bradbury (12), and P. P. Bliss (11).

The hymnal committee abandoned the all-purpose format because the Church Music Department was already publishing *The Church Musician.* This was a monthly magazine for choir directors, on the order of the Lorenz magazines, which contained an anthem and a choral arrangement of a new "Hymn-of-the-Month." The book *Hymns of Our Faith* by William J. Reynolds was issued as a companion to the hymnal in 1964 and became an important source book for American hymnology—and one of the first to treat thoroughly the authors and composers of the gospel songs.

A successor to the 1956 hymnal is the *Baptist Hymnal* (1975), edited by Reynolds, who succeeded Sims as secretary (director) of the Church Music Department in 1970. The contents of the new hymnal are simply organized under the headings God; God speaks; God's Work; God's People; Special Occasions; and Scripture Readings. The indexes are thorough, and a new *Companion to Baptist Hymnal* (1976), also by Reynolds, has added more valuable material to the growing literature on hymnology.

The divergent trends in twentieth-century hymnody were recognized by the hymnal committee and were dealt with by a special subcommittee for the inclusion of "new materials." The committee

> sought singable tunes with strength and character, avoiding awkwardness, difficulty, and dullness. . . . To strengthen the musical experience of congregational singing, more tunes for unison singing have been included, some tunes have been lowered to

more comfortable keys, and, in some instances, alternate tunes have been suggested to give more variety.[11]

The role of active church musicians in compiling the hymnal was recently emphasized by the editor, who said: "Fifty-five Southern Baptist authors and composers, most still living, contributed to the hymnal."[12]

The diversity of the contents in many late denominational hymnals is also demonstrated in the *Baptist Hymnal* (1975). There are fewer texts and tunes by the authors and composers in earlier hymnals. Probably the best illustration might be in the Index of Authors, Composers, and Sources. There are 435 sources which have only a single entry of a text or tune in the entire hymnal.

The index of Tunes shows a marked decrease in their multiple use. However, a few tunes, such as HYMN TO JOY, DIADEMATA, DUKE STREET, CWM RHONDDA, HYFRYDOL, KREMSER, ST. AGNES, ST. GERTRUDE, and ST. PETER maintain fixed multiple-text associations.

The major English authors remain: Isaac Watts (16); Charles Wesley (12); James Montgomery (5); Frances R. Havergal (4); and John M. Neale (4); William Cowper, William How, John Newton, and John Wesley (3 each).

The number of English tunes has also decreased sharply, with only Dykes, Barnby, Smart, and Sullivan making any significant contributions. Of particular interest is the work of Ralph Vaughan Williams. His arrangements of such traditional tunes as FOREST GREEN, SINE NOMINE, KING'S WESTON, and KINGSFOLD are used for eleven separate texts.

This latest *Baptist Hymnal* gives special attention to its own folk heritage. Early tune books such as Ingall's *Christian Harmony* (1805), Wyeth's *Repository of Sacred Music* (1810), Davison's *Kentucky Harmony* (ca. 1815), *Virginia Harmony* (1831), Walker's *Southern Harmony* (1835), and White's *The Sacred Harp* (1844) combine to contribute fifteen tunes. Most of these are reharmonized by Reynolds and Carlton R. Young from the original three-part vocal scores and are arranged to assure unison congregational singing. Many other tunes from these original sources have long been a part of the Southern hymnic heritage and have become a core of many Southern hymnals.

No single American author is especially prominent. Fanny J. Crosby retains thirteen texts, and B. B. McKinney has five texts with music. Other authors with at least three texts are Eliza E. Hewitt, Elisha A. Hoffman, Ed Seabough, and John G. Whittier. Of greater interest are those who created both text and music; in addition to B. B. McKinney, others are Gene Bartlett, John W. Peterson, Milburn Price, and William J. Reynolds.

American composers are also more numerous. B. B. McKinney leads with sixteen tunes, Reynolds has fourteen, and Charles Gabriel has eleven. Others with five to ten tunes are P. P. Bliss, William Bradbury, W. H. Doane, Thomas Hastings, William J. Kirkpatrick, Robert Lowry, Lowell Mason, James McGranahan, and George C. Stebbins. A list of composers with three or four would be too long to list here. However, at least twenty-two of the major contributors of texts and/or music lived and worked in the twentieth century, and many were still living at the date of publication.

A special characteristic of this hymnal is the inclusion of ten spirituals—not in a special section, but in their proper topical context. At least four of these were already established in other major hymnals, and the new additions are now a well-known part of our rich folk heritage. Even more commendable is the fact that many of these were arranged in 1907 by John W. Work, Jr. and Frederick Work, faculty members at Fisk University and long associated with the Jubilee Singers. Others were arranged by John W. Work III, also a professor at Fisk. Their arrangements present the spirituals in an unadorned simplicity and stylistic purity.

The German influence is also quite prominent. There are five translations by Catherine Winkworth, eleven selections from *Gesangbuchs,* and some fifty-six tunes or texts from German composers, arrangers, or translators of the Lutheran chorales.

The *Baptist Hymnal* (1975) is a studied presentation of the Baptists' hymnic heritage and contemporary creativity. It might also be a credible prediction of the future trends in Baptist hymnody. At this writing, Wesley L. Forbis, director of the

Church Music Department of the Baptist Sunday School Board, has announced plans for a new *Baptist Hymnal* and its projected release in 1991. A large group of church musicians, pastors, and college and seminary faculties is being asked to serve on various committees which will be responsible for the organization and contents of the hymnal. Recent hymnals published by other major denominations, as well as many all-purpose hymnals issued by the large independent publishers, will doubtless influence both the editorial format and the contents of this latest hymnal of Southern Baptists.

The preface to *The New Hymnal* (1916) of the Protestant Episcopal Church states the ideals of the Joint Commission for the selection and arranging of the hymns and tunes. This hymnal was designed as a companion for the Book of Common Prayer.

> These are hymns intended to voice our yearning for larger social service, for deeper patriotism, for a more eager obligation to the winning and maintaining of a free world, for a higher enthusiasm toward the unity and extension of Christianity. . . . There are hymns of objective adoration, august and distant, side by side with hymns that unburden the singer's heart and tell what God has done for him alone.[13]

The arrangement of the hymns is according to liturgical function and the Church Year: I. Daily Prayer (52 hymns); II. The Christian Year (250 hymns); III. The Sacraments and Rites (117 hymns); IV. Special Occasions (43 hymns); V. The Church (54 hymns); VI. Processionals (28 hymns); and, at the end, VII. Carols (17).

The Indexes are thorough. The First Line Index provides the author and date of the hymn. The Tune Index gives the meter, composer, and date of the music. A very significant segment of the hymnal is an Index of twenty-five hymns arranged for men's voices—in four parts, for either a quartet or men's chorus. The tunes are all familiar hymns of the period, and the melody is always assigned to the first tenor. American arrangements for men traditionally place the tune or melody in the second tenor part.

The Indexes reveal the hymns written in the early twentieth century, which should give expression to the desired "yearnings" of the commission.

"Father in Heaven, Who Lovest All"—Rudyard Kipling (1906)
"Father, Who on Man Dost Shower"—Percy Dearmer (1906)
"God of the Nations, Who Hast Led"—Elizabeth Wordsworth (1903)
"Lord of Hosts, Whose Mighty Hand"—John Oxenham (1915)
"O Master of the Sea and Sky"—Henry Burton (1905)
"Our Father! Thy Dear Name Dost Show"—Charles H. Richards (1910)
"Rise Up, O Men of God"—William P. Merrill (1911)
"We Build Our School on Thee, O Lord"—Sebastian W. Meyer (1908)
"Where Cross the Crowded Ways of Life"—Frank M. North (1905)
"Ye Watchers and Ye Holy Ones"—Athelstan Riley (1909)

The hymns by Kipling, Oxenham, Richards, Merrill, North, and Riley are repeated in *The Hymnal* (1940) and have become standard in many denominational hymnals.

The romantic emphasis upon the historical and the "unity" of Christianity are immediately recognized in the use of early Latin, Greek, and German hymnody. There are sixty-three Latin and Greek hymns. The principal translator was John M. Neale. Other translators were John Ellerton and Edward Caswall. There are sixteen plainsong sources, with most of the arrangements and accompaniments written by C. Winfred Douglas. The German texts accounted for more than fifty, with Catherine Winkworth's translations used for seven. The German chorale tunes were even more influential, with about eighty tunes from German composers or *Gesangbuchs*.

The English texts were, for the most part, written by clergymen, with 196 titled clergymen making contributions. Of special interest is that forty women poets are also represented in *The New Hymnal*. The major authors were Charles Wesley with eighteen texts, James Montgomery with seventeen, John Ellerton sixteen, Isaac Watts thirteen, and Bishop William Walsam

How with twelve. Cecil F. Alexander, the most prolific of the female writers, has eleven, and Reginald Heber was next with ten. The English authors were dominant throughout, with Henry Alford, Henry Baker, Horatius Bonar, Jane Borthwick, John Chandler, William C. Dix, Philip Doddridge, Frederick Faber, Frances R. Havergal, John Keble, Thomas Kelly, Henry F. Lyte, Richard Mant, John S. B. Monsell, John Newton, Thomas B. Pollock, Godfrey Thring, and Christopher Wordsworth each contributing at least five or more texts.

Nearly thirty Americans contributed at least one hymn to the collection. John G. Whittier's poems are used for four, and Bishop Arthur C. Cox and G. W. Doane have three each. Other noted American hymnists and poets included are Louis F. Benson, Phillips Brooks, William C. Bryant, George Duffield, Timothy Dwight, Washington Gladden, Thomas Hastings, Oliver W. Holmes, Julia Ward Howe, Francis Scott Key (a hymn and "The Star-Spangled Banner"), Samuel Longfellow, James R. Lowell, William P. Merrill, Ray Palmer, Samuel F. Smith (a hymn and "My Country 'Tis of Thee"), and Samuel Wolcott.

Although the tunes were widely distributed (thirty composers contributed three or more tunes), the English were a heavy majority. The use of multiple settings for the tunes was also prominent. John B. Dykes had thirty-five tunes with forty-five settings; Joseph Barnby had twenty-one tunes with twenty-seven settings; William H. Monk had twenty-one with twenty-three settings; and Arthur S. Sullivan had nineteen tunes with twenty-one settings. The most tunes by an American composer were by Horatio Parker, the noted American teacher and composer, and two of his tunes were used for additional texts. Sir John Stainer had thirteen tunes with seventeen texts, and Henry Smart had twelve of the most-used tunes for twenty texts. The distinguished English/American church musician T. Tertius Noble had eleven original tunes. At least fifteen additional English composers had three or more tunes.

Canon C. Winfred Douglas made the greatest contribution by an American composer, with three original tunes and twenty arrangements of plainsong and folk melodies. Lowell Mason had only eight tunes and William Bradbury only four. The prolific American writers of songs that "unburden the singer's heart" were still ignored in favor of the traditional, the functional, and the ancient texts and tunes.

In 1937 the General Convention of the Protestant Episcopal Church in the U.S.A. authorized the publication of a new hymnal and appointed a Joint Commission to preface it and report. Henry Judah Mikell of Atlanta was named chairman, and Dean Philemon F. Sturges of Boston was named vice-chairman. The report was made and accepted in 1940, and a historic hymnal in American church music went into publication—yet another in the midst of a national and international crisis.

The Commission began by surveying the 1892 and 1916 hymnals, with the expressed purpose of "holding fast that which is good." Special efforts were made to

> secure new hymns for children, and hymns which voice the social concerns of our day. Some of the latter group express the hope of a new world founded upon justice and expression of international brotherhood. The ecumenical movement, with its hope of Christian unity, has also received fitting recognition in the hymnal.[14]

The music for *The Hymnal* was prefaced by a mandate from the church for "a book suitable for congregational singing." Folk music was rated very highly because its survival indicated an enduring quality. In order to make the music more American, tunes were solicited in the United States and Canada, and forty-eight tunes "were chosen from over 4,000 manuscripts sent in anonymously to the commission."[15]

Some editorial innovations include the elimination of meter signatures because of the use of so many plainsong melodies with irregular rhythms; alternate tunes for the same text published directly beside the first tune; inclusion of valid and distinctive notation for tunes from different periods and styles; and directions relating to tempo and style of performance.

The arrangement of *The Hymnal* follows the liturgical functions of the texts—The Christian Year (111 hymns); Saint's Days and Holy Days (250); Thanksgiving and National Days (12); Morning and Evening (35); Sacraments and Other Rites of the

Church (44); Litanies (6); Hymns for Children (18); Missions (13); and General Hymns (35).

Choral Service Music comprises 141 musical settings of the Choral Service, the Canticles, and Holy Communion. Nine Indexes provide immediate access to all topical and liturgical texts, as well as authors, translators, and sources. The music is indexed by composers, arrangers, and sources, as well as by tunes and meters. First lines and "Hymns Suitable as Anthems" are also indexed.

A sensitivity to the church's heritage is most obvious in the selection of texts. There are forty translations of Latin texts, largely from the early saints. Forty-three are translations of German texts from the Reformation period, and five are from Greek. The major portion of these translations are the work of Robert Bridges, John M. Neale, Edward Caswell, Henry W. Baker, Catherine Winkworth, and C. Winfred Douglas.

The three major contributing authors remain almost the same as in the 1916 *Hymnal*—Charles Wesley (18), James Montgomery (14), and Isaac Watts (11). A list of authors having five or more includes Cecil F. Alexander, Henry W. Baker, Horatio Bonar, George W. Briggs, Percy Dearmer, Philip Doddridge, John Ellerton, Frederick Faber, Reginald Heber, Frederick Hosmer, William W. How, Thomas Ken, John M. Neale, John Oxenham, Thomas B. Pollock, Howard C. Robbins, F. Bland Tucker, John G. Whittier, and Christopher Wordsworth. Of these, Briggs, Dearmer, Oxenham, Robbins, and Tucker were active in the twentieth century.

The hymn tunes reveal an even stronger link with tradition. German sources, primarily from the Reformation period and the early *Gesangbuchs,* accounted for more than 130 tunes which were arranged in four-part chorale style. J. S. Bach's harmonizations represented 16 of these, and the *Gesangbuchs* provided 31 others. Johann Crueger has 10 original tunes, and there are 37 selected plainsong melodies. Many of the latter are harmonized with tasteful accompaniments for unison congregational singing. Early Psalters (Ravenscroft's, Scottish, Day's, and Est's) are the sources for fifteen more tunes. New harmonizations for these are by Leo Sowerby, C. Winfred Douglas,

David McK. Williams, David Evans, Ralph Vaughan Williams, and the brothers Martin and Geoffrey Shaw.

The multiple use of tunes is still quite prevalent, but confined mainly to the classic tunes of the early and middle nineteenth century. A total of ninety-three tunes are used with multiple texts. Three of these are used with four texts (REGENT SQUARE, OLD HUNDREDTH, and ST. FLAVIAN), and fifteen are used with three texts. Two Negro spirituals are included—"Were You There?" and MCKEE, arranged by Harry Burleigh for a literary hymn text.

The English musical heritage is still quite strong, and *Hymns Ancient and Modern* is still an effective influence. John B. Dykes is the major musical contributor, with twenty-five original tunes. Only two of these, however, are used with multiple texts. William H. Monk has twelve tunes and one arrangement of a traditional melody. Sir Arthur Sullivan has eight original tunes, two arrangements, and two tunes used with multiple texts. Henry Smart has seven tunes with two using multiple texts.

The use of traditional folk melodies is demonstrated most by the twentieth-century composers. Ralph Vaughan Williams has five original tunes, but eleven harmonizations of folk melodies. Martin Shaw has six tunes and three arrangements of folk melodies.

The forty-eight new tunes from Canada and the United States are most likely single entries, and by composers not yet in the mainstream of American church music. Three prominent Americans have three or more listings—Lowell Mason, T. Tertius Noble, and Horatio Parker. Other important American composers contemporary with the publication of the hymnal were Leo Sowerby, David McK. Williams, and C. Winfred Douglas.

After more than a decade of work, the Standing Commission on Church Music has, at this writing, issued *The Hymnal 1982*. Motivated by a "contemporary renaissance" in music and poetry, the Commission has assembled the most extensive collection of service music and hymns in twentieth-century church music. Amid their determination to assure "practicality and excellence," the Commission was burdened with much highly publicized controversy, centered around obscure and inclusive language, discriminatory gender terminology, a serious concern for world peace, and other issues related to the increasingly pluralistic nature of the contemporary church. The final result is a diversity of church music which includes plainsong, English chant, unison hymn tunes, unison and four-part settings with optional descants, Afro-American folk hymns, Southern folk hymns in unison and/or four-parts, and four-voice hymns in renaissance, classical, romantic, and contemporary harmonic idioms.

The Table of Contents indicates the organization and scope of the music and texts. The Service Music is listed first and indexed as S1—S288. The divisions include The Daily Office; The Great Litany; Proper Liturgies for Special Days; Holy Baptism; The Holy Eucharist (S76—S176); then Canticles (S177—S288). The Hymns follow, indexed as 1—720. The hymn divisions include The Daily Office (1—46); The Church Year (47—293); Holy Baptism (294—299); Holy Eucharist (300—347); Confirmation (348—349); Marriage (350—353); Burial of the Dead (354—358); Ordination (359); Consecration of a church (360—361); General Hymns, covering eleven subtopics (362—634); The Christian Life (635—709); Rounds and Canons (710—715); and National Songs (716—720).

Since a large body of the service music and hymns is published as a single line of plainsong, a folk tune, or a contemporary melody, two separate volumes of accompaniments are published for the organist. This assures unison singing by the congregation and/or choir and a freedom of style in the accompaniment, also allowing for more tunes and texts to be published in the available space. Many hymns are published consecutively, with two differing musical settings to allow for regional preferences. Meter signatures are omitted throughout, even in the most familiar settings. The relative time values of the notes dictate the flow of the text.

The hymn texts reflect a great commitment to high literary standards and to historical tradition, but at the same time an increasing awareness of the resurgence of hymn-writing in England and America. There are eighty-two Latin hymns, dating from the fifth to the late seventeenth centuries, and thirty-eight hymns taken directly from twenty-three of the Psalms. The translations and hymns of John M. Neale provide twenty-seven, many from the 1861 *Hymns Ancient and Modern*. The contemporary texts and translations of F. Bland Tucker bring an additional twenty-one. Most of the existing translations and texts have been altered to create a greater relevance to our contemporary society, for example, changing "Rise up, O men of God" to "Rise up, ye saints of God." The great English hymnists of the eighteenth century remain a dominant feature of *The Hymnal 1982*. Charles Wesley has twenty hymns included, and Isaac Watts has sixteen. Among the nineteenth-century hymnists, James Montgomery has ten, and Cecil F. Alexander has nine.

Special recognition is given in the Preface to Carl P. Daw, Jr. (b. 1944); Anne K. Le Croy (b. 1930); J. Waring McCrady (b. 1938); Charles P. Price (b. 1920); and F. Bland Tucker (1895-1984) for their translations, alterations, and many original texts. Other particularly noteworthy hymns and translations by twentieth-century writers would include George W. Briggs (1875-1959); C. Winfred Douglas (1867-1944); F. Pratt Green (b. 1903); and Brian Wren (b. 1936).

The texts and traditional melodies of six Afro-American spirituals are included: "Balm in Gilead" (melody only); "Go Tell It on the Mountain" (four-part arr. by John W. Work II); "Let My People Go" (four-part arr. by Horace C. Boyer); "Let Us Break Bread Together" (melody only); "Poor Little Jesus" (melody only); and "Were You There?" (four-part arr. by C. Winfred Douglas). Southern folk hymnody is also utilized, but primarily for its music. Seven tunes are taken from the *Southern Harmony* (1835), but only two are associated with their original texts: "Wondrous Love" and "Come Away to the Skies." "Wondrous Love" is in its original three-part harmonization, with the melody in the tenor. "Come Away to the Skies" uses the melody only, reharmonized by Jack W. Burnam (b. 1946). The other five melodies from the *Southern Harmony* have original texts or translations attached, and with a rare stylistic inconsistence, by Catherine Cameron (b. 1927), Reginald Heber, John M. Neale, and Erik Routley (1917-1982).

The musical diversity of the hymns might be emphasized best by their varied sources and composers. There are sixty plainsong settings of hymns which utilize all eight traditional church modes. Ralph Vaughan Williams contributed twenty-seven tunes and arrangements of traditional English tunes, and William H. Monk has twenty-one hymn settings. J. S. Bach has twenty settings of chorale tunes. Traditional English melodies are used with fifteen texts; thirteen tunes are from *Hymns Ancient and Modern;* and Lowell Mason has thirteen tunes and arrangements. Johann Cruger has ten chorales, and Orlando Gibbons provided ten settings. Many twentieth-century composers are led by Richard Proulx (b. 1937) with ten. Others with five or more include Peter Cutts (b. 1937), five; Richard W. Dirksen (b. 1921), seven; Craig S. Lang (1891-1971), seven; Martin F. Shaw (1875-1958), five; Charles V. Stanford (1852-1924), five; Cyril V. Taylor (b. 1907), five; David McK. Williams (1887-1978), five; and Alec Wyton (b. 1921), six.

Although a large number of alternate tunes are presented, the use of tunes with multiple texts has diminished drastically. Ninety-two tunes are used with two separate texts, and only eleven tunes are used with three. Of these eleven, the ones used more generally in other denominational hymnals are ABERYSTWYTH, DUNDEE, MOSCOW, and WAREHAM. Variety is added in many of these cases through changes of key or differing harmonizations.

The Hymnal 1982 is a monumental collection of hymns, tunes, and service music from the entire history of the Church and from many contemporary sources. The highest possible degree of theological integrity has been sought through extensive alterations of both old and new texts. At the same time, these changes have often enhanced the current relevance and poetic beauty of many of the hymns. In many cases, the retention of such traditionally poetic pronouns as *thy, thine, thou,* and *thee* has maintained a living relationship between so many parishioners and the great literature of the Church.

The Hymnal 1982 is probably so large and diverse that no

single congregation will find it totally useful or technically feasible. However, its musical diversity will permit each church to find the best possible material for an optimum choir and congregational participation in any special occasion or regular service of the church. The hymnal will undoubtedly be a valuable resource book for Episcopal church music for many years to come.

Although minimal changes are normally expected in new hymnals for liturgical churches, this has not been true of the hymnals published by the various synods of the Lutheran Churches in America. It is true that all Lutherans inherited a reasonably uniform liturgy, but linguistic and theological differences were too strong to allow any early common hymnal. After World War I, however, English gradually became the common language of their corporate worship, but the chorale remained the core of Lutheran church music. As each succeeding generation felt less transplanted, hymns written in English occupied a larger part of their hymnody. The next stage was the rise of the native Lutheran musician, trained in Lutheran colleges, with a thorough knowledge of the musical heritage, but now able to create new music for their contemporary worship.

A good point of reference is the *American Lutheran Hymnal.* This work of an intersynodical committee began as early as 1921, in response to an invitation from the Iowa Synod to all Lutheran synodical groups in America. Eventually the committee compiled and printed a provisional text edition in 1928 for study and revision. The final music edition (1930) of the hymnal contained chorales from each synodical tradition. Some of these were in earlier translations by Catherine Winkworth and Matthias Loy. The hymnal contained many hymns originally written in English. There were many new translations by H. Brueckner and Anna Hoppe, which were made in the 1920s. Original texts were also contributed by these twentieth-century translators.

Of particular interest to this study, however, were the many original English hymns and the English translations of early chorales and Latin hymns. James Montgomery heads the list with eight hymns, followed by Isaac Watts with seven, and

Charles Wesley with five. Authors with three or four texts were John Bowring, Edward Caswall, Philip Doddridge, Henry F. Lyte, and John M. Neale. A long list of other English hymnists included: Cecil F. Alexander, Sabine Baring-Gould, William Cowper, William C. Dix, John Ellerton, Frederick Faber, Frances R. Havergal, John Keble, John Newton, F. S. Pierpoint, John Rippon's SELECTION, Joseph Scriven, and Samuel Stennett.

American authors were limited to Katherine Lee Bates' "O Beautiful for Spacious Skies"; Phillips Brooks' "O Little Town of Bethlehem"; Joseph Gilmore's "He Leadeth Me"; Mary Ann Lathbury's morning and evening hymns, "Day Is Dawning in the East" and "Day Is Dying in the West"; and Samuel F. Smith's "My Country 'Tis of Thee."

Like the texts, the chorale tunes are dominant throughout. Many appear in their early "rhythmical" form, but the more familiar settings of the eighteenth and nineteenth centuries are printed alongside. Some chorale tunes are used with multiple texts and are assigned names other than their familiar text-associated titles (for example, ERFURT instead of VOM HIMMEL HOCH). Of these multiple-text chorale tunes, eleven are distinct bar-form (AAB) chorale tunes, and eight others are from German composers. The tunes TESCHNER (8 texts), NEANDER (6), and NICOLAI (6) are used for the most texts. The ever-present OLD HUNDREDTH, by Louis Bourgeois, is used for seven.

English composers are also used extensively, with more than twenty contributing twenty-nine tunes. Dykes and Sullivan have four tunes each, William H. Monk has three, and Henri F. Hemy two. Other English tunes are by Thomas Arne, Ithamar Conkey, William Croft, George J. Elvey, Orlando Gibbons, Frances R. and William H. Havergal, Edward J. Hopkins, F. A. Mann, William Tansur, and Samuel Webbe.

American composers provide thirty-six tunes. Lowell Mason leads with fifteen settings. He is followed by Bradbury's four tunes and William F. Sherwin's three. The most-used tune is WEBB (GOODWIN) with five texts. Other familiar American composers are Louis M. Gottschalk, Thomas Hastings, Robert Lowry, Louis Redner, George Stebbins, I. B. Woodbury, Samuel

A. Ward, and John Zundel. The *American Lutheran Hymnal* is a good indication of the significant trend toward an ecumenical body of hymn literature for corporate worship in America.

Probably the most significant hymnal for Lutherans in America was *The Lutheran Hymnal* (1941). Compiled by an intersynodical committee of four large synods, it was then published by Concordia Publishing House. The hymnal was a determined effort by the committee "to produce a hymnal containing the best of the hymnodical treasures of the Church, both as to texts and tunes, in accord with the highest standards of Christian worship."[16] One hundred sixty-nine pages are given to the liturgy, with appropriate musical chants, responses, and settings of the canticles and psalms. The hymns total 660 and are indexed as Adoration; The Church Year; Invitation; The Word; The Sacraments; Confession and Absolution; Confirmation; The Redeemer; Faith and Justification; Sanctification; Prayer; The Church; Cross and Comfort; Times and Seasons; The Last Things; Special Occasions; and Carols and Spiritual Songs.

The textual and musical heritage of the Lutheran chorale remains dominant, and the hymnal, with both service music and hymns, is entirely in English. The need for more translations was great, and the Index contains the names of eighty-seven translators. Thirty-three of these were active in the twentieth century. Although the majority were Americans of German extraction, the committee drew heavily upon existing translations of the chorales by some seventeen English authors, even as late as Percy Dearmer (1867-1936).

Original hymn texts in English included almost a hundred established English authors—even Watts, Wesley, and some psalms by Tate and Brady. Traditional American hymns were represented by less than ten authors—Louis F. Benson, Phillips Brooks, William C. Bryant, George Duffield, Timothy Dwight, Thomas Hastings, Francis S. Key, Ray Palmer, and Samuel F. Smith.

All of the service music is in the four-part style of English chant, and all hymns are also in the four-part harmonic style of the German chorale and the English hymn. The chorale is so dominant that many familiar English texts are set to an already familiar chorale tune.

Only nine of the musical settings are by familiar American composers—William Bradbury, Charles Converse, Thomas Hastings, Oliver Holden, Lowell Mason, Henry K. Oliver, Louis Redner, George C. Stebbins, and George J. Webb. The further Americanization of the Lutheran hymnals would require a new generation of native poets and musicians—many of whom were already in the Lutheran colleges in America.

Lutherans in America still had major obstacles to overcome before the *Lutheran Book of Worship* could be published. Foremost, the liturgical traditions were very similar, but each synod had a distinct hymnic and linguistic heritage. This was a special problem, since the congregational hymn was of basic importance to all Lutherans.

After *The Lutheran Hymnal* (1941), the *Service Book and Hymnal* (1958) was published by groups of Lutherans in Ohio, Iowa, and Texas. These groups would soon form The American Lutheran Church (1960) and the Lutheran Church in America (1962). Eventually, an Inter-Lutheran Commission on Worship was formed in 1966 by the Missouri Synod, The American Lutheran Church, and the Lutheran Church in America. After many years of dialogue between the component congregations, pastors, musicians, and theologians, the ILCW was able to publish the *Lutheran Book of Worship* (LBW) in 1978.

The LBW is a complete service book for the church year, lesser festivals and commemorations, prayers of the day, and the complete Psalter and Canticles with plainsong chants. The hymnal itself contains 547 hymns arranged according to The Church Year; The Church at Worship; The Life of Faith; and National Songs. The latter were limited to Samuel F. Smith's "My Country 'Tis of Thee," the anonymous "God Save Our Gracious Queen," and Charles T. Brooks' "God Bless Our Native Land"—all using the NATIONAL ANTHEM (AMERICA) tune; and Daniel C. Roberts' "God of Our Fathers" to the tune NATIONAL HYMN—without the two-measure fanfare introduction.

Richard Hillert served as music editor for the LBW, and Frederick Jachisch served as chairman of the Hymn Music

Committee. This is significant, since the LBW adopted many editorial innovations: (1) no meter signatures or tempo indications; (2) guitar symbols placed above specific hymns approved by the Hymn Music Committee; (3) almost half the hymns edited for unison singing, including many familiar and universal hymns already known in four parts. Many of the hymns have a single vocal line with a great-staff accompaniment; (4) up to four stanzas of text printed between the four-part staves; (5) all hymns in "familiar" English (for example, *Thee* and *Thou* are changed to *I* and *you*, as in "I Love Your Kingdom, Lord"); and (6) much more use is made of early Latin hymns and plainsong melodies—all of which required new translations, arrangements, and accompaniments.

The LBW is, first of all, an accommodation of the joint musical heritage of worship and a fusion of the diverse traditions of hymnody and chant. Fortunately, the bases for effective compromises were already at work in the music practices within the Lutheran Colleges in America. The final solutions were in the hands of such competent musicians as Richard Hillert (twenty-four arrangements), Jan O. Bender (one tune, twelve arrs.), Theodore A. Beck (eight arrs.), Carl Schalk (four tunes, thirty-one arrs.), Leland Sateren (five tunes, six arrs.), Dale Wood (four tunes, six arrs.), and Daniel Moe (two tunes).

The traditional translations of Catherine Winkworth (thirty) and the tunes of Martin Luther (twenty) were to be expected, but the lack of emphasis upon other German composers who are so prominent in other Protestant hymnals was unusual— Franz J. Haydn (two tunes), Johann M. Haydn (one tune), J. S. Bach (two tunes arranged), Robert Schumann (one tune), Beethoven (one tune), and Mendelssohn (three tunes).

The inclusion of a larger number of Scandinavian hymns required more contemporary translations. Notable twentieth-century scholars participating were Gilbert E. Doan (nine), Gracia Grindal (eight), Richard Massie (seven), and Jaroslav Vajda (three texts and six translations). The editors also borrowed heavily from the earlier English translations of the Latin hymns—Robert Bridges (three), Edward Caswall (seven), and John M. Neale (twenty-one). The English hymnists were well represented by Horatius Bonar (five), John Ellerton (five), Frederick Faber (three), Frances R. Havergal (five), Reginald Heber (five), John S. B. Monsell (four), James Montgomery (eight), John Newton (six), Isaac Watts (thirteen), and Charles Wesley (twelve). This use of so many hymns by Watts and Wesley is of particular interest.

The well-known American authors did not receive extensive acceptance, and most of these received only a single entry— George Duffield's "Stand up, Stand up for Jesus"; Harry E. Fosdick's "God of Grace and God of Glory"; Phillips Brooks' "O Little Town of Bethlehem"; William C. Bryant's "Look from Your Sphere of Endless Day"; Joseph H. Gilmore's "He Leadeth Me"; Washington Gladden's "O Master, Let Me Walk with Thee"; Mary A. Lathbury's "Break Thou the Bread of Life"; Samuel Longfellow's "Holy Spirit, Truth Divine"; William P. Merrill's "Not Alone for Mighty Empire"; Ray Palmer's "My Faith Looks up to Thee"; and Ernest W. Shurtleff's "Lead on, O King Eternal." The widely accepted gospel songs were all but eliminated. The one P. P. Bliss setting ("It Is Well with My Soul") had its refrain deleted.

The Negro spiritual is recognized with "Were You There?" (C. Winfred Douglas, Arr.); "Go Tell It on the Mountain" (John W. Work, Jr., Arr.); "Let Us Break Bread Together"; and the tune McKEE, arranged by Harry T. Burleigh and used as the setting for "In Christ There Is No East or West."

The English tunes are not endorsed as strongly as the English texts. Ralph Vaughan Williams leads with six tunes and ten arrangements. Barnby and Dykes follow with five and four respectively, and Sullivan and Maker have three each. The multiple use of tunes is not significant, but John Hatton's DUKE STREET and Rowland Prichard's HYFRYDOL are used with three texts each.

The Lutheran ILCW is effectively establishing their own composers, as has been cited. The other American composers used most are Lowell Mason (4) and William Bradbury (3). An important consideration of the American and English hymns and tunes was based upon the premise that most North American Lutherans no longer regard themselves as transplanted Europeans. The Anglo-American hymn tradition is given, therefore, a rightful and large place. More early American tunes are included than in previous hymnals; fewer late nineteenth century English tunes are included.[17]

Some twenty-six tunes are taken from the nineteenth-century American tune books, and many of these are from *Kentucky Harmony, Southern Harmony,* and *The Sacred Harp.* Originally in three parts (aTb), these tunes have been arranged or reharmonized—sometimes at the expense of the rhythmic or harmonic vitality of the original. Probably the best known of all these tunes at this date is NEW BRITAIN (AMAZING GRACE), using John Newton's text "Amazing Grace, How Sweet the Sound." The original setting in *The Sacred Harp* is in the key of C Major, giving the tenor melody a high g' as the top note. The version used most often in other hymnals is in G Major, giving the soprano melody a d" as the top note—a perfect fourth lower than the original key. The LBW lowers the key to F Major and reharmonizes it. On the positive side, the LBW deleted the anonymous fourth stanza and used Newton's original "The Lord has promised good to me."

Comments on the LBW by Episcopalian James Litton could well be made of other recent denominational hymnals.

> It will be a source of guidance for other future hymnals. It is also a reflection on the church as it finds itself in the late 1970's— aware of its changing and changed worship patterns, concerned about preserving a heritage; trying to recognize, cope with, and relate to the pressures of today's world.[18]

One striking recognition of today's world in the LBW is the inclusion of two worldwide favorites from the Graham crusades, "How Great Thou Art" and "Just As I Am."

10

The All-Purpose Hymnals

The major distributors of church hymnals through the middle of the twentieth century were the independent publishers. These companies produced books which contained songs especially appropriate for the church without professional music leadership—and with music for Worship, Children, Sunday School, Young People, Revivals, Patriotic, Thanksgiving, Christmas, and Mother's Day. The songs were also indexed as solos, duets, quartets, and choruses. These all-purpose hymnals were the church's music library.

A prime example of these books, and one which deserves special consideration, is *The Hymnal, Army and Navy*. Published by the United States Government Printing Office in 1942, it became the official handbook of worship and the musical resource book for all of the United States armed forces in World War II. Designed as an ultimate all-purpose book for Catholic, Jew, and Protestant, its contents were listed as Worship, Praise, Thanksgiving, Out of the Depths, the Magnificat, the Psalter, selected readings from the New Testament, various creeds, and prayers for all major occasions (including a prayer for mother). The copyright is 1941 by the A. S. Barnes and Company, Inc., but all rights were made available to the government without cost.

In the Preface, the editorial committee, chaired by Ivan L. Bennett, expressed the problems and difficulties in compiling such a book and stated the guidelines for the committee: "The Spiritual needs of the Army and Navy, the requirements of the chaplains, and meeting the requirements within the limitations of time, space, and funds available."[19] The task of including everything requested and desirable was impossible, but it was the committee's hope that it would provide the chaplains with the data essential for a fuller "congregational participation in public worship."

The hymn section contains numbers 158-623, with complete indexes, and a separate index of Processionals, Recessionals, and Hymns for Children. The contents of the hymnal comprise the better-known and most-used tunes of all major Protestant groups. Thus, the majority of tunes listed are by the more familiar composers: Joseph Barnby (9); William Bradbury (11); W. H. Doane (9); John B. Dykes (13); Lowell Mason (21); George C. Stebbins (9); Arthur S. Sullivan (8); traditional melodies (28); more than twenty chorales from the Lutheran tradition; and seventeen Negro spirituals, many of which have since been included in many denominational and independent hymnals. Hymns for Children lists twenty-eight; there are thirty-four Christmas carols; two hymns for Mother's Day; and ten solo and choral selections from the familiar sacred works of Beethoven, Fauré, Gounod, Handel, Mendelssohn, and Wagner. *The Hymnal* was easily the most "all-purpose" collection of music ever designed for religious worship and ceremony.

The texts also consist of the standard hymns as well as the more familiar gospel songs. Among the authors, Fanny J. Crosby appears most with fourteen, followed by Isaac Watts with thirteen, and Charles Wesley with twelve. The others which are most prominent are: Frederick Faber (9); Frances R. Havergal (7); Reginald Heber (6); James Montgomery (8); and John M. Neale with eight. The familiar gospel songs extended from Ira D. Sankey's collections to C. Austin Miles' "In the Garden" and George Bennard's "The Old Rugged Cross."

The limitations on the committee were staggering, but *The Hymnal, Army and Navy* became an important seedbed for ecumenical understanding and broadened the hymnic experience of the millions of young men and women who participated in "Divine Services" all over the world.

The lack of denominational hymnals which were available, or acceptable, to the smaller (and musically autonomous) churches in America gave the independent publishers a free hand in the marketplace. After the Sankey publications by Biglow & Main, Chicago publishers were in the center of the most intense evangelical activity in America. With an ear carefully tuned to the needs of the free churches, they became the most active in the field of "all-purpose" hymnals. One of these major companies was the Rodeheaver Company. During Charles Gabriel's tenure as music editor (1912-1932), the company published thirty-five songbooks, eight Sunday School songbooks, seven books for men's choruses, six for ladies' voices, ten children's songbooks, nineteen collections of anthems, and twenty-three cantatas.[20]

A typical Rodeheaver all-purpose hymnal might be *Victory Songs* (n.d.). Published around 1920, it was compiled by Rodeheaver and edited by Gabriel. *Victory Songs* was one of the widely accepted publications "For the Church, Sunday School, and Evangelistic Services." The complete subtitle cataloged the contents under "Church Hymns, Songs for Male Voices, Sunday School Songs, Revival Songs, Children's Songs, Solos and Choruses, and Responsive Readings." Used in the Billy Sunday campaigns, the book met the musical needs (and abilities) of a majority of small churches—especially in areas where the Sunday revivals had been held. It was printed in both round and shaped notes and orchestrated for strings, two clarinets, two cornets, two saxophones, trombone, and piano. It was attractive because local men's quartets had the same music which Rodeheaver used with his huge men's choruses. Also, local church choirs had the same large mixed choruses of the revival choirs, and soloists had the same solos and duets of Homer Rodeheaver and Virginia Asher—especially "The Old Rugged Cross" and "In the Garden." "Church Hymns" provided enough standard songs of worship and praise for the morning services, and the "Revival Songs" supplied the thrust of the evening "Evangelistic" service.

The Rodeheaver Company later acquired the Hall-Mack Company of Philadelphia and moved the corporate headquarters to Winona Lake, Indiana. The company continued with B. D. Ackley and C. Austin Miles as music editors. A long-continuing series of collections entitled *Gospel Solos and Duets*, originally compiled by Y. P. Rodeheaver (Homer's brother) and subtitled "Special Songs for Special Singers," went through many editions and provided much of the literature for the gospel radio and recording artists in the 1930s-1950s—not to mention the countless "specials" in local church services and revival campaigns.

The Rodeheaver Hall-Mack Company was acquired in recent years by Word, Incorporated, of Waco, Texas, and *Gospel Solos and Duets* became a precursor of some fifty-eight solo collections in the 1983 Word catalog. The majority of these published collections are the published music taken from LP or cassette albums featuring top solo artists and concert groups in the field of contemporary popular religious music. The title index of the collections lists more than two thousand song titles. A remnant of the Rodeheaver Hall-Mack acquisition appears as a single "Hymnal" entry, *Church Service Hymns,* an "all-time favorite church hymn book featuring the most popular hymns of the Protestant faith."

A distinct innovation by Word, Inc. is their recent (1983) release of *The Electric Hymnal.* It is being marketed as a kit, containing lyric slides for projection, two loose-leaf copies of the printed music, and one accompaniment cassette with "a full instrumental sound track and illustrated by inspiring multimedia visuals." A brochure advertises it as ideal for Sunday night services, camps, retreats, deaf ministries, retirement centers, outdoor services, and other services.

Hope Publishing Company, another Chicago-area company, issued *Worship and Praise* in 1929 with the subtitle "For Church and Sunday School." It, too, was published in both round and shaped notes and had orchestrations for eleven instruments in eight books. The topical index relates directly to its gospel contents. The "Christ" entries are divided into: Birth, Life and Ministry, Sacrifice, Resurrection, Ascension, and Second Coming. Another index is Choruses-Special, which refers to the short congregational choruses for youth or revival campaigns. The index of Choir Numbers contains the usual choir specials used by revival choirs in the Rodeheaver tradition.

One hymn in the Worship and Praise section is of unusual interest. "The Airman's Hymn," with text by William Runyan and music by George S. Schuler, was written in 1929, just two years after Charles Lindbergh's historic flight. It seems more than coincidental that both writers were associated with Moody Bible Institute, which was located within sight of the "Lindbergh Beacon" atop the YMCA building near downtown Chicago. Henry W. Foote also mentioned an earlier " 'Prayer for Airmen' in 1918"[21] by Kathryn Munro. Again, the date is important because of the exploits of American airmen in World War I. In spite of the unprecedented excitement created by the Lindbergh flight, the airplane never created a popular poetic image for the hymn or gospel songwriters comparable to earlier images from the sea. The advent of space travel has even spawned hymn competitions, but, as of this writing, none has captured the imaginations of the congregations or the gospel soloists.

In 1947 the Hope company published *Hymns of Praise*, edited by F. G. Kingsbury, which contained Hymnic Orders of Service, also known as "Sermons in Song." The topical index included Solos, Temperance, Conflict [the Church militant], Invitation, Heaven (24), Large Choruses (22), and Children's Songs. The breadth and established quality of the contents might be indicated by the large number of copyrights assigned to the Hope Company by Rodeheaver, Hall-Mack, Lorenz, Coleman, and E. O. Excell.

The Tabernacle Publishing Company, also of Chicago, published a series of hymnals entitled *Tabernacle Hymns* which were also printed in both round and shaped notes. When the *Tabernacle Hymns*, Number Three was published in 1936, it, too, was designed as an all-purpose hymnal for "Church and Sunday School." It was basically a collection of the better gospel songs, with a strong emphasis upon Solos and Specials, Invitation, Heaven (18), Children's Songs, and large choral arrangements. The inclusion of several short choruses, dating from 1914-1928, was a distinct feature of the series. When Tabernacle Publishing was later acquired by the Hope Company, the series of hymnals had reached *Tabernacle Hymns*, Number Five, in which the early work of John W. Peterson and Bill and Gloria Gaither appeared. The Hope Catalog (1983) still offers the Tabernacle publications *Hymns of Faith, The Service Hymnal,* and *Tabernacle Hymns,* Numbers Three and Five.

An assimilation of this gospel song tradition into the historic hymnic literature of Protestantism might have begun with Hope's *Worship and Service Hymnal* (1957). However, the all-purpose format still included forty-five "Choir Selections." An effective convergence of these elements might be Hope's *The Singing Church* (1985). This latest from Hope has its contents predetermined by the widespread acceptance and use of a majority of its texts and music. *The Singing Church* contains a large body of historical and traditional hymnody, solos, "choral classics," contemporary literary hymnody, one-line choruses, "Scripture songs," and many new songs already popularized through media exposure. The Foreword simply states that *The Singing Church* contains both old and new paraphrases of Scripture, as well as significant hymns from every period of the church's history. Also included are many new songs growing out of the folk influences of the 1950s and 1960s. These

new examples of popular hymnody began to appear in fresh literary and musical styles, written by such individuals as Ralph Carmichael, William and Gloria Gaither, Andrae Crouch, Kurt Kaiser, Don Wyrtzen, Ken Medema, and Mark Blankenship. Even more recently, we witnessed an explosion of new hymns in more traditional forms by authors in both America and Great Britain—Margaret Clarkson, Bryan Jeffery Leech, Timothy Dudley-Smith, Fred Pratt Green, Brian Wren, Erik Routley and Fred Kaan—a number of them are contained in this book.[22]

A new editorial feature of *The Singing Church* is the addition of a specific verse of Scripture as the basis for each gospel song or hymn. Another is the comprehensive indexing of the contents (fifty pages) into the following categories: Scripture readings; scriptural allusions in each hymn; tunes alphabetical and metrical; authors, composers, and sources; and topical and alphabetical indexes of all hymns. The topical index of the hymnal is: God the Father; Jesus Christ; The Trinity; The Church; The Gospel; The Christian Life; Life Eternal; Special Times and Seasons; and Service Music.

The diversity of the contents of *The Singing Church* requires a ten-page index of authors, composers, and sources, and no period or group of authors or composers constitute a dominant feature. After Charles Wesley's eighteen hymns, Isaac Watts' fourteen, and Fanny J. Crosby's eleven come ten Negro spirituals. After John M. Neale's nine translations and James Montgomery's seven hymns, the authors who drop to six each are: P. P. Bliss, Margaret Clarkson, Timothy Dudley-Smith, William J. Gaither (words and music), Frances R. Havergal, Elisha A. Hoffman, John Newton, John W. Peterson (words and music), and Catherine Winkworth (translations). The point of greatest interest here is that Clarkson, Dudley-Smith, Gaither, and Peterson have contributed almost half of the hymns of this final group, and all are contemporary. Authors with four or five hymns are, for the most part, from the nineteenth or early twentieth centuries: Horatius Bonar, William W. How, Henry F. Lyte, and John G. Whittier—then Americans Ralph Carmichael, Avis M. Christiansen, Andrae Crouch, and Gloria Gaither are all from the middle and late twentieth century. The breadth of sources is further emphasized by the fact that fifty-five authors have only two or three texts, and there are only four Latin text translations. The remaining texts are from authors who contributed only one hymn to the collection. No other American hymnal examined has so much material written by contemporary poets, and no other seems to have dared publish so much new material for congregational worship.

The trend toward a more comprehensive hymnal with music by American composers is particularly noticeable, and the multiple use of hymn tunes is minimal. REGENT SQUARE is used for five texts, and AUSTRIAN HYMN, DIADEMATA, LANCASHIRE, and ST. THOMAS are used with four texts each. After these only twenty-one tunes are used with two or three texts. Among the well-known English and American composers, William J. Kirkpatrick and Lowell Mason have ten settings each; Henry Smart and Ralph Vaughan Williams have nine each; John B. Dykes has eight; William B. Bradbury and W. H. Doane have seven each; P. P. Bliss has six; George Elvey, James McGranahan, John Stainer, and Daniel B. Towner have five each; George C. Stebbins has four; and Joseph Barnby, George F. Handel, and William F. Monk have three each. The use of folk and traditional tunes is extensive, with thirty-three tunes classified as American traditional or from early American tune books; twenty-six tunes are from early English tune books; and twenty-nine are German traditional or from early *Gesangbuchs.*

The trend toward contemporary composers is strong, with thirty-one composers (twenty-one American and ten English) who were active in the twentieth century but died before 1960. Twenty-nine composers (twenty-six American, two English, one Canadian) were living at the date of publication (1985).

Another trend often cited by hymnologists is that contemporary authors write for traditional tunes, and contemporary composers write for traditional texts. *The Singing Church* has highlighted what may be a coming trend—an increase in the number of writers (forty-five) who have created both words and music. These were led in the early years of this century by Alfred H. Ackley, George Bennard, Charles H. Gabriel, Donald S. Marsh, C. Austin Miles, and William M. Runyan. The most prominent among the more recent writers might be Richard K. Avery, Charles F. Brown, Ralph Carmichael, Andrae Crouch, William J. Gaither, Ken Medema, John W. Peterson, and Erik Routley. Although the main themes of most of these writers has been in the area of personal Christian experience, the best efforts of each are the ones included in *The Singing Church.*

The "choral classics" listed are arrangements of Albert Hay Malotte's "The Lord's Prayer," Olive Dungan's "Lord, Make Me an Instrument of Thy Peace," John Stainer's "God So Loved the World," DuBois' "Christ, We Do All Adore Thee," and Peter C. Lutkin's "The Lord Bless You and Keep You." Although continuing, to a degree, the all-purpose hymnal, *The Singing Church* is an exemplary compilation of works from the varied trends which are shaping Protestant worship in the late twentieth century.

Another serious effort by the Hope Publishing Company to promote the literary trends in contemporary hymnody is their *Hymnal Supplement* (1984). This small hymnal was designed to make available to American parishes and schools a number of these [English pastors Fred Pratt Green, Fred Kaan, and Brian Wren] as well as others whose hymns have spread a song heard 'round the world. This includes the contributions of Timothy Dudley-Smith, Malcolm Williamson, Peter Cutts, Tom Colvin, Erik Routley, John Wilson, R. T. Brooks, David G. Wilson, and Michael Baughen, as well as Canada's Margaret Clarkson.[23]

The Americans cited were Richard Avery, Donald Marsh, Alec Wyton, Richard Dirksen, Jane Marshall, Austin Lovelace, M. Lee Suitor, John Ness Beck, and Emma Lou Diemer. This "explosion" of new literary hymns could be the renewal and fusion of Scripture and meaningful contemporary poetry. The most significant factor could well be the return of the clergy to the expression of their theology and Christian experience in a medium for the people to sing. It is only when our Scriptures can be understood in contemporary parables and poetic images that theological truth can become a living congregational worship experience.

Notes

1. Foote, Henry W., *Three Centuries of American Hymnody* (Cambridge: Harvard University Press, 1940), p. 135, citing Dearmer's *Songs of Praise Discussed*, p.5.

2. Ives, Charles E. *Essays Before a Sonata* (New York: The Knickerbocker Press, 1920), p.95.

3. Stevenson, PCMA., p.129.

4. Ibid., p.128.

5. Diehl, Katherine Smith, *Hymns and Tunes—an Index* (New York: The Scarecrow Press, Inc. 1966), p.xx.

6. *The Methodist Hymnal*, Carlton R. Young, Ed. (Nashville: The Methodist Publishing House, 1966), p.v.

7. Personal letter from Carlton R. Young, July 16, 1987.

8. *The Hymnal*, Clarence Dickinson, Ed. (Philadelphia: Presbyterian Board of Christian Education, 1933) p.iii.

9. *The Hymnbook*, David Hugh Jones, Ed. (Philadelphia: John Ribble, Publishing Agent, 1955), p.5.

10. *Baptist Hymnal*, W. Hines Sims, Ed. (Nashville: Convention Press, 1956), p.v.

11. *Baptist Hymnal,* William J. Reynolds, Ed. (Nashville: Convention Press, 1975), p.viii.

12. Reynolds, William J., "10 Years Later, Reynolds Pleased with Hymnal." Ft. Worth: *Southwestern News,* John Earl Seelig, Ed., April, 1985, Vol. 43, No.8., p.5.

13. *The New Hymnal* of the Protestant Episcopal Church. Cortland Whitehead, Chairman of the Joint Commission (New York: The Church Pension Fund, The H. W. Gray Co., 1916), p.v.

14. *The Hymnal* of the Protestant Episcopal Church in the U.S.A., Bishop Henry Judah Mikell, Chairman of the Joint Commission (New York: The Church Pension Fund, 1940), p.iii.

15. Ibid., p.v.

16. *The Lutheran Hymnal,* The Evangelical Lutheran Synodical Conference of North America (St. Louis: Concordia Publishing House, 1941), p.2.

17. *Lutheran Book of Worship,* Inter-Lutheran Commission on Worship, Eugene Brand, Director (Minneapolis: Augsburg Publishing House, 1978), p.8.

18. Litton, James, "An Episcopalian Looks at the *The Lutheran Book of Worship*," *Church Music,* Carl Schalk, Ed. (St. Louis: Concordia Publishing House, 1979), p.93.

19. *The Hymnal, Army and Navy.* Ivan L. Bennett, Ed. (Washington: U.S. Government Printing Office, 1941), p.3.

20. Reynolds, William J., *Hymns of Our Faith* (Nashville: Broadman Press, 1964), p.295.

21. Foote, Henry W., "Recent American Hymnody," *The Papers of the Hymn Society of America,* Lindsay B. Longacre, Ed. (New York: The Hymn Society of America, 1952), p.4.

22. *The Singing Church,* no ed. (Carol Stream, Ill.: Hope Publishing Company, 1985), p.2.

23. *Hymnal Supplement,* no ed. (Carol Stream, Ill.: Agape, 1984), p.3.

Part IV:

Mass Communications

11

Radio

It is not possible to comprehend the rapid transitions in church music during the second quarter of this century apart from the world's most revolutionary advance in communications—radio. A new song could be in the ears of America before the ink was dry on the manuscript. It was an instrument of instant distribution of communal musical styles and performance practices. After the first radio broadcast of the Harding-Cox election returns by the Westinghouse station KDKA, Pittsburgh, November 2, 1920, other electric firms quickly followed suit. At the end of 1921 eight stations were operating in New York, New Jersey, Massachusetts, Chicago, and Los Angeles. The construction of home receiving sets began a "boom" in 1921-22, which was followed by a huge increase in transmitting stations.

> By Nov. 1, 1922, 564 broadcast stations had been licensed to operate. A classification made in Feb. 1923 showed that about half the stations licensed up to that time were associated with radio or electrical concerns. Next in importance came educational and religious institutions, newspapers and publications and department stores.[1]

The educational possibilities of the "radiophone," however, were paramount in the mind of David Sarnoff in 1922 as he already envisioned a National Broadcasting Company network as a nonprofit organization financed by annual contributions of 2 percent of the gross incomes from the sales of radio equipment. As late as 1929 Owen D. Young affirmed that NBC's aim had never been to make money. Publicly owned radio was

140

another early option which the City of New York chose (WNYC) as a public-service gesture to its citizens. The rapid growth of the industry is best emphasized by an excerpt from a speech by Secretary of Commerce Herbert Hoover in October 1924:

> 534 stations are in operation, making radio available to every home in the country. The sales of radio apparatus have increased from a million dollars a year to a million dollars a day, . . . and the radio audience probably exceeds 20 millions.[2]

This pressure of increasing requests for the licensing of broadcasting stations was not brought under control until the Radio Act of 1927, which established the Federal Radio Commission, with members to be appointed by the President. The NBC network was established in 1926, and CBS followed in 1927. From this point the sponsored program and the commercial potential of radio became dominant. As the networks grew locally produced programs became less profitable, because the network revenues were passed down proportionately to each affiliated station. By 1948, 60 percent of all radio advertising revenues were derived from these national and regional advertisers. "Of one great network's total advertising revenues, 37.5% came from six sponsors."[3]

The early appeal of radio to religious institutions and churches constituted a biblical missionary mandate: "And this gospel of the kingdom shall be preached in all the world for a witness to all nations" (Matt. 24:14). Radio was viewed as the instrument of literal fulfillment of this prophecy, and when WLW, Cincinnati increased its power in 1934 to half-a-million watts, their responses from around the world were verification of the prophetic possibility.

In the early years religious programming was local, for the most part, and utilized local talent of all kinds. Probably typical of most stations was WSB, Atlanta, the South's first station. In March 1922 "it was thrilling to tune in to three essays read by Girl Scouts, a five-minute talk on applied psychology, or a performer playing a saw with a violin bow."[4] The *Atlanta Journal* was the original owner of WSB, but both were sold to James M. Cox in 1939—the same Cox whose defeat for the presidency was reported on the first radio broadcast from KDKA in 1920. In addition to the original license to broadcast news and entertainment, WSB went in heavily for "Sabbath sermonizing."

> The Baptists and the Methodists refused an offer to have their services broadcast, as they didn't want a microphone defiling their pulpits. But, Dr. J. Sproles Lyon, pastor of the First Presbyterian Church, saw the possibilities in the new medium and quickly agreed. As a result, WSB became the first station in the nation to present a complete church service on Easter Sunday, 1922.[5]

Other commercial stations were soon broadcasting both morning and evening services until the prime-time offerings of the new networks became more attractive financially. Daytime reception was then limited to morning services from nearby stations.

After the networks took over the prime afternoon and evening periods, the local stations retained control of the morning and late-night hours. With an eye toward local sponsors, a popular feature of local programming was the gospel quartet. Until the 1950s, a regional or local quartet often appeared daily as a morning or noontime program. Some the favorites featured by these quartets included: "Farther Along," "Precious Lord, Take My Hand," "Royal Telephone," "Will the Circle Be Unbroken?," "A Closer Walk with Thee," "Precious Memories," and "Peace in the Valley."

The early educational/religious stations had distinct purposes. In some cases they had endowments or financial support from direct contributions or the sale of music or religious books. James D. Vaughan's station WOAN (Tennessee's first) sold gospel music, maintained its own eleven-piece band, and provided news of gospel music and musicians. A more distinct pioneer in religious broadcasting was WMBI (Moody Bible Institute) of Chicago. Located in a prime commercial area, the station had to share time and broadcast frequencies with other stations. When the Radio Act of 1927 was passed,

> there were 733 stations licensed under the old law, and these stations had to be accommodated on 89 wave channels. To make

the problem more complex, several hundred applications were on file to erect new stations.[6]

The program logs of WMBI in 1927 show Bible Reading, Family Worship, Organ Music, Hymns, Telephone Requests, and lots of "Music." A unique offering was a "Radio School of the Bible"— one of the early attempts at teaching a formal class via radio. The music programmed was largely a continuation of the Sankey and Rodeheaver literature, but also utilized a large body of new songs being issued by the Chicago publishers. The textual emphasis remained upon the personal religious experience, but within a context of theological and scriptural validity. As the middle of the century approached, the programs broadened to include a broader spectrum of standard hymns, anthems, and oratorios.

The major networks presented programs which featured church music rather than preaching or morning worship services. During the 1920s and 1930s, "Smilin' Ed McConnell," singing hymns and gospel songs and playing his own accompaniments on the piano, was almost typical. In the 1940s, E. Power Biggs presented live organ concerts each Sunday morning and featured classical, romantic, and contemporary organ music. Biggs introduced the concerts with his own arrangement of J. S. Bach's "Sheep May Safely Graze." Complete oratorios were often presented in the 1940s and 1950s by the New York Philharmonic and the NBC Symphony and featured the Westminster Choir under John Finley Williamson or the Robert Shaw Chorale.

The longest ongoing network program featuring traditional church music has been "Music and the Spoken Word," produced by the Mormon Tabernacle Choir since 1929 and sponsored by CBS since 1932. Its direct influence upon church music in America has been strong and continuous. These broadcasts were created, written, and announced by Richard L. Evans for forty-one consecutive years (1930-1971), "without vacations, without ghost writers."[7] His opening announcement, "Once again we welcome you within these walls with music and the spoken word from the crossroads of the West," and his sign-off, "Again we leave you within the shadows of the ever-lasting hills. May peace be with you, this day and always" remain to this day in the voice of J. Spencer Kinard. Although the voice has changed, the style and format also remain—announcing the organ solos and the choir numbers, with a three-minute nonsectarian message in between.

The story of the musical concerts originating from the Mormon Tabernacle should rightfully begin with the organ. The first organ was built by Joseph H. Ridges, an English cabinet-maker who had gone to Australia to prospect for gold, but came to America after his conversion to Mormonism. This first organ, built in Australia, was shipped to America in 1857. It was then hauled by wagons from San Bernardino, California, to Salt Lake City and installed in the old adobe tabernacle. Brigham Young then asked Ridges to build a new organ and install it in the new tabernacle under construction. Both the new tracker organ (32 ranks) and the new tabernacle were completed in 1867. The organ was rebuilt by the Kimball Organ Company in 1901, and a tubular-pneumatic action was installed, allowing the console to be detached and moved some fifty feet from the organ chamber. After the installation was completed, organist John J. McClellan began giving daily concerts for the public, featuring the organ works of J. S. Bach, Mendelssohn, orchestral transcriptions, and popular favorites of the period.

The organ was again rebuilt and serviced regularly by the Austin Organ Company in 1926 and 1940. They installed a new electro-pneumatic action, dependable wind chests, thirty-three additional stops, and a four-manual console with pedal board. In 1945 the Aeolian-Skinner Company was asked to redesign the organ, under the direction of G. Donald Harrison, and in consultation with the Tabernacle organist, Alexander Schreiner. The new organ incorporated the classic elements of Baroque design, which were being rediscovered in the writings of the eighteenth-century builders. The result was "an American classic organ, with tonal resources appropriate to virtually every type of music. The Tabernacle organ is a unique instrument and may well be his [Harrison's] masterpiece."[8] The organ contains eleven thousand pipes, comprising 188 stops, and a console of five manuals and pedals.

After McClellan, the organist responsible for the musical tradition already established at the Tabernacle was Edward P. Kimball, a student of McClellan who became his assistant in 1905 and later accompanied the first radio broadcast in 1929. Two other young organists, Frank Asper and Alexander Schreiner, were appointed in 1925. This new team would "launch the historic series of radio network broadcasts which would make the music of the Tabernacle Choir and organ accessible to virtually every home in the United States."[9] Asper studied in Germany and the New England Conservatory. Schreiner was German-born, but did his advanced study in France, under Widor and Vierne. In addition to their work with the choir, they performed thousands of recitals, did many solo radio broadcasts, published volumes of organ music, wrote many hymns, helped produce the *Latter-Day Saints Hymnal*, recorded many albums of organ music, and helped produce the first stereophonic recordings. Asper and Schreiner alternated the traditional daily recitals, the choir rehearsals, and the broadcasts.

At the turn of the century, the Mormon Tabernacle Choir had already gone from regional to national prominence under the leadership of Evan Stephens. They had toured America's major cities, won choral competitions, and made some early recordings for the Columbia Phonograph Company in 1910 using the "acoustical process" developed by Thomas A. Edison. After Stephens' retirement, Anthony C. Lund became the Choir's first Utah-born director. Lund made the first "electrical" recording of the Choir in 1927 for Victor and launched the unprecedented radio broadcasts in 1929. After Lund's death in 1935, J. Spencer Cornwall was appointed as the Choir's tenth director. This team of Cornwall, Richard Evans, Frank Asper, and Alexander Schreiner was to become familiar to every music-loving household in America.

J. Spencer Cornwall brought to his directorship wide experience in public-school music and was supervisor of music in the Salt Lake City school system. He also brought a fresh approach to programming, which included the first Negro spiritual. He continued to attend music clinics in the summer, particularly those of F. Melius Christiansen. These afforded a working acquaintance with other choir directors from colleges, high schools, and churches from all over America. He worked constantly to improve the quality of the Choir's performances, to broaden the repertoire, and to develop a choral library of more than 950 compositions.

Their most devoted audience, however, came from their recordings. These ranked among the highest in sales in the field of classical music. They were among the first to record on the new LP records, and with the Philadelphia Orchestra they produced the first high-fidelity, multiple-track stereophonic recording. The first demonstration of this sound system was given at Carnegie Hall in April 1940. The writer was overwhelmed a short time later by the same demonstration in the Eastman Theater in Rochester, New York. The Choir remained a continuing reflection of the vision and musicianship of J. Spencer Cornwall until his retirement in 1957.

The current staff of the Mormon Tabernacle Choir is Mormon-born, and they represent a harvest of their own musical heritage. All have earned doctorates in music from the Eastman School of Music, Brigham Young University, or the University of Oregon. John Longhurst has his D.M.A. under David Craighead at Eastman; organist Robert Cundick has a Ph.D. in composition under Leroy J. Robertson at Brigham Young; and Jerold Ottley, who was named director of the Choir in 1975, earned his doctorate at the University of Oregon.

Like Cornwall, Dr. Ottley brought his experience as a music educator and a member of the faculty at the University of Utah. His background as a music educator quickly brought a renewed emphasis upon the refinement of the choral sound, primarily through small vocal workshops taught by Mrs. JoAnn Ottley. He also brought an emphasis upon basic musicianship and an expansion of the repertoire in two directions—the performance and recording of lighter excerpts from the American musical theater, and a new emphasis upon more contemporary choral works by major American composers. The new staff has established itself through effective leadership, musicianship, and a harmony of spirit. All of this is apparent since the new dimension of television has been added. The visual impact of the massive performances portrays vividly the depth of spirit in "Music and the Spoken Word."

No major denomination grasped the potential of a radio ministry as quickly and as well as the Lutheran Church, Missouri Synod. When their Concordia Seminary moved to an entirely new campus in 1926, the faculty and students enjoyed an academic utopia of Tudor-Gothic buildings overlooking a beautiful wooded area of suburban St. Louis. In May 1927, the Seminary's radio station KFUO (Forward, Upward, Onward) also moved into a new building with four studios and reception and control rooms and was completed as an outright gift from the Lutheran Layman's League. The new quarters, with its twin-towers antenna, was the fulfillment of a dream by a Concordia professor of Old Testament with a Ph.D. (1929) in Semitics from Harvard, Walter A. Maier. Thousands gathered for the dedication, and in Maier's principal address, he said:

> In our church today only the towers transmit the Christian message on a regular basis. God grant that this is only the beginning, that some day many other such spires of steel may radiate Christ even as structurally they point to heaven.[10]

As early as 1923 Maier had alerted his church to radio's potential, and the new KFUO transmitter would fuel his dream of a coast-to-coast "Lutheran Radio Hour" on one of the newly formed networks of NBC or CBS. After discussing this possibility with his colleagues on the radio committee of KFUO in the fall of 1929, the committee resolved that "Dean Fritz and Dr. Maier confer in person with the officials of the various networks at New York for the purpose of having Lutheran religious radio programs broadcast over the chains."[11]

At that time NBC was already donating time for religious broadcasts to Protestants, Catholics, and Jews. The Protestant programs were sponsored by the Federal Council of Churches and featured S. Parkes Cadman and Harry Emerson Fosdick. Further, as a matter of policy, NBC would not schedule religious programs on a commercial basis. CBS was still accepting paid religious programs, but the cost was forty-five hundred dollars for a thirty-minute program over a network of thirty-two cities. The radio committee of KFUO decided in April 1930 to opt for a half-year of weekly programs and to turn again to the Lutheran Layman's League for help. At the convention of the LLL in May 1930, the League adopted a resolution "to sponsor a national Lutheran Radio Hour over the Columbia Broadcasting System beginning in the fall,"[12] with Walter A. Maier as speaker.

The broadcasts were scheduled for Thursday evenings at 10:00, Eastern Time and were to premiere on October 2, 1930, from station WHK in Cleveland. This was arranged "so that the Cleveland Bach Chorus could provide Lutheranism's finest music for the occasion."[13] When cued "On the Air," director F. W. Strieter and the chorus responded with "A Mighty Fortress," and David Ross, the CBS announcer, superimposed "The Lutheran Hour—Bringing Christ to the Nation from Coast to Coast." The chorus also presented chorales from Bach's *Mass in B Minor* and *St. John Passion*. The sermon was appropriate for the deepening depression, with its agnosticism and a popular movement toward atheism.

After only two months on the air, Dr. Maier and the LLL were receiving more mail than most of radio's top secular shows and more than any other religious program. At the conclusion of the series in June 1931, CBS had "received more letters at its New York headquarters concerning the Lutheran Hour than in response to any other network program."[14] In spite of this tremendous response, the depression forced the LLL to discontinue the contract in the fall of 1931.

During the next three and one-half years, Dr. Maier was a frequent guest speaker on "The Lutheran Hour of Faith and Fellowship," over a seven-station network in Michigan and Indiana. Sponsored by the Detroit Lutheran Pastoral Conference, the Detroit Radio Committee was determined to resume the national "Lutheran Hour" with Dr. Maier as speaker, this time over the new Mutual network. The LLL added their support to the plan. The need for immediate cash to underwrite the contracts was guaranteed by William S. Knudsen, president of the Chevrolet Division of the General Motors Corporation. The broadcasts would also originate from Knudsen's own Epiphany Church in Detroit.

The second series of the national "Lutheran Hour" was aired on February 10, 1935, with the following format:

Opening Chimes and Organ—Mr. Carl Munzel
Announcement—Brace Beemer [the original "Lone Ranger"]
"Beautiful Savior"—Detroit Bach Chorus, Prof. Eduard Ossko,
    Director
Prayer—Dr. Walter Maier
Chorale—Bach Chorus
Address—"Comfort for a Critical Day"—Dr. Maier
Chorale—Bach Chorus
The Fellowship Period—Pastor Edward H. Bucheimer
The Lord's Prayer
The Closing Theme [Beautiful Savior] and Station Announce-
    ment—Chorus and Brace Beemer[15]

After a successful season, the LLL decided to sponsor another series (1935-1936), using part of the Mutual Network. It would consist of one shortwave station and nine AM stations, with powerful WLW, Cincinnati as the central control station. The actual broadcast, however, could originate from the studios of KFUO on the campus of Concordia Seminary. Studios B and C were used by Dr. Maier and Reinhold Janetzke, the announcer. The Concordia Chapel was to be used by the Seminary Lutheran Hour Chorus. The new series was announced as "The Lutheran Hour—Bringing Christ to the Nation!" The chorus signed on with "A Mighty Fortress," which would thereafter be the theme of "The Lutheran Hour."

The fourth season opened with thirty-one stations, which included Denver and nine California stations. There was no way to accurately estimate the listening audience, but the LLL received 90,000 cards and letters during the season. The outlets doubled the next year (1937-1938) to sixty-two, and the mail increased to 125,000. The network now included the South and the far Northwest. Half of the budget came from individual contributions, and the other half from church congregations and societies within the Lutheran Church.

The 1939-1940 series was launched amid war in Europe and a rapid buildup of American forces as a backdrop. A major technical advance was the "electrical transcription," which was high in fidelity and could be mailed out to independent stations to be aired at their convenience. This added seventy-two outlets for a total of 171 stations. With the United States almost saturated, the "Lutheran Hour" now looked to international outlets. This had been the dream of Dr. Maier from the very first. The door opened when Clarence W. Jones, director of the "Voice of the Andes," station HCJB in Quito, Ecuador, offered their facilities for English and Spanish broadcasts of the "Lutheran Hour." "Thus the Hour's foreign program department was born, and Spanish became the first of fifty-nine languages in which the broadcast was eventually aired."[16] The sign-on was officially changed to "Bringing Christ to the *Nations,*" and fifty-two more foreign stations joined the international network. The total number for the season reached 346; the letters exceeded a quarter million; and the weekly audience was estimated at ten million.

The most dramatic increases came during World War II and the early postwar years. As of 1950 quantities of mail arrived from 120 countries and territories, and the broadcasts were originating in 55 of these lands in thirty-six languages. Counting the transcription outlets, "the enterprise now embraced 1,236 stations."[17] The budget had also increased to an annual $1.5 million.

The war itself became a factor in the world outreach of the "Lutheran Hour." The electrical transcriptions were mailed to more than a hundred major American military installations for their local use, as well as to the fifty- and hundred-watt radio transmitters which served large concentrations of troops overseas. It was perhaps a prophetic coincidence that at 7:30 AM on the morning of December 7, 1941, the "Lutheran Hour" was broadcast over KGMB, Honolulu. It was being heard by many servicemen aboard ships and in Scofield Barracks. After "A Mighty Fortress," Dr. Maier began: "In a critical moment like the present, when our country gropes on the jagged edge of long protracted warfare. . . ."[18] As the "Amen" concluded the program, the "infamy" of Pearl Harbor was beginning.

As "A Mighty Fortress" became the familiar symbol of "The Lutheran Hour" in many countries, it was banned by Hitler and became a symbol of resistance in Europe. The impact of the great hymn was demonstrated on the occasion of President Franklin D. Roosevelt's death in April 1945. The famed Forty-fifth Infantry Division was moving through Southern Germany. As Chaplain William E. King reported to me, he received orders to halt the advance long enough to hold a brief memorial service for their Commander in Chief. They came into the city of Miesbach, which offered no resistance. The German S.S. troops had already moved out, but not before warning the natives of the brutality of the American troops. The streets were empty. The civilians were locked inside their houses. Colonel King located the mayor and asked to use the empty church for the brief memorial service—which included the singing of "A Mighty Fortress." As the service ended, a young soldier hurried to report to the chaplain that the church was surrounded by the civilian population. As King went outside to confront the people, the mayor came forward, extended his hand, and welcomed the Forty-fifth Division to their city, saying they feared nothing from an army that sang their "Mighty Fortress." The hymn had been forbidden by Hitler for years—and had just conquered a city!

Throughout this long period of growth, the format of the "Lutheran Hour" changed very little. The most familiar sound was the male chorus, made up of Concordia Seminary students. Their spirited performance of the opening theme was, to a great degree, responsible for its tune EIN' FESTE BURG being the best-known and possibly the most-published hymn tune in the world. No less Lutheran and almost equally well known was the hymn "Beautiful Savior," which was used by F. Melius Christiansen and his St. Olaf's Choir for two generations and became one of the most-performed a cappella arrangements of any hymn in the English language. The St. Louis A Cappella Choir, under the direction of Dr. William B. Heyne, brought the musical heritage of the Lutherans to the attention of all Evangelicals. And the "Lutheran Hour" Chorus, directed by E. W. Schroeter, made many of the chorales a familiar element of Christian worship throughout the world. The "Lutheran Hour" used music as Martin Luther envisioned it—the handmaiden of theology.

After Dr. Maier's death in 1950, the "Lutheran Hour" continued in its best traditions. In recent years, the choirs from many Lutheran colleges have been featured, but always in the traditional program format. These college choirs have brought a highly professional quality to the music. They, too, have featured the chorale, but have added the best of the historical music literature of the church. They have also brought into focus many fine choral works by contemporary American composers. In a 1985 broadcast they used the Negro spiritual "Balm in Gilead" and a Virgil Thomson arrangement of a Southern folk hymn—adding a living continuity to "Bringing Christ to the Nations."

As of this writing, the "Lutheran Hour" is carried by almost 1,300 radio stations. Special Easter and Christmas radio series are carried by an additional 350 stations. The current speakers are Dr. Oswald Hoffman (a student of Dr. Maier) and Wallace R. Schultz.[19]

Television was adopted early by the LLL, and they have sponsored a regular series, "This Is the Life." Their Christmas and Easter specials are carried by almost one hundred TV stations. "Yeshua," a five-hour miniseries, was produced in 1984 and aired over the CBN cable network. "The series uses art, archaeology, drama, music, and interesting narration to tell the story of Jesus' life, death, and resurrection."[20] A distinct musical development took place in a 1982 Easter special, "The Crosswalk," that featured "contemporary Christian music." Using the music of well-known Christian pop artists, "Crosswalk" has become a "leader in the field of syndicated Christian radio music programs. . . . 'Crosswalk' is heard on more than 300 stations throughout the United States and Canada."[21] A special television feature for children, "Easter Is" stars the cartoon character Benji and his dog Waldo and is in its eleventh year. It is currently booked by sixty TV stations.

After the major radio networks were established and electrical transcriptions were developed, a nationwide radio ministry became possible without the aid of a denominational sponsor. The most immediate appeal was to the evangelists, and none was more successful in radio evangelism than Charles E. Fuller. "The Old Fashioned Revival Hour" came as an outgrowth of his affiliation with the Bible Institute of Los Angeles (BIOLA), which owned KTBI, one of the earliest radio stations in the Los Angeles area. As chairman of the board of trustees at BIOLA until 1931, Fuller had already become aware of radio's potential as a teaching and preaching medium. His early experience in broadcasting was the live broadcasts of his morning and evening services over KGER from Calvary Church in Long Beach. Other early broadcasts by Fuller included a Radio Bible Class over a western network of CBS and a Sunday School Hour on Saturday evenings over KFI, Los Angeles. To support these latter broadcasts, a nonprofit organization called the Gospel Broadcasting Association was organized in a meeting at BIOLA in May, 1933. The board consisted of prominent business and professional men and included Dr. Stewart McLennan, pastor of the First Presbyterian Church of Hollywood. The GBA retained office space on the eighth floor of the BIOLA building.

In 1934 the GBA arranged a one-hour "Heart to Heart Hour" on Sunday evenings over KNX, Hollywood. Harold Alexander, the singing circuit rider, led the singing. The plan was to have a live audience and to originate from the one-thousand-seat auditorium in the Women's Club on Hollywood Boulevard. The advanced publicity announced plans for an "Old Fashioned Revival." The attendance was so poor, however, the program was moved to the KNX studio and was called "The Radio Revival Hour."[22] With the move into the studio, a choir became necessary, so the choir of the Fountain Avenue Baptist Church volunteered their services. A Mr. Miller directed the choir, but people were still invited to attend and participate in the live broadcast.

In June 1936 KNX came under CBS management and followed the network's policy of no "paid" religious broadcasts. Fuller promptly changed to the new "electrical transcriptions," which he began mailing out to a growing network of independent radio stations. In order to solicit new stations, Fuller flew to major cities during the week for mass meetings, then returned to Hollywood for the Sunday recording sessions.

Late that same year (1936) the Mutual Broadcasting System was formed, and the GBA was able to get on the new network in January 1937. The program was scheduled on Sundays and the network extended as far as Chicago. In October the network was extended to the East Coast, and included thirty stations. At this point, the name was changed to "The Old Fashioned Revival Hour," and Fuller invited the Goose Creek Quartet and their pianist, Rudy Atwood, of "The Country Church of Hollywood" to join the music staff. The quartet became an integral part of the musical format, and Atwood's gospel piano playing became the role model for all revival pianists who heard him. His recorded hymn improvisations are still available and are heard often on hymn and gospel radio programs. With the live network program, Leland Green was asked to assemble and direct a professional choir, and George Broadbent was at the newly developed electric organ. Atwood and Green were both graduates of BIOLA. Green took graduate degrees at the University of Southern California, directed high school choirs at Garden Grove, and became music supervisor in the public schools of Pasadena. Both Atwood and Green remained with "The Old Fashioned Revival Hour" until after Charles Fuller's death in 1968.

The Mutual network continued to expand. At the end of 1938 the total had reached 128 stations. One year later, the total was 152, and "The Old Fashioned Revival Hour" had an estimated weekly audience of ten million.[23] As Mutual continued to expand, the GBA kept contracting for the entire network, which reached 456 stations in the fall of 1942.

Another major change took place in 1939. A group of friends in Long Beach asked the GBA to use their municipal auditorium in order to have a larger live audience for the broadcast. Originally, they used the small downstairs hall (a thousand seats); but as the war erupted, it became necessary for them to move into the main auditorium in 1944. The Long Beach Memorial Auditorium thus became the home of "The Old Fashioned Revival Hour" for the next twenty years.

The theme song "Jesus Saves," sung by the choir and audience, gave a live "presence" to the broadcast. The quartet and the solos by Leland Green satisfied the interest in "special music," and the piano artistry of Rudy Atwood was a constant musical highlight. When Fuller travelled to cities for his mass meetings, Atwood was always a main attraction. Because of the audience reaction to Fuller's solo introduction of the chorus "Heavenly Sunshine" (a text variation on the refrain to H. J. Zelly's gospel song, "Heavenly Sunlight"), Fuller's version became a theme of "The Old-Fashioned Revival Hour." It also became a favorite among evangelical congregations all over America.

"The Old Fashioned Revival Hour" contributed little that was new or constant in American Protestant church music. However, its timely appearance during the most stressful period of the century (the Great Depression and World War II) reaffirmed the distinctiveness of the American gospel song and its preeminence in the musical life of the evangelical Christian. Charles Fuller removed any doubts about the vitality of revivalism in America, and the donations made through the GBA provided the funding for a major conservative theological seminary in California which bears his name. "The Old Fashioned Revival Hour" also provided the basic organizational structure for the various "electronic churches" which began to flourish after the war and prepared the way for the most far-reaching and widely received evangelistic efforts in the history of Christianity—the Billy Graham crusades.

The thrust of independent network radio remains a major element of religious broadcasting. Denominational "Hours" quickly followed the lead of the Lutherans, with local stations opting for transcriptions, then later for tapes to be broadcast on Sundays—often as a public service during early morning hours or late evening. A typical one might be "The Baptist Hour," which began in 1941. The original format which ran for many years was a miniature morning worship service, complete with a small professional choir singing special hymn arrangements, an anthem, a frequent solo, and a short sermon by one of the denomination's prominent pastors. The Baptist support for this new radio ministry was rapidly expanded when the Radio Committee of 1941 became the Radio Commission of the Southern Baptist Convention in 1946, then the Radio and Television Commission in 1953. The headquarters was moved from Atlanta to Fort Worth in 1955, and an international communications center, with state-of-the-art audio and video recording studios, was completed in 1965. The special hymn arrangements and anthems heard on "The Baptist Hour" became standard repertoire in many denominations throughout the listening areas.

In the 1960s, the programming was directed toward diversification. Two new programs, "Master Control" and "Country Crossroads," were designed in a magazine format, with an initial sign-on and content not unlike a secular program. "Country Crossroads" features an interview with a top country-and-western guest musician, who gives a personal Christian testimony as a climax to the show. Other specialized radio programs were designed for children, teenagers, athletes, and the black community. "By 1969, they [Southern Baptists] were originating a broadcast somewhere in the world on the average of every three minutes."[24]

"The Baptist Hour" and "Country Crossroads" are, at this writing, still prominent releases on Sunday radio. "Country Crossroads" maintains its original format, with celebrity interviews and personal testimonies. "The Baptist Hour" has now introduced the informal conversation of a magazine format and has added personal counseling by correspondence, special prayer requests, and a free gift to all who write in. The music is now provided by a special men's chorus called "The Singing Churchmen," composed of ministers of music from Baptist churches; an "Alleluia" signature with orchestra and chorus, and using the "Ode to Joy" theme from Beethoven's Ninth Symphony; and many recordings of popular contemporary gospel artists. The thrust remains basically evangelistic, but the sermons are more often directed toward the conflicts of contemporary Christian life.

12

Television

Radio has been almost relegated to the local audience, since the emergence in the 1960s and 1970s of television as the primary medium for the "electronic church." The video recordings developed so rapidly that magnetic videotapes could be distributed as readily as the old electrical transcriptions and audiotapes of the 1940s and 1950s. Early television was limited almost entirely to local live telecasts of the morning worship services. The technology of the videotape transformed America's living rooms into a visual sanctuary of the electronic church.

Billy Graham and Oral Roberts pioneered the field, and each had his own distinct visions and techniques for attracting financial support from the multitudes who joined their television congregations. Graham's early use of the live crusade as the format for his television ministry remains to this day. Originally conceived as a promotional device, a crusade was filmed, then, after editing, the films became the format for a one-hour television replay of a recent crusade. However, one of the most appealing elements for the live audience (and the television congregation) was practically eliminated in favor of the celebrity soloists and testimonies—that is, the congregational singing and the choir specials.

Oral Roberts used the appeal of the faith healer in a revival tent in 1954. His success at media healing and fund raising were so phenomenal that by 1969 he had built Oral Roberts University and was originating his television ministries from a completely modern television studio on campus. He, too, had a continuous flow of celebrity guests, and a musical format designed, written, and orchestrated by the best writers in the field of contemporary gospel.

The major influence upon general church music in the twentieth century by the Graham and Roberts television ministries has been limited to solo gospel literature, the standardization of a few congregational hymns, and the choral collections edited by Cliff Barrows, which have been cited earlier. The main thrust of these television music programs has been to attract and hold listeners rather than establishing guidelines for worship in the local church. This normally reduces the musical format to its commercial common denominator—the new and fresh and/or the favored familiar. Some of their followers, however, have been more successful in their efforts to create a sanctuary in the living room, as well as eliciting the financial support necessary for its sustenance.

One of the earliest and most successful to launch such a concept was Rex Humbard of Akron, Ohio. In 1952 Humbard founded a church with the specific goal of broadcasting the services on radio and television.

> Starting on an Akron TV station, the weekly televised service was financed primarily by the membership of the new church as a ministry to those who, because of age or illness, could not attend a church service. Today [1979] . . . the Akron church has become the "Cathedral of Tomorrow," with several thousand members, ten pastors, choirs and musical groups in profusion, Bible studies, and specialized ministries.[25]

The building seats five thousand and was designed to meet the technical needs of television. Its stage area is large enough to accommodate television crews, choirs, orchestra, and members of the Humbard family who participate in the service. In this setting, Humbard successfully assumes the role of "your TV pastor," and a communion service is held annually with the television audience participating in their own living rooms.

Another television pastor who has been successful at creating a living-room sanctuary is Jerry Falwell, who attributes his conversion to the "Old Fashioned Revival Hour" of Charles Fuller. Falwell's ministry originates from the Thomas Road Baptist Church (and Liberty Baptist College) in Lynchburg, Virginia and is termed the "Old Time Gospel Hour." The music features revival hymns by the congregation, solo and choir specials, and a sermon—all originating from the church sanctuary. The scenario, plus his personal directness and authoritative style, creates a pastoral atmosphere. It has, at the same time, catapulted him into a position as spokesman and leader of the "Moral Majority" political movement. The music is both traditional and contemporary gospel, utilizing well the musical resources of the college students.

A sharp contrast to any of the other major television ministers is Robert Schuller, who, in a 1986 conversation on camera with Billy Graham, related his own commitment to Christ in one of Graham's early crusades. The most pronounced influence upon his life and ministry through the "Hour of Power," however, was Norman Vincent Peale and his book *The Power of Positive Thinking.* Schuller, like Peale, is a member of the Reformed Church in America.

Sent by his denomination to Southern California in 1955 to build a congregation, Schuller rented a drive-in theater in Garden Grove for ten dollars a week, held services in the first drive-in church, and urged people to "come as you are, pray in the family car."[26] In June 1957, Peale made a guest appearance at the "open-air church" and became the role model for Schuller's ministry of Christian optimism through "Possibility Thinking." His creed: "When faced with a mountain, I will not quit. I will keep on striving until I climb over, find a pass through, tunnel underneath or simply stay and turn the mountain into a gold mine, with God's help."

The "Hour of Power," launched in 1970, is "now aired (at a cost of about $8 million last year, according to church officials) on some 190 TV stations in the United States, Canada, and Australia, as well as the United States Armed Forces Network" [1983].[27] According to the Arbitron ratings, Schuller is viewed in more homes than any other television evangelist but trails at least one other gospel evangelist in number of actual viewers with 2.7 million.

The living-room sanctuary of the "Hour of Power" is the famed Crystal Cathedral in Garden Grove, California, built at a cost of nearly $20 million. It is equipped with the million-dollar Hazel Wright organ, which has an additional million-dollar endowment for its continued tuning and maintenance. The congregations of the Crystal Cathedral contribute $4 million annually to the ministries, and the television audiences contribute an additional $30 million.

In sharp contrast to the informal conversation or authoritative proclamations of so many televangelists, the services from the Crystal Cathedral present worship as a dramatic ritual, with robes, anthems, and traditional hymnody. The music directors have all been nationally recognized organists and choral directors, who have provided standard congregational hymns and serious contemporary anthem literature. The organ music is taken from standard concert and church literature, from J. S. Bach to our contemporary composers of serious organ music for the church. The guest musicians appearing each Sunday might be a leading baritone from the Metropolitan Opera singing a sacred art song, a college a cappella choir, a children's string orchestra, or a contemporary gospel artist.

The Crystal Cathedral's pageants at Christmas and Easter are imitated by large urban churches throughout America and have become a major theatrical presentation of the great Christian festivals. The diversity of the music produced on the "Hour of Power" might well be representative of urban denominational church music in America, and the style of its production a model for all in the 1980s.

The electronic church has many other major prophets with significant followings, whose television productions are models of music and preaching for countless local churches where live telecasts of worship services are produced every Sunday. Worthy of note are Richard DeHaan's "Day of Discovery"; Pat Robertson's "Full Gospel" 700 Club and the Christian Broadcasting Network; James Robison's "Truth"; and another aggres-

sive young preacher, Kenneth Copeland—all of whom emphasize a daily walk with God.

If one could view all of the live television worship services
and listen to the radio broadcasts of worship services, only then
could one assess the impact of the electronic "models" upon
current church music practices. Another handle for the re-
searcher would be a record of the total sales of hymnals, choral
music, solos, and taped accompaniments reported by the current publishers of church music. Even this fails to account for
the thousands of repeat performances of the classic anthem and
solo repertoire used Sunday after Sunday.

The future of religious television is already with us. The electronic church is no longer dependent upon time purchased
from the secular stations. Television stations offering predominantly religious and family programming "are growing at the
rate of one per month in the United States."[28] And hundreds of
cable TV systems are offering all-religious channels. Religious
broadcasters have already expanded their operations to earth
stations and communications satellites. Robertson's CBN was
the first, but following in quick succession were PTL ("Praise
the Lord") from Charlotte, North Carolina; Trinity Broadcasting Network from Santa Anna, California; and LeSea Broadcasting of South Bend, Indiana. Satellite broadcasting is bringing
about a further fulfillment, many believe, of Matthew 24:14:
"And this gospel of the kingdom shall be preached in all the
world for a witness to all nations"—and now simultaneously!

Notes

1. Lanterman, Walter F., "Broadcasting," *Encyclopaedia Britannica*, Vol.
IV (Chicago: Encyclopaedia Britannica, Inc.), p.212.

2. Ibid., p.213.

3. Siepmann, Charles A., *Radio, Television and Society* (New York: Oxford
University Press, 1950), p.9.

4. McDougald, Worth and Stewart, Lynda. *Welcome South Brother, Fifty
Years of Broadcasting at WSB* (Atlanta: Verlan Industries, Inc., 1974), p.14.

5. Ibid.

6. Getz, Gene A., *MBI, The Story of Moody Bible Institute* (Chicago: Moody Press, 1969), p.283.

7. Calman, Charles Jeffrey and Kaufmann, William I., *The Mormon Tabernacle Choir* (New York: Harper and Row, 1979), p.87.

8. Ibid., p.93.

9. Ibid., p.79.

10. Maier, Paul L., *A Man Spoke, a World Listened* (St. Louis: Concordia Publishing House, 1980), p.85.

11. Ibid., p.112.

12. Ibid., p.114.

13. Ibid., p.115.

14. Ibid., p.119.

15. Ibid., p.166.

16. Ibid., p.178.

17. Ibid., p.347.

18. Ibid., p.216.

19. *BCTN Magazine*, Walter E. Cranor, ed. (St. Louis: Lutheran Layman's League, March 1985), Vol. IV, No.2, p.12.

20. Ibid., p.2.

21. *BCTN Magazine*, June 1985, Vol. IV, No.4, p.2.

22. Fuller, Daniel P., *Give the Winds a Mighty Voice* (Waco, Texas: Word Books, 1972), p.106.

23. Ibid., p.136.

24. Coleman, Lucien, "The Southern Baptist Convention and the Media," *Review and Expositor*, Vol. LXXXI, No. 1, Roy L. Honeycutt, ed. (Louisville: Southern Baptist Theological Seminary, 1984), p.22.

25. Armstrong, Ben, *The Electric Church* (Nashville: Thomas Nelson Publishers, Inc., 1979), p.83.

26. *Los Angeles Times*, May 29, 1983.

27. Ibid.

28. Armstrong, p.100.

Part V:

Church Music Education

13

The Bible Institutes

Until the growth and expansion of the free churches in America, the training of church musicians was largely by an apprentice system within the institutional churches themselves. The choirboys became the organists, composers, and conductors for each succeeding generation. The other alternative was the use of other professional musicians as part-time performers in the choir loft on Sundays.

The evangelical expansion in America through Revivalism now created demands for musicians with new commitments and new skills in conducting volunteer choirs, composing new music, and leading congregational singing. The singing schools provided the basic musical needs of the small church, but the choirs and congregations of mass evangelism required specialized training in leadership, vocal instruction, band and orchestral instruments, and large publishing firms to provide the literature.

The cumbersome organization of the institutional churches often made the study of church music a source of controversy and ideological division. At the turn of the century, no uniform denominational standards were in practice, and few of the established institutions of higher learning were authorized, or qualified, to train musicians for the growing demands of church music. Granted that music had enjoyed a high curricular priority in the denominational liberal-arts colleges, yet it was more often a basic cultural pursuit rather than professional training for the practice of church music. The paid quartet still reigned in the urban choir loft. It remained the task of the independent institutions, with the support of private individuals and industry, to lead the way in creating the necessary professional training for the church musician.

At this point (1909), an unusual and realistic assessment of the status and future of church music was provided by the book *Practical Church Music* by Edmund S. Lorenz of Dayton, Ohio. The book was based upon a series of earlier lectures before the theology students of Union Biblical Seminary and Vanderbilt University. Relying upon his "thirty years of active service in practically every relation to the music of the church service, and under the most varied conditions," Lorenz's purpose was to "render Christian workers more efficient in their use of music in religious work."[1] The topics covered were: I. The Minister's Musical Preparation; II. The Minister's Hymnological Preparation; III. Congregational Singing; IV. The Management of Church Choirs; and V. Practical Applications of Church Music.

Of unusual interest to this study was Lorenz's survey of "Music in Theological Seminaries." He upbraided the seminaries for their pure scholarly pursuits, at the expense of more directly pastoral subjects—homiletics, elocution, Sunday Schools, hymnology, and church music. He spoke specifically of Yale as "one of the best of our American seminaries" (and where he received his own B.D. degree in 1883), as a school where a theological student

> can receive the best possible instruction in Sanscrit, Syriac, Arabic, philosophy, sociology, physiological psychology, and many other branches of no particular value, but, in spite of the magnificent Lowell Mason Music Library, which until recently lay in the East Divinity Hall unused and unexploited, and practically uncared for, he can get no musical instruction that will have any practical bearing on his management of a church and its services.[2]

He added that the same was true at Union Theological Seminary in New York, but cited efforts on the part of Congregational seminaries in Hartford and Oberlin and the Presbyterians' Western Theological Seminary in Allegheny, Pennsylvania, to create interest in church music. "Unfortunately the naturally academic interest in abstract standards in these pioneer efforts greatly lessens their practical value."[3] He commended the work of Dr. Daniel B. Towner at Moody Bible Institute as "the most practical and helpful courses in church music in this country, if not in the world . . . primarily intended for singing evangelists, it is equally valuable for regular pastors."[4]

Practical Church Music was so prophetic in its methods that it could easily have been used as a textbook for the organization and administration of the graded choir programs as they were set up after World War II. In a day when quartets still occupied the urban lofts, Lorenz contended that

> the ideal choir, after all, is the chorus choir made up of the best voices in the congregation. Twenty voices of moderate range and melodiousness can do more to lift the spirit of the worshipper than the best trained quartet in the land.[5]

Only a few men like Charles Alexander and Homer Rodeheaver would understand so well the psychological effectiveness of the volunteer choir for many years to come. However, a few musician-educators would soon capture Lorenz's vision and channel his ideas into a graded program of children's choirs, junior choirs, youth choirs, adult choirs, and a comprehensive instrumental program in church music.

It was almost inevitable that in such a free society, among so many free churches, Dwight L. Moody's new interdenominational Moody Bible Institute (1889) should place great emphasis upon the musical skills necessary for the students to become "leaders, singers, and organists" to "assist evangelists and pastors, and do a work on mission fields, both at home and abroad."[6] Moody, with his high regard for the gospel song, is reputed to have said that Ira D. Sankey sang more people into the kingdom of God than did he [Moody] through preaching.

H. H. McGranahan was the first director of music at the Institute. Daniel B. Towner, whose ambition had been to be a concert and oratorio soloist, succeeded him (1893-1919) and developed a music curriculum by 1895 which included "notation, sight reading, harmony, solo and part singing, vocal training, conducting, normal training for teachers, and composition.'"[7] E. O. Sellers, who assisted Towner for five years at MBI, said of him:

> as a teacher he certainly was without a peer. He is gratefully remembered by literally thousands of his students now scattered in every part of the world. . . . The directors of music in probably a majority of the Bible institutes and theological seminaries were instructed by Dr. Towner, or have felt the impact of his life and service.[8]

Among Towner's students who became church music educators, composers, and directors were Charles M. Alexander, Homer Hammondtree, Harry D. Loes, W. Plunkett Martin, I. E. Reynolds, George S. Schuler, E. O. Sellers, H. E. Tovey, and J. B. Trowbridge. Towner's musical contributions included many hymnals, choral collections, textbooks, anthems, and about two thousand gospel songs. Some of these have already been cited, and some of his song settings play a continuing role in evangelical church music.

By 1906 MBI offered three optional majors: Bible, Bible/Music, and Music. The straight music program was designed especially for students planning a full-time ministry through music. The music curriculum was enlarged again in 1928 according to President James M. Gray's concept of "Our New Adventure in Music." The music major now included advanced theory, counterpoint, history of music, and hymnology. The student could use either a keyboard- or vocal-performance emphasis.

This new emphasis upon performance was also carried over into the choral ensembles. Choral groups had been functioning as instructional units since 1895; but, as a performing group, a choir was not organized until 1921. The gospel song, in the meantime, had been suffering the abuses of overpopularity and became the subject of a controversy known as "the gospel song versus the hymn." Gray, seeking to give balance to his "model" services conducted at 4 PM each Sunday, wanted a choir selected from the student body. This was the origin of the Auditorium Choir, under the direction of a faculty member, Guy Latchaw. He was succeeded by Alfred Holzworth, who presented the group in concert in various churches in the Chicago area. Talmage J. Bittikofer—formerly with the Moody Memorial Church but he had joined the faculty in the early thirties—became its director until 1946. The repertoire of the choir now included the standard anthem and oratorio literature of the day.

When James Davies took over the Auditorium Choir in 1946 the name was changed to The Moody Chorale, and its members went on its first extended tour in 1947. That same year Donald Hustad succeeded Davies and, under his leadership, the Chorale developed an international reputation as one of the finest musical organizations in the country. From 1948 to 1965 The Moody Chorale "participated in 37 extended choir tours, singing in 43 states and 6 Canadian provinces."[9]

One important additional ensemble was The Moody Institute Singers, a small, semiprofessional group directed by Bittikofer, which was presented nationwide by the NBC radio network live from the Merchandise Mart Building from July 1935 to April 1936. This was a program of special hymn arrangements by Emil Soderstrum, who was a member of the NBC music staff in Chicago.

The academic emphasis at MBI since World War II has been toward curriculum development and eventual accreditation by the National Association of Schools of Music. The 1983-84 catalog offered curricula leading to a diploma in Church Music or in Christian Education/Music. The Bachelor of Arts and the Bachelor of Music are also offered, and students are allowed to major in piano, organ, voice, orchestral instrument, or composition. The music courses conform to the NASM degree requirements, but for the Bachelors Degrees the student is required to transfer fifty-four hours of acceptable college credits or take two years of subsequent study in a conservatory or college-level school of music. A strong emphasis is placed upon applied performance, and all history and theory requirements meet the standards of NASM. The diploma program was accredited in 1983, and the overall purpose maintained to provide the orientation necessary to become a successful church musician in the total spirit of the Institute's motto from 2 Timothy 2:15: "Study

to shew thyself approved unto God, a workman that needeth
not to be ashamed, rightly dividing the word of truth."

The Bible Institute of Los Angeles (BIOLA) was quick to
follow the lead of the Moody Bible Institute. It was founded in
1908 by Lyman Stewart (founder of the Union Oil Company)
and T. C. Horton for the training of lay Christian workers. The
curricula soon expanded into the training of professional Christian ministries and, in 1912, named Reuben A. Torrey (from
MBI) as dean.

For many years, BIOLA was housed in The Church of the
Open Door in downtown Los Angeles. From the outset BIOLA
was in the forefront of the gospel-song movement on the West
Coast. Herbert E. Tovey served as head of the music department from the early 1920s until the late 1940s.[10] As the curricula continued to grow the Institute's program became a
four-year course in the 1940s, leading to degrees in Theology,
Christian Education, and Sacred Music. In 1949 the Institute
became Biola College. Further growth brought about the move
to a new seventy-five-acre campus in La Mirada, California, in
1959, and the college became Biola University.

The present offering in the Department of Music, with Dr.
Jack Schwarz as chairman, is the professional Bachelor of Music
degree, with majors in applied music, composition, and music
education. The faculty became "convinced that church music
belonged on the graduate level" and dropped the B.M. major
in church music in 1970.[11] Consequently, the Graduate School
now offers the Master of Music in church music. All work is
accredited by NASM, and the commitment to its early Christian
posture remains strong—a "comprehensive Christian college of
arts, sciences and professional studies."

Another Bible institute, and an early entry into the field of
church music, was the New Orleans Baptist Bible Institute. In
1919 Ernest O. Sellers, a former assistant to Daniel B. Towner,
was named the first Professor of Sacred Music. He served until
1952 and taught such diverse courses as sightreading, harmony,
counterpoint, music history, conducting, hymnology, practical
church music, music and psychology, and directed a general
chorus and a men's chorus—a near duplication of the Moody

curriculum. The music enrollment at the Bible Institutes was so predominantly male that a balanced mixed chorus was difficult to maintain. Instruction in applied music was in organ, piano, and voice culture. A course called normal training was offered for those planning to go into teaching. Sellers also published two of his own texts—*Elements of Notation and Conducting* and *How to Improve Church Music.*[12]

From 1919 to 1932 the Institute offered a Diploma in Music and a Bachelor of Gospel Music. After 1936 the Diploma in Music was retained, but a Bachelor of Religious Education and a Master of Religious Education were offered with a major in music. The choral ensembles were reduced to one mixed chorus which met for one rehearsal each week.

Another MBI graduate, W. Plunkett Martin, succeeded Sellers as director of the Music Department in 1945, and in 1946 the Southern Baptist Convention changed the name of the Bible institute to New Orleans Baptist Theological Seminary. The degree offerings were changed again in 1951 to the Bachelor of Sacred Music and Master of Sacred Music. The B.S.M. was reserved for those students who already had a college degree in some field other than music. The Diploma was continued for the benefit of students who did not have a college degree. Now that the institute had become a seminary, the trend in the curricula was toward the uniform requirements in theory, history and literature, and applied music as set forth by the National Association of Schools of Music. In 1953 the department was changed to a School of Sacred Music, and again in 1960 to a School of Church Music. NASM accreditation of the Master of Church Music was received in 1966, and a Doctor of Musical Arts was approved in 1979. Majors on the M.C.M. are in theory/composition, church music education, music history and hymnology, and performance (piano, organ, voice, and conducting). The major for the D.M.A. is church music, with prescribed supporting areas in research, musicianship, music history and literature, and performance. The growth of denominational ministries in music has not only provided the facilities, but an adequate number of students to support the educational program.

14

The Seminaries

The evangelistic expectations of the early twentieth century brought about other duplications of the curricular programs of the Bible institutes in denominational institutions. One of the earliest to follow the trend was Southwestern Baptist Seminary in Fort Worth, Texas. In 1915 L. R. Scarborough, president of the seminary, hired Isham E. Reynolds to head a new department of Gospel Music. As a young man, Reynolds had attended singing schools led by A. J. Showalter and J. B. Herbert and was a former student of D. B. Towner (1907-08) at MBI. After his appointment, Reynolds sought Towner's aid in setting up the new program for the training of pianists, organists, and, especially, directors of congregational and choral singing in Baptist churches and revival campaigns.

Reynolds also focused his attention on the goal of improving music in the individual churches. In his *Manual of Practical Church Music* (1923), he reiterated much of Lorenz's earlier (1909) ideas and anticipated John F. Williamson's "Manifesto" of 1925. The Department of Gospel Music became a School of Church Music in 1921 and began offering degrees in church music. In 1926 a prominent ranching family in West Texas built the beautiful and functional Cowden Hall to house the school. The design was complete with soundproof studios, practice rooms, classrooms, rehearsal rooms, an organ, and a recital auditorium. The renovation in 1960 made no changes in design but added air conditioning, two new organs, and a music library.

Early in his tenure Reynolds began working to establish both state and Convention-wide departments of church music in the

Southern Baptist Convention. These would provide and be responsible for: the training of church musicians; the publication of church hymnals and choral music; the organization of graded choirs and church orchestras; and the development of summer leadership conferences in church music at the denomination's summer assembly grounds in Ridgecrest, North Carolina. This summer conference would be the Baptist counterpart of Rodeheaver's Practical Training School at Winona Lake, Indiana.

In 1925 Reynolds asked the Southern Baptist Convention to appoint a committee to bring a recommendation for the advancement of music in Southern Baptist churches. In 1926 he proposed to the Texas Baptist convention

> that this convention go on record as being in favor of the Sunday School Board of the Southern Baptist Convention giving careful consideration, at its earliest convenience, to the advisability of establishing and fostering a Church Music Department for the purpose of improving the musical conditions in the stated church, Sunday School and BYPU [Baptist Young People's Union].[13]

He did personal surveys to support his proposals. It was not until 1935, however, that the Sunday School Board [the publishing agency for Southern Baptists] asked B. B. McKinney, a former student and faculty member at Southwestern Seminary, as well as a prolific writer of gospel songs, to come to work at the Board. His duties were to be

> editor of all music offered, accepted, and considered for publication in our books, periodicals, and programs; songwriter and contributor to our publications; author and compiler of songbooks, director of music at training schools, assemblies, and conventions.[14]

In 1941, after hearing John Finley Williamson's Westminster Choir and being impressed with a similar musical potential in Baptist churches, T. L. Holcomb, the secretary-treasurer of the Sunday School Board, recommended to the Executive Committee of the Board that a Department of Church Music be established. The committee approved his recommendation; and when he polled the total membership of the board by mail, they gave him unanimous approval. The individual states quickly followed suit by establishing their own departments of church music in order to implement the total denominational programs and objectives. The oldest Southern Baptist seminary at Louisville, Kentucky, inaugurated its own School of Church Music in 1944, and all three seminaries experienced phenomenal growth in church music education soon after World War II.

National accreditation for Schools of Church Music became a primary objective during the 1950s. However, the National Association of Schools of Music had no category or standards for the evaluation of the programs in seminaries and Bible colleges. The door began to open when the Texas Association of Music Schools, an organization of more than fifty schools and departments of music, adopted standards in theory, history, and applied music which were the equivalent of NASM requirements. Southwestern Seminary's School of Church Music was admitted, and Dean Campbell Wray served as president of the Texas organization.

It was not until 1964 that Southwestern Seminary received NASM accreditation, but soon thereafter the other two Baptist seminaries at Louisville and New Orleans were also accredited. Approved were the B.C.M., M.C.M., and D.C.M. degrees. At this writing, however, all are changing their graduate degrees to the standard M.M. and D.M.A., which are the more uniform terminal degrees offered by Schools of Music. All three seminaries require similar cores of study in music and offer majors at the master's level in Performance (organ, piano, voice, instruments, and conducting), Theory and Composition, Musicology, and Church Music Education. All require a considerable amount of additional studies in theology and religious education in order to better prepare the students for spiritual leadership in the church.

The growth pattern in these three seminaries began about 1956-57, when they enrolled 303 majors in church music—some at the Bachelor's level and some at the Master's level. During the 1983-84 school year they enrolled 678 full-time equivalent students. Since a majority of seminary students are part-time students, this FTE number would translate into approximately an eight-hundred accumulated student enroll-ment.

As an important factor in the continuing education for gradu-ates active in church music, each of the seminaries offers an annual workshop featuring national specialists in church music education, conducting, choral methods, choral and organ litera-ture, solo recitals, and choral concerts. These annual workshops bring an additional six to eight hundred church musicians to the campuses each year for a week of intensive study and inspira-tion.

Isham E. Reynolds dreamed of a Convention-wide Depart-ment of Church Music which might sponsor a week's summer music conference at Ridgecrest, North Carolina. He could never have imagined four weeks of music conferences—two each at Ridgecrest, North Carolina, and Glorieta, New Mexico. Attendance at each of these weeks now runs between eighteen hundred and three thousand choir directors, organists, pianists, their families, and a few church choirs. The conferences consist of classes in organ, piano, theory, conducting, hymnology, music for all graded choirs, instrumental ensembles, organ re-citals, and oratorio and cantata performances each evening of the conference week.

One of the earliest and most advanced programs in church music was initiated by Union Theological Seminary in New York City. After its founding in 1836 "as early as 1837 Abner Jones had been appointed Instructor in Sacred Music."[15] He was followed by such familiar names in church music as George F. Root, Lowell Mason, Thomas Hastings (father of a future president of Union), and Gerrit Smith, "a founder of the Ameri-can Guild of Organists who gave the Guild its name and became its first warden."[16] Smith's successor in 1912 was Clarence Dickinson. A native of Indiana and a graduate of Northwestern University (B.A. and M.A.), Dickinson studied under Peter C. Lutkin and continued his studies in Paris and Berlin. He had also served as organist/director at St. James in Chicago. He and his wife, Helen A. Dickinson (Ph.D. from Heidelberg Universi-ty), proposed in January 1928 that Union Seminary establish a graduate School of Sacred Music in order to enable their students to "be efficient helpers in the work of Sunday Schools and young people's societies, and give them a background in the Bible, Church History or Theology."[17] The Dickinsons laid out a curriculum which was approved, and the School of Sacred Music opened the following autumn.

Dickinson arranged for the performance of two oratorios each year, to be conducted and accompanied by students. An active composer himself, he also scheduled performances each spring of original organ and choral compositions by student composers. Graduates of the school were not only accepted as organists and directors but were sought by other schools and colleges as well. A program of high academic quality was not too difficult to achieve, since so many distinguished teachers were available in New York. This grew into the Doctor of Sacred Music degree in 1941.

The Dickinsons were able to exert an international influence upon church music through their writings, music arrangements, compositions, and recitals and lectures abroad. His edition of *Historical Recitals for Organ,* sacred choruses and anthems, and his *Technique and Art of Organ Playing* (1921) became a well-known text for organ students. He was also editor of the *Hymnal* (1933) of the Presbyterian Church.

Other distinguished faculty who exerted strong influences upon American church music were C. Winfred Douglas, Miles Farrow, Harold B. Gibbs, T. Tertius Noble, Hugh Porter, Franklin W. Robinson, and Edwin J. Stringham. Union Seminary's School of Sacred Music was discontinued in 1973. This will be discussed at some length in "Robert Handy's forthcoming history of Union Seminary, which [was scheduled to] be published in Fall or Winter 1986 by Columbia University Press."[18]

15

Church-related Colleges

German immigrants brought two great traditions to America, which have made an indelible mark upon all American church music—their music and their high regard for education. The pioneers made great financial sacrifices in order to establish institutions of higher learning. It was through these colleges that they preserved best their most cherished heritage—their music. The most immediate heritage was the chorale; but through their churches and colleges, they quickly expanded this heritage to include the oratorio, cantata, and instrumental music.

This Lutheran heritage in American church music was nowhere as strong or more influential than in the life and work of F. Melius Christiansen (1871-1955) at Saint Olaf College in Northfield, Minnesota. Indeed, the work of Melius and his two sons, Olaf and Paul, has in recent years been termed the "Christiansen Tradition." The longevity of the tradition spans a period from 1903 to late in the century and has created one of the major influences upon twentieth-century Protestant church music in America.

Born in Larvik, Norway, F. Melius Christiansen was from a musical family and began his early music instruction on the violin, piano, and organ. He was fortunate to have good teachers and had dreams of a career as a concert artist. Since his early training was instrumental, he played in a small amateur symphony, copied parts from the conductor's score, and played the organ at the Lutheran church. In the small town of Larvik he was also immersed in the folk music of Norway.

While Christiansen was a young man, Norway was in a period

of political and religious upheaval. Pietism and Revivalism had united the common people of Norway in a search for a more personal religion. Politically, a nationalistic spirit had brought about a revolt against the four-hundred-year rule of Norway by the Danes and the Treaty of Kiel (1814) which was to transfer the Danish control of Norway to Sweden. On May 17, 1814 a constitution was adopted by a group of Norwegians, and May 17 was proclaimed Norway's Independence Day. This pervasive nationalism and the holiday itself would eventually be a strong factor in the life and musical career of F. Melius Christiansen.

After graduation from public school, Melius set up a private studio in Larvik and continued his work as copyist. But the "America Fever" had already claimed his brother Karl, and Melius had become infected. In anticipation of a move to America, he gave violin lessons to two Mormon missionaries in exchange for English lessons.[19]

In October 1888 Melius set sail for America. After landing in New York he went to Oakland, California, where he had relatives, but California failed to provide the environment for a career in music. He then went to his brother Karl in Washburn, Wisconsin, where he received the security and encouragement necessary to launch a music career in America.

His first music position, at age nineteen, was in the small town of Marinette as director of the Scandinavian Band. He taught piano, violin, and organ and became the organist and choir director for Our Savior's Lutheran Congregation. He also began composing for his choir. In 1892 a member of a men's quartet persuaded Melius to come to Augsburg College in Minneapolis. Here his abilities were soon discovered, and he became director of the Augsburg Chorus and teacher of theory and singing. He later became organist and choir director at Trinity Lutheran Church. The intellectual environment at Augsburg helped him to formulate his ideas on music and to fully justify his decision to pursue a musical career.

He continued his own musical studies at Minneapolis' Northwestern Conservatory, and composition became an increasingly important facet of his musical life. On May 17, 1894 (Norwegian Independence Day),

> a chorus of Lutherans combined in the largest auditorium of
> Minneapolis and sang a composition by Christiansen and Urseth
> [a poet at Augsburg] called "velkomstsang" (song of welcome)
> written for the occasion.[20]

The dramatic increase in the immigrant population of Minneapolis provided more private pupils, and his first collection
of twelve *Korsange* was published later in 1894. In 1896 he and
Urseth collaborated in the production of a monthly bulletin of
choral music. For greater freedom and a higher degree of performance quality, he organized a special choir at Trinity Lutheran called *Nordlyset* (north light) with no circumstances or
controls but his own.

Christiansen returned to Europe in 1897 for graduate study
at the Royal Conservatory of Music in Leipzig, Germany. His
main interest at the Conservatory was his violin study with
Hans Sitt, but he also studied piano. The director of the Conservatory was Arthur Nikisch, who had appeared in Minneapolis
with the Boston Symphony in 1890. After his graduation in
1899 Christiansen returned to Minneapolis and the Northwestern Conservatory. He was now a member of the faculty as
teacher of violin and eventually became head of the string
faculty. He also resumed his post at the organ of Trinity Lutheran Church and conducted a Norwegian singing society. He
composed for the male chorus and frequently appeared as a
violin soloist featuring the works of Bruch, Grieg, and Wieniaw-
ski.

Upon the recommendation of Paul G. Schmidt, a member of
the faculty and a former member of Christiansen's male chorus
in Minneapolis, F. Melius Christiansen joined the faculty of
Saint Olaf Lutheran College in 1903. His musical responsibilities were primarily to direct the band. But he also directed the
Choral Union (a choir combining the church choir and some
college students) in a cantata and played a solo violin recital. In
the spring semester of 1904 he produced a music festival on
May 17 and 18. Besides the obvious focus upon Norway's Independence Day, the prospectus was not devoted entirely to the

festivities, but stated the aim of the festival was to decry the low standards of church music.

> The flashy superficial music of the hour requiring no specially developed taste to be appreciated. . . . It is a deplorable fact that this low standard of taste is kept up and encouraged by the broadcast spreading of hymn-books and songbooks published by individuals who, if they are not led by mercenary motives are at any rate activated by the mistaken idea that they must cater to the taste of the public.[21]

The article then contends that it is the responsibility of our educational institutions to counteract these tendencies. The prospectus also included an article entitled "The Educational Value of Music." An excerpt states

> That it is a fallacy to consider music of less importance in education than science or mathematics or literature or athletics is readily seen when it is pointed out that the study of music produces all the results that these can give.[22]

It is of great interest to note that on the afternoon of May 17 "the traditional baseball game was played" by these immigrants and first-generation Americans. The festival then featured a band concert in the evening, playing a *Norwegian Rhapsody* by Christiansen which was based upon Norwegian folk melodies. The finale of the festival was *The Creation* by Haydn. The chorus was made up of 110 voices, and Christiansen engaged professional soloists and an orchestra from Minneapolis—all of this from a small college of "roughly three hundred and fifty students."[23] The 1905 festival featured Handel's *Messiah,* also with an orchestra.

Christiansen's early years at Saint Olaf were filled with the typical curricular frustrations of music educators—music for credit, ensemble credits, applied music, public appearances, and tours. His band had its first tour in 1905 with limited effectiveness. Thereafter, Professor Paul G. Schmidt was assigned as manager of tours and continued in this capacity until Christiansen's retirement.

In May of the same year, Saint Olaf sponsored a choral group from Christiana [Oslo], Norway. The element of nationalism again became an important factor in Christiansen's musical career. While the group was visiting Saint Olaf, word was received that Norway had declared herself free from the union with Sweden, and a king was to be chosen for Norway. Music for the visitors included the *Norwegian Rhapsody* for the band and a band arrangement of the Norwegian national anthem. The result was an invitation to the band to visit Norway in the summer of 1906. Such an opportunity was sensational in its effect, and the ensuing tour was an overwhelming success. Norway had just crowned a new king, and patriotism was at a new high.

After the tour, Christiansen returned to Leipzig for a year of postgraduate study. He devoted most of his efforts to the study of the chorale and folk music. Another interest was the study of more theory with Gustav Schreck and the observation of his rehearsal and performance techniques with his choir at the St. Thomas School. Admittedly, Schreck and his singers had a profound influence upon Christiansen, and he was determined to bring to America some of the ideals and techniques which he had absorbed.[24] Another influence, particularly in conducting, was the book *Der Moderne Dirigent* by Arthur Laser. The book was written about the virtuoso conductor Hans von Bulow.

Upon his return to Northfield, he formed the St. Olaf Lutheran Choir as a joint venture of his church and the college. This was the organization which was to develop an international reputation and provide a major body of twentieth-century choral literature for evangelical Christianity in America.

The establishment of a choral tradition was achieved in his own lifetime, but its continuation was the work of two sons, Olaf C. and Paul J.—very much in accord with Lutheran tradition in Europe. Olaf C. Christiansen was born in 1901 and grew up in the collegiate environment of Saint Olaf, where his musical training was primarily instrumental. When he was nineteen he was named band director, dean of men, and athletic director at a small teachers' college in Mayville, North Dakota. The year's experience determined his choice of music as a career—and he met his future wife, Ellen Beatrice Kjos. His spring concert on

May 18 featured Ellen as a vocal soloist and her brother Neal [sic] as clarinet soloist.[25] Neil was to become the principal publisher of Olaf's music. In spite of his success in instrumental music, the major musical influence in his life was the Saint Olaf Lutheran Choir.

After Ellen's graduation in 1925 she and Olaf were married, and he went to New York to study opera. After the year in New York he accepted a teaching position in Flint, Michigan, where he taught junior high school for a year and then moved to the junior college. The experience developed strong convictions about music in the public schools and provided a variety of musical experiences while at the junior college. There he directed the a cappella choir and the annual opera and taught theory, madrigals, and public-school music methods. His work also extended to the high school, where he directed the second band, taught choral classes, and coached gymnastics and golf. His civic activities included playing bass clarinet in the symphony, soloing in opera and oratorio performances, and directing music at the Central Methodist Church.

At the end of his third year (1929) he was asked to join the faculty at Oberlin College. There he taught choral conducting, a madrigal group, and private voice, and founded the Oberlin A Cappella Choir. He was also the conductor of the Musical Union Choir, which performed the major oratorios of J. S. Bach, Cesar Franck, Charles Gounod, Felix Mendelssohn, Horatio Parker, and Gabriel Faure. This choir met one night each week. The new college environment was most stimulating. He edited the *Oberlin Choir Series*, published by Neil A. Kjos, and enjoyed his association with Normand Lockwood, a recent winner of the Prix de Rome in composition. Another strong influence was the frequent visits to the campus by Nadia Boulanger, Lockwood's former teacher in Paris.[26]

In 1939 Olaf returned to New York to pursue the M.S.M. degree at Union Theological Seminary. His principal instructor was Clarence Dickinson, and his voice teachers were Marshall Bryant and Douglas Stanley. His work with Stanley affected his approach to choral techniques. He became, above all else, concerned with "correct singing." On one occasion he is quoted to have said to his choir: "If you are going to sing until you are seventy, you [sic] better build it up now, so you won't have to quit when you are thirty-five."[27]

He returned to Saint Olaf Lutheran College in 1941 to succeed his father and assumed the responsibilities for the choir and music department in 1943. In spite of the war, the choral program was maintained, and they were able to make short tours. Except for the choir at Saint John's Church, Olaf's life followed closely that of his father. A major change was the extension of the choral literature to include the masters of the Renaissance and works of the major contemporary American composers. A major technical advance was his constant effort to fuse the physiological and psychological functions of the human voice. The analysis and control of breathing, the diaphragm, the tongue, the epiglottis, and the larynx all became the tools and technique of vocal development.

His choice of literature continued to be sacred, but with an increased emphasis upon the quality of the text, then upon the appropriateness of the musical setting. His concerts were designed as though the texts were a liturgy rather than a chronological presentation of musical styles.

An important point in Olaf's preparation of a score for performance was adjustments which were often made in the score itself. Though published scores are usually considered sacrosanct by conductors (and composers), Olaf did not hesitate to make editorial adjustments in a score to enhance structural clarity, harmonic balance, emphasis upon the inner parts, or textual emphasis demanded of the musical setting.

The total concert repertoire of the Saint Olaf Choir was compiled by Frederick A. Schmidt for the years 1913 to 1967, and the years 1912 and 1968 were added by Albert Johnson. These compilations provide a valuable survey of the composers and works performed before hundreds of thousands in both Europe and America.[28] J. S. Bach was listed most often during the entire period. Eight of his works were programmed by F. Melius, and five of these were continued by Olaf. Among the works written by F. Melius, seventy-eight titles were listed. Of these, forty-seven were dropped from the repertoire, and thirty-one were continued or introduced by Olaf. Twenty-three works by Olaf were programmed from 1943 through 1968. Eleven works by Paul were performed by F. Melius.

Although Melius' scores were devoted almost entirely to the Lutheran chorale, one arrangement of a hymn common to both German and English hymnody deserves special mention. "Beautiful Savior," with the tune erroneously designated CRUSADERS' HYMN in English hymnals, first appeared in the *Muensterisch Gesangbuch* (1677). The English translation by Richard S. Willis appeared in his *Church Chorals and Choir Studies* in New York (1850). The tune was then termed ST. ELIZABETH because Liszt had used it in his oratorio by the same name.[29] Perhaps the universal appeal of both tune and text was a factor, but because of its sensitive choral harmonies and its superb use of contrapuntal lines by F. Melius Christiansen, "Beautiful Savior" became one of the best known (and most performed) works in all of American a cappella choral literature. It first appeared on the 1912 concert, and it is noted in Schmidt's compilation that it appeared almost every year thereafter—if not programmed, then almost surely as an encore.

Of passing interest, when one is considering an international touring choir from America, is the fact that only one Negro spiritual was listed—H. T. Burleigh's "Deep River." It was the European audiences that later insisted upon spirituals and American folk songs from the Westminster Choir and influenced the format of their concerts thereafter.

The Russian composers Tschesnikoff, Tchaikovsky, and particularly Gretchaninoff were featured regularly by both F. Melius and Olaf. The choral works of Grieg, as one might expect, were also programmed regularly. The graduates of Saint Olaf were represented most often by Morton J. Luvaas with seven numbers. Among other contemporary American composers, Olaf programmed works by Jean Berger, Normand Lockwood, Don Malin, and Katherine Davis. Olaf also featured earlier works by J. P. Sweelinck and Heinrich Schutz.

The third member of the "tradition" is Paul J. Christiansen (born 1914). Paul graduated from Saint Olaf, did graduate work at Oberlin under Lockwood, then transferred to Eastman

School of Music, where his teacher was composer/teacher Bernard Rogers. Before completing his graduate studies, he went to Concordia College in Moorhead, Minnesota, as head of the Department of Music and director of the college choir. Through his activities as composer, conductor, and choral clinician, he has also contributed to an even greater expansion of the Christiansen "tradition" and its widening influence upon American church music.

The work of the Christiansens was nurtured and fell upon fertile soil. A study of thirty-four Lutheran colleges revealed that by 1900, four had glee clubs, five had choral unions, and two had oratorio societies.[30] As early as 1880 Olaf Olsson organized the Handel Oratorio Society at Augustana College and Seminary at Rock Island, Illinois. Another society was organized at Bethany College in Lindsborg, Kansas, in 1882 and was open to citizens of the community. Here, only twelve years after the first settlers arrived in Lindsborg, they began rehearsing Handel's *Messiah*.[31] Other societies were organized soon after the turn of the century. After *Messiah,* other favored works were Mendelssohn's *Elijah, St. Paul,* and *Hymn of Praise;* Brahms' *German Requiem;* Handel's *Israel in Egypt;* Haydn's *Creation;* and J. S. Bach's *B Minor Mass* and the *Passion According to St. Matthew*—a solid German heritage.

The choral unions were a joint organization of church and college choirs. Some of the early choral unions were organized at Saint Olaf as the "Lutheran Choir" (1900); Luther College (1889); Dana College (1914); Concordia at Moorhead (1917); Augustana at Sioux Falls (1921); and Augsburg (1922).

One of the greatest musical influences upon American church music came as a result of the firmly established a cappella tradition. After F. Melius Christiansen's "Lutheran Choir" of 1911, twenty-eight Lutheran colleges established a cappella choirs—twenty-five of these before 1939 and World War II. The early impact of this choral concept upon John Finley Williamson and his Westminster Choir compounded the influence upon American church music. Another important assist was given by the publishing firms of Neil A. Kjos, Augsburg, and Concordia.

The constant touring of these choirs created more college a

cappella choirs, and the movement moved down to the high schools of America. This made it possible for the churches to appropriate the inspiration, the techniques, and the musicianship developed in the colleges and public schools. At this writing, many adult and youth choirs go on tours and mission trips; participate in choral festivals; present oratorios, musical dramas, and operas; and attend summer workshops for directors and their choirs.

Another major influence of the Christiansens was their summer Choral School for conductors—first held at Winona Lake, Indiana, in 1935, then finally locating at both Lake Forest, Illinois and Chambersburg, Pennsylvania. After the retirement of F. Melius, Olaf took over the choral school, and Paul began his own summer workshops. Thousands of conductors attended these clinics for inspiration, conducting, choral techniques, and to survey the ever-increasing choral literature available from the music publishers.

After all aspects of this new a cappella tradition have been examined, probably the most important effect might be the development of a distinctly American style of choral music and a new school of conductors and composers of church music. The early years had to depend upon the music of J. S. Bach and the original arrangements of chorales and folk hymns by F. Melius Christiansen, but in the 1940s the entire literature was expanded to include Renaissance composers and the Romantic works of the Russians. "The negro spirituals were sung by a few of the [Lutheran] choirs, but there was no evidence of any increase in the use of this type of folksong material during this period."[32]

After World War II, the choral directors who had graduated from Saint Olaf went out to organize and promote choral music in other Lutheran colleges. They made significant changes in literature and style. They amplified the Lutheran heritage through the use of more music from the Baroque and Renaissance periods. Another contributing factor was that church music and choral programs were growing at such a pace that the music of contemporary American composers which was designed especially for the a cappella chorus was demanding more attention from the conductors. This rapid expansion of choral publications in the 1950s extended the performance literature to include many contemporary American composers such as Jean Berger, Alan Hovhaness, Normand Lockwood, Austin Lovelace, Daniel Moe, Lawrence Morton, Lloyd Pfautsch, Frank Pooler, Leland Sateren, Randall Thompson, Virgil Thomson, and Gordon Young. Many of these composers had also emerged from the Lutheran colleges or the Lutheran traditions already apparent in secondary schools and even state universities.

The extension of this a cappella style to the high schools and to the church youth choirs brought about two distinct styles of music for young voices. The choral works of Noble Cain exemplified the tradition in its romantic richness of harmony. He achieved this through the division of the chord parts into six or eight voice parts, thereby substituting a thick harmonic texture for the richness of the mature adult voices. But the average church choir of young voices did not contain enough capable voices for such divisions, so the composers resorted to an organ accompaniment which provided intensity and richness of harmonic texture, and then gave the young voices more unison, two-, and three-part scores with more rhythmic energy and simple imitative structures. Particularly effective in this style are the works of Austin C. Lovelace. Neither of these styles necessarily represented an abandonment of European and American choral traditions, but were often a way for the composer to artistically adapt choral music to the musical hazards of the sound-deadened postwar sanctuaries and public-school auditoriums.

On a similar level in the spectrum of church music education, another choral director, church musician, and music educator from Dayton, Ohio, entered the scene—John Finley Williamson (1887-1964). After receiving a diploma in voice from Otterbein University in 1911, Williamson's church music career began in 1912 at the First Evangelical United Brethren Church in Dayton. His recruiting technique for his volunteer choir was "Wouldn't you like to sing in a choir? If you'll sing in my choir, I'll give you [voice] lessons free."[33] He also taught hymnology, public speaking, and church music at Dayton's Central Theological Seminary. His church choir soon grew to fifty voices, and he expanded it to the entire community as the "Dayton Chorus" of sixty voices. This larger chorus gave concerts in nearby communities and served as the resident chorus for the Winona Lake Chatauqua Assembly in 1917. The formal concert program for the choir that year included eight choral selections which might be termed representative of the better works of American composers and publishers of the period: Dudley Buck's "God Is Our Refuge" and "Rock of Ages"; Bantock's "On Himalaya"; Cooke's "Strike, Strike the Lyre"; Alcock's "Voix Celeste"; Stewart's "Bells of St. Michael's Tower"; Neidlinger's "The Silent Sea"; Roberts' "Seek Ye the Lord"; and closed with Handel's "Hallelujah Chorus." The program was interspersed with three solo groups by Hilbert Kratzer, tenor.[34]

Three years later Williamson moved to the Westminster Presbyterian Church and a long working relationship with the pastor, Dr. Hugh I. Evans. The paid quartet had been well entrenched at Westminster and became a source of controversy as Williamson began shaping his volunteer choir program. His new church choir made its first appearance at the morning service on September 5, 1920, and sang two anthems by Dudley Buck—"God Is Our Refuge" and "Rock of Ages." The church had to remodel to accommodate the choir, and the choir had difficulty finding a place to rehearse—four nights each week!

The following summer Homer Rodeheaver invited the choir to serve as the resident choir and Williamson to teach at his Practical Training School for Christian Workers at Winona Lake, Indiana. The choir participated again in 1922, and Williamson returned to teach in 1923 and 1924. He also served as the local music chairman for Billy Sunday's Dayton revival. These trips to Winona Lake were the first appearances outside Dayton for the first Westminster Choir.

The 1922 concert contained works by American composers Clarence Dickinson, F. Melius Christiansen, Harry Rowe Shelley, and Ethelbert Nevin. The choir opened with J. S. Bach's "Christians Be Joyful" and closed with Rossini's "Inflammatus" from the *Stabat Mater*. Christiansen's choirs were a profound influence upon Williamson. For years, almost every program by the Westminster Choir included works by Christiansen; Williamson limited his choirs to fifty or sixty voices; he insisted upon their singing by memory; and he programmed only sacred a cappella numbers.[35]

Plans for the choir went much further. In 1922 they also sang in Pittsburgh, Cleveland, and Detroit. In 1924, after a successful tour in Chicago, Mrs. Harold E. Talbott became the official sponsor of the Westminster Choir tours. By the end of 1925 the choir had sung in Carnegie Hall, New York; Symphony Hall, Boston; Academy of Music, Philadelphia; Orchestra Hall, Chicago; and Carnegie Hall, Pittsburgh. In 1925 Mrs. Talbott also held a competition for the best a cappella composition for mixed chorus by an American composer. The judges included the recently appointed director of the Eastman School, Howard Hanson, and Earl V. Moore, dean of the School of Music at the University of Michigan.

The year 1925 was probably of greatest importance to church music because of Williamson's opportunities to declare his "manifesto" in two important national forums. The first was the General Assembly of the Presbyterian Church in the U.S.A., held in Columbus, Ohio, in May. The appearance by the choir and Williamson's presentation were arranged by his pastor, Dr. Evans, for the purpose of establishing "a Commission on Church Music to study the problem of church music within our denomination, and steps to be taken to make music a greater instrument for the expression of Christian Worship."[36] Williamson presented his program for church music and the choir performed, but no steps were taken to establish the Commission—just a recognition of his good work and an encouragement to other churches to use Westminster as a model program. The quartet still controlled the choir loft.

The other major event was the national convention of the Music Teachers National Association, which was held in Dayton in December. Williamson was asked to present his program for music education in the church, with its benefits for the individual, its service to the community, and a program of worship for the church. The plan included a department of music in each church, with a junior choir (ages six to twelve), intermediate choir (ages twelve to eighteen), and an adult choir. Churches with over six hundred members would have a high-school choir (ages sixteen to twenty-one), an adult choir to start at age twenty-one, an orchestra in every church, a free voice lesson every week for each member of the adult choir, and a leader of the highest character.

The plan, as it was working at Westminster Presbyterian, was reported in the *Dayton Journal* as

> the beginning of a new era of church music. . . . marked last nite [sic] when five choirs of Westminster Presbyterian Church, making a chorus of more than 200 voices, assisted by the Civic orchestra, presented Gaul's "Holy City" at Memorial Hall to an audience which filled the place to overflowing.[37]

The *Practical Church Music* (1909) of Edmund S. Lorenz was finding realization in his own hometown.

The professional quartet did not go away, and qualified leaders to build a Westminster program were not available. The only creative alternative was to start a school for the preparation of "Ministers of Music"—a term coined by Dr. Evans and Williamson to be conferred upon its graduates.

In April 1926 Williamson entered into a contract with the church for the use of its facilities for such a school. Thus, the Choir School formally opened on September 13, 1926, with sixty students from fourteen states and a faculty of ten. The cost of operating the school was underwritten by Mrs. Talbott, and no tuition was charged the first year. The following year a tuition charge of $150 was made, and the rental on the church was $1,800.

By the fall of 1928 the school had eighty students and a faculty of twelve. The church's facilities were already inadequate. Dr. Evans and Mrs. Talbott were working on a plan to purchase the Dayton Country Club, when a committee from the Ithaca (N.Y.) Conservatory of Music presented a formal invitation to Williamson to move the Choir School to Ithaca. The school would retain its name, and its director, get a new building, and have the authority to grant the Bachelor of Music degree. The Westminster Choir School moved to Ithaca the following September. But as early as 1932 the school had fifty-four graduates employed by churches in eighteen states, and sixty-one churches in the Ithaca area were being served by student directors. The Ithaca connection was already inadequate.

The Westminster Choir School moved to Princeton, New Jersey, in the summer of 1932, after working out academic relationships with the Princeton Theological Seminary, the Princeton Chapel, the university, and the First Presbyterian Church. The following spring, Mrs. J. Livingston Taylor became the school's second major sponsor by donating $350,000 for the building of the complete facilities for the choir school. The cornerstone was laid in January 1934, and in August the deed for the campus and four Georgian-style buildings were transferred from Mrs. Taylor to the Westminster Choir School.[38]

In June 1928 Mrs. Talbott signed a tour contract with Albert Morini, a Viennese manager, for an extensive European tour. The Europeans, notwithstanding, proved somewhat skeptical of an American choir singing sacred choral literature to European audiences. In 1934, soon after moving into the new campus, the choir made a second European tour which was successful beyond their expectations. Morini had convinced Williamson that Europeans wanted to hear distinctively American folk songs, ballads, and spirituals. The concerts thereafter featured concert arrangements of spirituals, cowboy ballads, and other folk songs.

After moving to the new campus Roy Harris joined the faculty and launched the Contemporary American Music Festivals of 1936 and 1938. The categories were chamber music, organ, and a cappella choral works. Among the three hundred entries, twenty-two works were premiered at the first festival. The judges for the competitions were Paul Boepple (faculty), Carl Engel, Roy Harris (faculty), Quincy Porter, and Edgar Varese.

Another major event of 1934 was the invitation from Leopold Stokowski to perform J. S. Bach's *B Minor Mass* with the Philadelphia orchestra. The performance was repeated in New York and Princeton. This was the first of 162 performances of forty major choral works with symphonies in New York City, Rochester, Baltimore, and Philadelphia. One hundred twenty-five of these were with the New York Philharmonic. The most noted conductors included Leopold Stokowski, Bruno Walter, Dimitri Mitropoulos, Artur Rodzinski, Eugene Ormandy, Arturo Toscanini, John Barbarolli, and Leonard Bernstein. Many of these performances were American premieres, and many were the first American recordings of major works for chorus and orchestra.

One of the more important legacies of the Choir School was in the field of choral publications. Several series were generated by Williamson and the faculty. The first was *The Westminster Choir Series* from 1931-1945. It consisted of forty-two pieces, primarily from the Renaissance and Baroque periods, and was published by G. Schirmer. Six works entitled *John Finley Williamson Series* were published by Carl Fischer. These contained three classics and three contemporary pieces. A third series, *The Westminster Choir College Library* (1950-1957), was edited by Normand Lockwood (faculty) and published by the Theodore Presser Company. The series was later resumed (1962) with David Stanley York as editor. The Choir School also provided a unique addition to the available choral literature by housing the Drinker Library of Choral Music (1943). This consisted of 365 major choral works made available to churches, schools, and choral organizations on a rental basis.

The roster of distinguished faculty is impressive. In addition to those mentioned, we would include Elaine Brown, Julius Herford, George Lynn, Alexander McCurdy, Paul Nettl, Carl Parrish, Feri Roth, Robert Stevenson, and Carl Weinrich.

World War II was difficult for all schools of the arts, and Westminster was no exception. While enrolled in a special military training school at Princeton University, I was privileged to attend the First Presbyterian Church, where Dr. Williamson was directing a very small choir, and to attend the Princeton Chapel where Carl Weinrich was organist. There were many echoes of the prewar vespers and choral activities, but the lull was very temporary, for the emergence of church music as an academic discipline and church ministry was hardly imaginable in those bleak years. The greatest years for church music were about to begin and were brought about by the total dedication of men like John Finley Williamson.

The educational explosion of the postwar years strained the facilities of the renamed Westminster Choir College. In an effort to expand, the college purchased a ninety-five-acre estate just outside Princeton, with a thirty-two-room residence. Williamson was dreaming of a summer "Tanglewood" with the New York Philharmonic, and attempts were made to sell the existing campus. Unfortunately, no buyer was found, and they had to settle for a new $400,000 men's dormitory on the original site.

At Dr. Williamson's retirement in 1958 the College had an enrollment of 350 students from thirty states. Although a majority of these would work as ministers of music, many would become college voice teachers and choral directors. This compounded the influence of John Finley Williamson and the choral literature which he espoused.

Williamson's retirement, the musical expansion of the denominational seminaries, and the entry of many state universities into the field of church music brought about some changes in the curricula at the Choir College. Although the offerings are still limited to keyboard, vocal, and choral majors, the aims are now "to serve the churches, schools, and the community." By 1961 students could major in performance or music education at both the Bachelors and Masters levels. Changes notwithstanding, the Westminster Choir College "continues to maintain its original commitment to the church and to choral music."[39]

. By 1984, under the presidency of Dr. Ray E. Robinson, the catalog reported an enrollment of nearly four hundred undergraduate and graduate students, and six choirs constituted a nucleus for the choral curricula. The Westminster Choir College continues to be a major influence upon the music ministries in the Protestant churches of America.

From the ranks of active church musicians and church music educators, the creation and performance of our most functional church music has continued throughout this century. As Dudley Buck was a dominant force at the turn of the century, Leo

Sowerby (1895-1968) was to make major contributions to the hymnody, organ literature, choral music, and church music education from the 1920s to his death. It could be said that Sowerby was a prototype of a new professional church musician —or perhaps an extension of the organist/director of years past. It was the rise of church music as an academic discipline of higher education which brought to the choir loft and organ bench the professor/organist; the professor/composer; and the professor/choir director.

Leo Sowerby was first the composer—his violin concerto was programmed by the Chicago Symphony in 1913, and he was awarded the Prix de Rome in 1921. He joined the faculty of Chicago's American Conservatory in 1917 and was an assistant to Eric DeLamarter at the Fourth Presbyterian Church. He was later appointed to succeed John Wesley Norton as the organist/choirmaster of Saint James Episcopal Church (1927), one of the most influential Episcopal churches in America. It was a post formerly held by Dudley Buck, Peter Lutkin, and Clarence Dickinson.[40]

As the teacher of young composers at the conservatory, he was influential in shaping their concepts of the functions of music in public worship, as well as the development of a personal musical style. He himself wrote hymn tunes, anthems, service music, cantatas, oratorios, and organ music for every facet of the Episcopal liturgy. He served on the Joint Commission for the *Hymnal 1940* at the request of Canon Winfred Douglas. With a mandate to make the music more "suitable for congregational singing,"[41] many nineteenth-century tunes were dropped and replaced by plainsong, psalm tunes, and chorales. Sowerby also corrected and improved minor details in the harmonizations. He contributed two new tunes—PALISADES and TAYLOR HALL —and harmonized three existing tunes. A later edition of the *Hymnal* (1961) added Sowerby's *Communion Service in D*. Because of the quality of the work and its wide acceptance, *Hymnal 1940* became the model format for a long series of denominational hymnals published after World War II.

Sowerby, as an educator/church musician, became deeply involved in the shaping of an emerging ideology for church music and church musicians. In April 1941 he went to Washington, D.C.

> to participate in the second annual church music conference
> sponsored by the Washington Cathedral. . . . He called his paper
> "Ideals in Church Music," in which he traced the origin and
> progress of church music from early plainsong, through the
> Reformation period up to the current situation.[42]

At the conclusion of the conference, several choirs from the Washington area combined in the performance of his *Te Deum Laudamus* in D minor. Two years later, he repeated the lectures at St. Bartholomew's Church in New York City, where his friend and composer David McK. Williams was organist and choirmaster. At the conclusion of his lectures, Searle Wright gave a recital of Sowerby's organ works. The Seabury Press published his *Ideals in Church Music* in 1956 as "an official statement prepared for the Joint Commission on Church Music."[43] A basic premise of the lectures was:

> The basic idea underlying all the music of the Church is that it
> is performed as an act of praise, worship, prayer, or thanksgiving
> directly to God. How wrong, then, is the thought that the people
> who come to worship must expect that they will be entertained
> by the music.[44]

The little book was destined to become required reading for students in many schools of church music.

Sowerby's denominational influence was enhanced through his work at the Wa-Li-Ro summer conference for church music at Put-in-Bay, Ohio. Founded in 1937 as a training camp for boy choristers from Episcopal churches, Sowerby became a regular member of the staff in 1954 as a lecturer and assisted in the training of the choirboys. He returned each year until his death in 1968 and wrote eleven anthems for the Wa-Li-Ro staff and choristers.

Leo Sowerby remained at the American Conservatory and Saint James until 1962. In that same year, Saint James became the Episcopal Cathedral for the Diocese of Chicago. The rededication of the church was the occasion for the writing and performance of his *Te Deum Laudamus* in E-flat. The event also marked his resignation from the conservatory and Saint James, to become the director of a new College of Church Musicians, which was to be a part of the Washington Cathedral complex. This College represented an ambitious undertaking in the ideal environment of the Cathedral. The twenty-one members of the initial governing board included such distinguished musician/ educators as Dr. Robert Baker, Dr. Samuel Barber, Dr. E. William Doty, Dr. Howard Hanson, and Dr. Earl V. Moore. Besides Sowerby, the other members of the faculty were Paul Callaway, Richard Dirksen, Leonard Ellinwood, and William Workman. The studies included plainsong and hymnody; anthem repertory; music for various services of the church; service playing; improvisation; composition; analysis; orchestration; and organ study. In June 1966 the College of Church Musicians conferred Master's degrees upon its first graduates.[46]

Sowerby's administration of the college was not without problems, but his composition was now focused almost entirely upon choral music. The years 1965 and 1966 were his most productive, with forty-four pieces. The anthem now became his largest catalog of compositions with eighty-five.

His position at the college carried great denominational prestige and made it possible for him to travel widely as lecturer and conductor. An added honor which came to him was his election as a Fellow of the Royal School of Church Music (F.R.S.C.M.) at Surrey, England, in 1963. The launching of the College of Church Musicians showed great promise and attracted a substantial endowment. However, after Sowerby's death in 1968 the denominational colleges and seminaries began to monopolize the professional training of church musicians. According to a recent conversation I had with a member of the board, the endowment is used to support a fellow who normally has completed a graduate degree in music and who serves the Cathedral as an apprentice.

Sowerby's music was a pioneering effort in twentiety-century church music. Revolting against the Romantic, stylized, and predictable harmonic control of music, he characterized the modern church musician as a seer and prophet. He believed that "venturesomeness is the most vital quality in art, as in living; and it is this element of venturesomeness that is always in evidence in the work of the modern church musician."[47] At the same time, he was vehemently opposed to the experimental use of jazz or other popular idioms in church music. He contended that jazz is for entertainment, and that excluded its use in worship.

His sacred choral works are not given to experimentation. They are vocally idiomatic and project strong text declamation. His organ works are equally idiomatic, but virtuosic to a degree that churches without a very competent organist are not able to utilize much of his choral literature. Jones' summation of the anthems concludes that "Sowerby's goal was to praise God with this music and it becomes a worthy instrument in the hands of the initiated and competent musician whose desire is also to please God and worship Him."[48]

An interesting facet of this study is Jones' list of all the anthems used at Saint James Church in Chicago during Sowerby's tenure (1927-1962). Of twenty composers who had four or more anthems or responses performed, fourteen were late-nineteenth- or early-twentieth-century composers, and only two of these were American—Horatio Parker (7) and Eric DeLamarter (4). Six were from the sixteenth, seventeenth, or eighteenth centuries—J. S. Bach, William Byrd, Orlando Gibbons, George F. Handel, Palestrina, and Henry Purcell. The single composer with the most anthems used was the Irish organist Charles Wood, with eleven. The only other Americans who had more than one anthem listed were: Harvey Gaul (3), Peter Lutkin (3), H. A. Matthews (2), T. Tertius Noble (3), and Dudley Buck, a former director at Saint James (2).

The anthems used most often by Sowerby are of equal interest. It was not surprising that Handel's "Hallelujah Chorus" was used thirty-seven times. Next was J. S. Bach's "Break Forth, O Beauteous, Heavenly Light." The third most used was shared by Samuel Wesley's "Lead Me, Lord," Charles Wood's "This Sanctuary of My Soul," and Cesar Franck's "Psalm CL." There were nine additional anthems which were used more than twenty times. These were by Mark Andrews, J. S. Bach, E. C.

Bairstow (2), D. S. Bortniansky, Brahms, Edward Elgar, Charles Wood, and Samuel Wesley.

The American composers of church music and the concurrent a cappella trends in choral music were minimized at Saint James in favor of the English traditions. In turn, Sowerby's expertly crafted choral music, with its complex organ accompaniments, has been largely by passed by the influential conductors and institutional educators in church music.

16
Curricular Development in Graduate Schools

The seminaries with denominational support were in a preferred position to take the lead in the training of church musicians. With budgeted financial support from their constituency, they had the opportunity to establish and promote a music ministry that was now education oriented. As late as 1952 Fink reported that "leaders in religious work are today realizing that the training of the church musician is a specialized endeavor requiring broad preparation in both theology and music."[49] His study examined the status (1952) of church music training through published catalogs, ministers, and full-time ministers of music. His study was limited to those seminaries accredited by the American Association of Theological Schools. At that time, of the 107 schools listed by the AATS, only five offered a curriculum in music at the graduate level. They were:

(1) San Francisco Theological Seminary, San Anselmo, California; (2) Union Theological Seminary, New York, New York; (3) The Southern Baptist Theological Seminary, Louisville, Kentucky; (4) New Orleans Baptist Theological Seminary, New Orleans, Louisiana; and (5) Southwestern Baptist Theological Seminary, Fort Worth, Texas.[50]

According to Fink's study, the preferred undergraduate preparation for graduate study in church music was either a B.A. degree with a Music major or the B.M. degree with a major in Music Education. The possibilities for making up deficiencies in music were fairly uniform, and a heavy emphasis upon biblical and doctrinal studies was in all curricula. The academic distinctives included such courses as Sacred Music Literature, History of Church Music, Hymnology, Worship, Vocal Techniques, and Choral Conducting. Since the graded choirs had become a basic concept of the music ministry, courses in Church Music Methods and Administration became parallel to graduate studies in Music Education. Fink cited an interview with Dr. W. E. Welsh, minister of the East Dallas Christian Church, in March 1951:

> The minister of music should be more than an organist or choir director; his place in the church and religion goes beyond these functions. He is an educator or teacher, ministering to the congregation through religious music, which work involves a teaching ministry.[51]

Although deeply rooted in the experience of the Bible institutes, these expanded curricula also represented a distillation of the earlier writings of Clarence Dickinson, Edmund S. Lorenz, Waldo Selden Pratt, Isham E. Reynolds, Ernest O. Sellers, and John Finley Williamson. Because of pending accreditation, the standards for musicianship were already being taken from the *By-laws and Regulations* of the National Association of Schools of Music.

The conclusions from Fink's study were that training in basic musicianship should precede graduate study in church music and that there was little uniformity in other areas which were deemed essential background studies for the ministry of music. A summary of these needs included: "(1) spiritual preparation and general background, (2) basic musicianship, (3) applied music, (4) sacred musicianship and church music pedagogy, and (5) theology."[52]

It was shortly after Fink's study that NASM began the accreditation of degrees in church music and admitted seminaries to full or associate membership. It was then, through the experience and influence of existing curricula and the *By-laws* of NASM, that both uniformity and denominational flexibility would be brought to the training of ministers of music.

The rapid expansion of graduate studies in church music reached a high degree of uniformity in the middle 1960s. A new study of graduate programs offered in 1964-1965 by William L. Hooper began with the ten seminaries listed in the directory of AATS which now offered graduate programs in church music. The study now included eighteen schools of music accredited by NASM which now offered the Master's degree in Church Music. These eighteen were colleges, universities, and conservatories. Some maintained a denominational affiliation, some were privately endowed and independent, and some were state-supported universities. Since the Fink study in 1952, five additional seminaries were offering graduate work in music. Almost all of the colleges and universities that had added church music were following the curricular standards of NASM. Their degree requirements were consistent with other graduate programs which required a minimum of thirty or thirty-six hours of credit. Their degree plans also emphasized performance majors in organ or voice.

The AATS had not set any standards for degrees in church music, so the seminaries followed the musical standards set by NASM. Thus some striking differences appeared in the curricula of the seminaries and the schools of music.

> The degree programs in church music offered by the seminaries
> . . . were initiated in response to [the] need of the churches for
> theologically oriented musicians. The educational philosophy of
> the seminaries has been that of preparing servants for the
> Church who will and can minister through music.[53]

The additional requirements in theology and Christian education increased the seminary degrees to a minimum of fifty and a maximum of sixty-four semester hours. In the various seminaries, the required nonmusic courses ranged from ten to thirty-eight hours and electives from one to twelve hours.

Among the ten seminaries, some offered the Master of Sacred

Music and some the Master of Church Music. As stated earlier, many are now using the more universal Master of Music. As terminal projects for the degree, eight of the ten seminaries required a recital, seven a thesis, six a composition, and only three written and/or oral comprehensive exams. The terminal project was determined by the student's major field of study.

Many differences also appeared in the music requirements of the seminaries and the schools of music. The greatest differences occurred in the field of music theory. The seminaries might require simply Advanced Theory, Choral Arranging, Composition, or Electives in Music Theory. The music schools were more specific in requiring Counterpoint, Stylistic Analysis, Canon and Fugue, or Theory Seminar.

The seminaries required Conducting (and some offer it as a major), while only seven of the eighteen schools of music required conducting in their degree programs. The requirements in Music History were equally diverse. Both generally required Musicology and allowed electives, but the schools of music often specified particular courses which were probably common to other graduate programs, such as Music of Bach, Oratorio Literature, Music of the Baroque, and Organ Literature.

In the area of specific courses in church music, the seminaries were more strict (for example, Church Music Administration, Music for Children, or Contemporary Church Music). The schools of music tended to treat this material more generally in seminars, surveys, or church music philosophy. Both emphasized organ and voice, and some seminaries allowed a piano or instrumental principal. Some seminaries also added courses in organ design and pedagogy in organ, voice, and diction. Such courses in methods and materials emphasized the multiple role of the minister of music as teacher, performer, and conductor.

Hooper summarized these comparative curricula in church music:

> The majority of the master's degrees in church music in the [18] graduate music schools of this study were basically applied music degrees, while the majority of the master's degrees in church

music in the seminaries in this study were basically vocational church music degrees.[54]

He also surveyed 219 graduates of the ten seminaries regarding the adequacy of their training. The three areas in which the graduates expressed their greatest needs were (1) laboratory experience in graded choirs, (2) administration, and (3) choral arranging.

The rapid growth of church music as an academic discipline has created curricula so varied that any attempt at music accreditation by the AATS would be very difficult. The seminaries will undoubtedly continue to structure their curricula to meet the needs of their denominational constituency, but continue within the musical standards of NASM.

As churches adopted the educational concept of graded choirs and instrumental ensembles, the "ministries" of the minister of music were expanded. He now assumed the added functions of educator and administrator, as well as choral director and leader in worship. His role as educator required that he extend his own skills to the training of lay assistants to conduct and give vocal instruction to children of various age levels. Since liturgical services limit, to a degree, the participation of many of these ensembles in the worship service, the nonliturgical churches have been able to better utilize some of these musical resources.

17

Continuing Education

The major denominations quickly established Departments, Commissions, or Boards to assist in this in-service training of leaders for these programs of music education in the individual churches. These plans for continuing education are carried out through state, regional, and even national conferences and workshops. The classes include advanced and refresher courses in conducting, choral literature, vocal instruction, theory, hymnology, and instrumental ensembles. A continuing development is an increase in denominational publications which contain more music and instructional materials.

The United Methodist Church published the *Music Ministry* magazine as an aid to the selection of literature and the maintenance of a music program. The Lutherans have *Church Music* from Concordia Publishing Company. Southern Baptists began publishing *The Church Musician* in 1950, with articles of interest and help to choir directors, plus a study of the "Hymn of the Month," to be studied and featured some time during the month. Following the format of the Lorenz magazines, a hymn arrangement and choral music were included, and the music portion could be removed and preserved in the choir library. After *The Church Musician* surpassed 100,000 circulation in the 1960s, a separate *Junior Musician* and *Youth Musician* were issued in order to accommodate the minimum choir programs.

As of 1970 *The Church Musician* was restricted to special articles for choir leaders and to instrumental music for winds, strings, and handbells. Individual parts were included so that the instruments could be used with the congregation or choirs or independently in the worship service. One of the most distinctly church oriented of these has been the handbell choir. Almost all medium and large churches maintain a bell choir alongside their vocal ensembles. Bell ringing is probably unsurpassed as a rhythmic discipline, and its sound has been enthusiastically accepted in the sanctuaries of almost all Protestant congregations.

A significant factor in continuing education and professional fellowship has been the organizations of ministers of music. The Methodists organized a National Fellowship of Methodist Musicians (NaFOMM). Baptists organized a Southern Baptist Church Music Conference in 1957, which has a current (1985) membership of nearly one thousand. This SBCMC has an annual meeting in June each year, with a program format emphasizing performances by seminary, college, and church choirs (each number listed gives the name of publisher), a new anthem commissioned and published for the conference, and devotional and instructional papers on church music. The annual proceedings are then published for the membership. A *Southern Baptist Church Music Journal* (since 1984) is now published annually with feature articles and reviews of recent books on church music. The current editors of the Journal are musicologists Hugh McElrath and Harry Eskew.

The central functions of music among all Protestants have remained almost constant, but with differing emphases. Music is an *aid* to worship. Music is a *means* of worship. Music is a *method* of proclamation of the gospel. This is eloquently expressed by Don Collins in his study of prevailing practices in church music education:

> as an aid to worship, the church has used music to assist the worshipper to experience the presence of God and to imbibe the requirements of His will. Music is a means of worship because through it, Christians have a vehicle for directly expressing their thoughts and emotions. . . . the particular musical item should gather and express the emotion, the frame of mind, and the liturgical action of the moment.[55]

The growth of dominant musical and educational practices initiated within individual churches, has often dictated and will continue to dictate curricular changes in the colleges and seminaries preparing young men and women for this growing Christian ministry.

Notes

1. Lorenz, Edmund S., *Practical Church Music* (New York: Fleming H. Revell Company, 1909) p.11.
2. Ibid., p.131.
3. Ibid., p.132.
4. Ibid.
5. Ibid., p.250.
6. Getz, Gene A., *MBI, The Story of Moody Bible Institute* (Chicago: Moody Press, 1969) p.140.

7. Ibid.

8. Ibid., citing Sellers, E.O., *Evangelism in Sermon and Song*, p.70.

9. Ibid., p.153.

10. Personal interview with Dr. Gordon Hooker, Ret., November 19, 1984.

11. Personal letter from Dr. Schwarz, dated April 25, 1983.

12. Redden, Sally Jean, *A History of the School of Church Music at New Orleans Baptist Theological Seminary* (1919-1966). MCM Thesis, NOBTS, New Orleans, 1968.

13. Spigener, Tommy R., *The Contributions of Isham E. Reynolds to Church Music in the Southern Baptist Convention between 1915-1945*. MCM Thesis, SBTS, Ft. Worth, 1962, p.63.

14. Ibid., p.70.

15. Coffin, Henry Sloane, *A Half Century of Union Theological Seminary*, 1896-1945 (New York: Charles Scribner's Sons, 1954), p.170.

16. Ibid., p.171.

17. Ibid., p.172.

18. Personal letter from Seth Kasten, Ref. Librarian, UTS, November 30, 1985.

19. Johnson, Albert Rykken, *The Christiansen Choral Tradition: F. Melius Christiansen, Olaf C. Christiansen, and Paul J. Christiansen*. Ph.D. Dissertation, The University of Iowa, 1973, p.65.

20. Ibid., p.76, citing Bergmann, Leola Nelson, *Music Masters of the Middle West*, p.59.

21. Ibid., p.99.

22. Ibid., p.98.

23. Ibid., p.97.

24. Ibid., p.118.

25. Ibid., p.292.

26. Ibid., p.308.

27. Ibid., p.321.

28. Ibid., pp.525-547.

29. Reynolds, William J., *Hymns of Our Faith* (Nashville: Broadman Press, 1964), p.42.

30. Neve, Paul E., *The Contributions of the Lutheran College Choirs to Music in America* (Ann Arbor: University Microfilms, 1967), pp.35-36.

31. Ibid., p.43.

32. Ibid., p.80.

33. Wehr, David A., *John Finley Williamson (1887-1964): His Life and Contribution to Choral Music*. Ph.D. Dissertation, University of Miami, 1971, p.19.

34. Ibid., p.23.

35. Ibid., p.53.

36. Ibid., p.59.

37. Ibid., p.57.

38. Ibid., p.87.

39. Catalog of Westminster Choir College, 1982-1984, p.3.

40. Jones, Raymond D., *Leo Sowerby: His Life and His Choral Music* (Ann Arbor: University Microfilms, 1973), p.192.

41. *Hymnal 1940* (New York: The Church Pension Fund, 1943), p.iv.

42. Jones, *Leo Sowerby*, p.177.

43. Ibid., p.178.

44. Sowerby, Leo, *Ideals in Church Music* (Greenwich, Conn.: Seabury Press, 1956) p.17.

45. Jones, Leo Sowerby, p.208.

46. Ibid., p.217.

47. Ibid. p.162, quoting "The Compleat Choirmaster," an unpublished lecture, November 1, 1961 for the Joint Commission on Church Music.

48. Ibid., p.313.

49. Fink, Fred W., *Graduate Music Curricula in Protestant Theological Seminaries of America*. M.M. Thesis, Southern Methodist University, 1952, p.1.

50. Ibid., p.5.

51. Ibid., p.30.

52. Ibid., p.72.

53. Hooper, William Loyd, *The Master's Degree in Church Music in Protestant Theological Seminaries of the United States*. Ph.D. Dissertation, George Peabody College for Teachers, 1966, p.77.

54. Ibid., pp.145-146.

55. Collins, Don L., *Principles and Practices Prevailing in Church Music Education Programs of Selected Protestant Churches of America*. The Florida State University, 1970, pp.53-54.

Part VI:

Recent Developments

18

Publishers and Composers

Any study of Protestant church music in twentieth-century America must give adequate consideration to the composers and to the music available to directors of the choral groups. With the rapid growth of graded choirs after World War II, a major problem was finding appropriate music for choirs at all levels. Since the Lorenz graded publications have already been treated as an important indication of the practice of church music at the turn of the century, it is worthy of note that these choir magazines are still in publication at this writing. The editorial responsibilities for the *Choir Leader, Choir Herald,* and *Volunteer Choir* were carried by Edmund S. Lorenz himself into the 1930s. His assistant editors included Carrie B. Adams, L. O. Emerson, J. S. Fearis, Charles H. Gabriel, Marie Hine, William J. Kirkpatrick, Mrs. C. H. Morris, Roy Nolte, J. A. Parks, H. W. Petrie, and Ira B. Wilson.

The most productive of his composer-editors, however, was Emma L. Ashford (1850-1930). She was a church organist from age twelve, a member of Dudley Buck's choir at Saint James in Chicago, and for forty years a teacher and composer in Nashville, Tennessee. Her compositions number three hundred anthems, fourteen cantatas, fifty solos, and seven collections of organ music. According to the *Choir Leader* of January 1931, the best known of these works are the solo "My Task" and the anthem "Lift up Your Heads." After Lorenz's own compositions, Mrs. Ashford was the largest contributor to the magazines.

The magazine articles continued to be informative and helpful to choir directors and organists. Many were reprints from

208

other sources but were authoritative and as diverse as vocal techniques by D. A. Clippinger, E. P. Hiland, or John Finley Williamson; articles on hymnody by Frank Metcalf and Homer Rodeheaver; discussions of how composers write music and questions on theory by B.C. Unseld; and even articles on choir parties.

An interesting poll of 119 choir directors, published in *The Choir Leader* for June 1930, recorded the twenty-five "best" and "most-used" anthems of 1929. A list of the composers cited most indicates the style and content of church music as practiced at that point—Ashford, Heyser, Petrie, and Wooler. The texts of these fifty anthems were about equally divided between Scripture and familiar hymn texts. The "best" and "most used" were "More Love to Thee, O Christ" and "A Pilgrim's Journey" respectively. The latter was an arrangement of the folk tune *Londonderry Air*. The adaptation of familiar folk or classical tunes was quite appealing in this period, both in hymnals and choral settings. The *Herald* and *Volunteer Choir* also had their polls of "best" and "most-used" polls of 239 directors. Their choices leaned strongly toward the hymn and gospel song texts. Carrie B. Adams and Ira B. Wilson were the "most used" in the *Herald*. Charles H. Gabriel and Wilson were the "most used" in the *Volunteer Choir*. Music for special days and seasons was continued in all of the magazines, and Gabriel's "Mother of Mine" was voted among the best in the 1929 *Herald*.

As stated earlier, the three magazines remain in publication at this writing, and they have been joined by the *SAB Choir*. This latest magazine meets the vocal needs of both the youth choir and the small adult choir with very limited male voices. Each magazine has its own editor, and all materials have simple keyboard accompaniments. Hugh S. Livingston, Jr. is editor of the new *SAB Choir*, and a most interesting number in the October 1984 issue is his arrangement of Ashford's "My Task"— and indexed as "One of Lorenz's most popular anthems in a fresh, updated arrangement." Other composers who are prominent in the current magazines are Lani Smith, Gordon Young, Ellen Jane Lorenz, James Mansfield, Robert J. Hughes, and Franklin Ritter.

The tremendous growth of church music in the decades after World War II is indicated in the expansion of what is now the Lorenz Corporation. The separate divisions now include the Lorenz Publishing Company; Heritage Press; Laurel Press; The Sacred Music Press; Roger Dean Publishing Company; Sonshine Productions; Triune Music, Incorporated; and exclusive distribution for the publications of The Choristers Guild and the American Guild of English Handbell Ringers, Incorporated.

The Lorenz catalog now contains extensive offerings in keyboard music, instrumental music, choral octavos, cantatas, youth musicals, music and music education materials for children, choral collections, handbell music and materials, recordings and tapes for teaching and accompaniments, and vocal solo collections.

Another large independent publisher, but distinctly directed toward the free churches of German and Scandinavian origin, is the Augsburg Publishing House of Minneapolis. A modest choral catalog of 1948-49 listed less than one hundred anthems in the choral library, with nine compositions by Paul Christiansen, seventeen by Leland Sateren, and eighteen arrangements of traditional choral literature by Oscar Overby. Dorothy and Gunnar Malmin had thirty sacred songs for treble voices. Less than ten of these were chorales, and the remainder were original texts or hymns familiar to most Protestant congregations. The principal body of choral music in the 1948-49 catalog was the *St. Olaf Choir Series,* consisting of more than two hundred fifty "Sacred Anthems for Mixed Voices, Composed and Arranged by F. Melius Christiansen." A few standard composers whose music was not arranged were Bach, Barnby, Beethoven, Goss, Gounod, Grieg, Mendelssohn, Mozart, Schubert, Schumann, Vulpius, and Wagner.

Other special college choir series were the *Augustana,* the *Dana,* and *Northland,* edited by Carl Youngdahl, Gunner Malmin, and Margrethe Hokanson respectively. The three series combined contained only thirteen numbers, but of special import were three Negro spirituals in the *Dana Choir Series,* edited by Malmin—"Steal Away," "Crucifixion," and "Swing Low, Sweet Chariot."

Augsburg's 1970-71 catalog was a thirty-six-page volume which indexed books and pamphlets for Choir Directors, Singers, Organists, Soloists and Music Teachers, Hymns, Worship, and History. The choral music was contained in pages 7-29 and included large Choral Works, Choral Collections, Choir with Instruments, Anthems, a Special Anthem Series of German Carols, Scandinavian Carols, Choral Settings of Psalms, and the Augsburg Concert Series. The focus of the books is indicative of the growth and metamorphosis of Lutheran church music in the two previous decades. Topics included a translation of Wilhelm Elmann's *The Changing Voice; Choral Conducting; The New Song* by Leland Sateren; *Problems in Conducting* by Daniel Moe; *The Development of Lutheran Hymnody in America;* and *The Lutheran Church-Its Basic Traditions* by Johannes Riedel.

Large choral works were featured by Jean Berger, Paul Fetler, Normand Lockwood, and Ronald A. Nelson. The Choral Collections had Unison Hymns with Descants; Unison Chorale Anthems for Adult or Junior Choir; Hymns for Men; and a large selection of Anthems for Choir with Instruments. But the largest single listing was Anthems for Mixed Voices, with more than four hundred entries. A majority of the composers were educators and church musicians from the many Lutheran colleges of the Midwest—Paul Christiansen, Paul Fetler, Kenneth Jennings, David Johnson, Paul Mantz, Daniel Moe, Ronald A. Nelson, Knut Nystedt, Frank and Marie Pooler, Leland Sateren, and Robert Wetzler. A significant number of anthems, however, were from composers who were active church musicians from other denominations—William Hooper, Austin Lovelace, Gordon Young, and Philip Young. The *St. Olaf Choir Series* by F. Melius Christiansen was continued, and a few of the titles were rearranged by his son Olaf. The current director of the Saint Olaf Choir, Kenneth Jennings, has arrangements and original compositions. Paul continued the Christiansen tradition with the most single entries.

Especially noteworthy is the work of Marie Pooler in the field of children's choirs. This new emphasis brought forth several anthems combining junior and adult choirs, as either Unison with SATB or SA with SATB combinations. Of equal interest is a number of works by David Johnson which feature folk melodies and hymn texts from the South, augmenting the traditional folk literature from Germany, Norway, and Sweden, used so extensively in the Lutheran choral tradition. The texts are also more ecumenical, drawing more heavily from traditional English hymnody.

One of the most dynamic elements in the Augsburg catalog is probably expressed in *Contemporary Worship I—Hymns,* a collection of twenty-one new hymns with twenty-six new musical settings. Leading this move toward a more contemporary text and a more academic contemporary harmony were David Johnson, Daniel Moe, Knut Nystedt, and Leland Sateren. The continuation of this effort resulted in several new additions to the *Lutheran Book of Worship* (1978).

A similar, and major, independent publisher is the Neil A. Kjos Music Company, formerly based in Chicago, but presently in San Diego. Founded in 1936, "its first publication was the *Pitts Voice Class Method,* by Carol Marhoff Pitts. Its publication followed the establishment of the Christiansen Choral School in Ephraim, Wisconsin about the same time."[1] The company now comprises eight music divisions, which include the Tuskegee Music Press, Pallma Music Company, and the Parks Music Company (formerly the J.A. Parks Music Company of York, Nebraska). Kjos became the sole distributor for the Parks Company in 1950 and inherited an incredible catalog of almost 400 listings of secular TTBB and TTB titles and almost 150 items of sacred TTBB and TTB. There were nearly 200 secular SATB choruses; more than 200 sacred SATB anthems; and more than 50 sacred three-part and two-part anthems. Approximately 60 percent of all this music was composed or arranged by Parks. His experience as editor for E. S. Lorenz is apparent in his choice of texts and his arrangements of the standard romantic composers. His texts were largely from better-known hymns and romantic religious poetry and included special music for Thanksgiving, Christmas, Easter, Patriotic, Children's Day, and Mother's Day.

The 1950 Kjos catalog of choral and instrumental music had more than five hundred listings of Sacred and Secular Choral

Music, and nearly one hundred titles of Christmas Music. The Kjos catalog also carried the huge *St. Olaf Choir Series*, the *Augsburg Choral Library*, and the *Augustana, Dana,* and *Northland* colleges' choir series. All three Christiansens were prominent in the titles as both composers and arrangers; but at this point, Max and Beatrice Krone and Morten Luvaas appeared more often as arrangers of folk music and the classics. Bach and Handel were abundant, and the Russian choral composers were in great demand—probably encouraged by the popular appeal of the touring Don Cossack men's chorus in years past. Their "Hospodi Pomilui" by Lvovsky was performed by almost every college choir.

The Krones, associated with the University of Southern California for many years, were holding workshops in Music Education nationwide. In the rapid expansion of public music education and graded choirs in the churches, they popularized folk music from around the world. As of this 1950 catalog, the Krones had collected and edited fifteen books of folk songs and descants and two grade-school collections entitled *Growing Up with Music.*

Another symptomatic category of church music at this date was the inclusion of many titles from the Renaissance. The music of Des Pres, Hassler, Ingegneri, Morley, Palestrina, and Tallis were frequent entries, but J. S. Bach remained the most used of all historic composers.

A catalog of forty-nine titles under "Choral Music for Special Occasions" was given almost entirely to Thanksgiving and patriotic—with no Children's Day or Mother's Day.

Two decades later the 1970 SATB sacred octavo catalog contained about 650 anthems, almost 200 Christmas selections, and more than 100 Easter octavos. The trends of 1950 were expanded and now included an even larger representation of American composers. Olaf and Paul Christiansen and Max and Beatrice Krone remained as the most prominent composers. However, the list of native Lutheran composers was now featuring Stanley Glarum, Sven Lekberg, Don Malin, Gerhard Schroth, and Peter Tkach. Composers listed often in other catalogs were now in Kjos'—Jean Berger, Noble Cain, Theron Kirk,

Normand Lockwood, Austin Lovelace, Richard Willis, Carlton Young, and Gordon Young. The most distinct addition to the Kjos catalog was spirituals. There were forty-five, arranged by eighteen different composers. The most significant, however, were thirty issued for SATB, SSA, and TTBB under the Tuskegee Music Press, and arranged by Professor William L. Dawson of the Tuskegee Institute in Alabama. Many of these are standard repertoire for most college and high school choirs and are in the music libraries of many churches. Dawson's "Ev'ry Time I Feel the Spirit" became a favorite choral theme of the Billy Graham crusades.

Important issues of historical cantatas and oratorios by Handel and Purcell emerged, along with many sacred collections for mixed, treble, and male voices. Perhaps the most farsighted addition was a catalog of anthems with instrumental accompaniments.

The 1983 Kjos catalog expands the list of American composers and is very innovative in design. Each title is charted by accompaniment, special voicing, solos, instruments accompanying, grade level, and price. The section on books contains choral texts and methods by Olaf Christiansen, Kenneth Jennings, Leon V. Metcalf, Peter D. Tkach, and Ruth Whitlock. Texts in Music Theory, Ear Training, and Music History are offered for secondary and college classes. Arrangements of Baroque, Classical, and Romantic music (especially Russian) are continued, but the list of composers contains more contemporary college teachers, church musicians, and free-lance composers. Among those with multiple listings are John B. Auberlen, Bob Burroughs, Dede Duson, Robert Jordahl, Lena J. McLin, and David Stocker. This 1983 Kjos catalog indicates clearly the scope and diversity of contemporary church music in America and is a reliable source of stylistic trends in its literature.

One of America's major publishing firms, which has helped to determine the performance literature of church music in this century, is G. Schirmer, Incorporated / Associated Music Publishers, Incorporated of New York. The company has multiple subsidiaries, plus the sole distributorship for many foreign companies: G. Ricordi; Breitkopf and Haertel; Editions Salabert;

Faber Music, Ltd.; and the AMP Library of Russian-Soviet Music.

The G. Schirmer holdings require separate catalogs for the many categories of instrumental and vocal music. The current *Vocal and Choral Music* (1983-84) has almost eight hundred entries in SATB voicing, and almost two hundred additional listings for SAB, SA, TB, and Unison voicings. It also contains more than thirty choral collections and nearly two hundred cantatas, oratorios, and masses. There are more than three hundred octavos for Christmas and almost as many for Easter.

The catalog of Vocal Solos is a strong distinctive for G. Schirmer, with more than four hundred items. A large percentage of these are sacred art songs first popularized by Dudley Buck. The major holdings in this genre are works of the American composers: Ole Speaks (8), Albert Hay Malotte (5); Virgil Thomson (5); Dudley Buck (4); Pearl Curran (3); David Guion (3); John J. Niles (4); F. Flaxington Harker (3); and John Prindle Scott (3). Additional Americans, many of whom are contemporary, include: Ernest Charles, John Corigliano, Cecil Effinger, Austin Lovelace, Carl Mueller, William H. Neidlinger, James H. Rogers, and Harry Rowe Shelley. Many solos in the catalog are from the sacred cantatas and oratorios of J. S. Bach, George F. Handel, and especially Felix Mendelssohn. The familiar English composers Gaul, O'Hara, and Stainer appear, but the genre is almost as American as the gospel song. These solo art songs continue to occupy a prominent place in Protestant worship in America, and a majority continue in the repertoire of college voice students.

Sacred octavo music offered by G. Schirmer consists of music from the Renaissance, Baroque, Classical, and Romantic composers, many of which have been translated and arranged for American church and concert choirs. Probably the outstanding offerings from the American traditions are from the folk hymnody of the South, featured in arrangements by Van Camp, James Cram, Walter Ehret, John J. Niles, and the Robert Shaw and Alice Parker series. These original tunes were taken from the *Southern Harmony, The Sacred Harp*, the collections of

George Pullen Jackson, and the early spirituals of the Fisk Jubilee Singers.

The most prominent composer and arranger of church music for G. Schirmer was Carl Mueller with nineteen octavos. Among contemporaries, L. Stanley Glarum has twelve and Lloyd Pfautsch has eight. Early twentieth-century American composers are still represented by J. V. Roberts ("Seek Ye the Lord"); Harry R. Shelley ("Hark, Hark My Soul"); James H. Rogers ("Great Peace Have They"); David Guion ("Prayer"); John P. Scott ("Come Ye Blessed"); F. Flaxington Harker ("How Beautiful upon the Mountains"); and Noble Cain ("In the Night, Christ Came Walking"). More contemporary sacred octavos by American composers are from Samuel Adler, Jean Berger, John Corigliano, Theron Kirk, Sven Lekberg, Normand Lockwood, Leland Sateren, Virgil Thomson, and Elwyn Wienandt.

Numerous sacred cantatas and oratorios are listed by the major Baroque, Classical, and Romantic composers. Many significant works by American composers are also listed: Dudley Buck's *The Coming of the King;* Cecil Effinger's *The St. Luke Christmas Story* and *Cantata for Easter;* James Gillette's *The Divine Mystery;* William H. Neidlinger's *Followers of the Stars;* Lloyd Pfautsch's *God with Us;* and Virgil Thomson's *The Nativity, As Sung by the Shepherds.*

There are special choral series by noted directors and arrangers: the Robert De Cormier Choral Series; the Morris Hayes Choral Series; the Robert Shaw Choral Series; and the Gregg Smith Choral Series. These represent extensive holdings in folk hymns, spirituals, and folk music from around the world. G. Schirmer is, in effect, a contemporary clearinghouse for church music from major publishers and Christian traditions in Europe and America. An important result is a trend toward more universal and ecumenical expressions of the Christian message throughout all Protestantism.

The current catalog of the E.C. Schirmer Company of Boston is primarily choral, with almost eighteen hundred titles. These include many large works for voice or chorus with orchestral instruments and/or electronic tapes. Like other publishers, they feature a large group of composers who are published almost exclusively by E. C. Schirmer. The catalog lists more than sixty editors and arrangers of classical and folk literature. Renaissance music is especially prominent, with almost twenty composers listed. Palestrina alone has twenty-two titles and Victoria [Vittoria] has thirteen. The Baroque is represented most by J. S. Bach through chorales and choruses from his cantatas and oratorios. The classical period, led by Haydn and Mozart, does not comprise a significant amount of literature. The Romantic period is strongly represented by more than ten Russian composers. The largest single body of choral music is in the neo-Romantic collection of folk hymnody and Christmas carols. These collections have thirteen regional sources, and the carols have sixteen national origins.

The strongest emphasis in the E. C. Schirmer catalog is the contemporary American composer. Americans have contributed many major choral works as well as anthems and arrangements. Among these are: Howard Boatwright (*Canticle of the Sun* and *The Passion According to St. Matthew*); Richard Felciano; Libby Larsen (a recent addition to the catalog); Matthew N. Lundquist; Kirke Mechem; Alice Parker (*An Easter Rejoicing, Gaudete, The Martyr's Mirror,* and *A Sermon from the Mountain*); Daniel Pinkham (eighty-six titles and nine major works); Conrad Susa; and Randall Thompson (*A Feast of Praise, Mass of the Holy Spirit, The Nativity According to St. Luke, The Peaceable Kingdom, Requiem,* and *The Testament of Freedom*).

One of the more interesting segments of the catalog is listed as "Hymns and Spirituals," but has only fourteen titles. Only two of these are spirituals—"Ride on, King Jesus," arranged by Elliot Forbes, and "You May Bury Me in the East," one of the most successful of the early Fisk Jubilee songs, as arranged by John Work.

Two of the most influential publications of the E. C. Schirmer Company have been *The Concord Anthem Book* and *The Second Concord Anthem Book,* both edited by Archibald T. Davison and hymnologist Henry Wilder Foote. The two collections contain some of the best performance editions of the historic choral literature of the church and have helped to strengthen its influence upon our twentieth-century choral worship. The original edition contained ten anthems from the Renaissance, thirteen baroque (Bach, Handel, and Purcell), and thirteen Romantic—which included eight Russians. A third volume, compiled by Victoria Glaser and edited by Henry Clough-Leighter, was also without any American composers.

Throughout the first half of this century, the American liturgical churches remained under the strong musical influence of their European traditions. This was especially true of the Episcopal Church. An example of this pervasive influence is in the catalogs of the Oxford University Press. With its main office in London, the company opened an office in New York City and became a major distributor of anthems and service music for the Episcopal Church of America. The dominant influence in hymnody has already been noted.

The musical offerings have been almost totally English. The 1923 collections of service music contained multiple settings by E. C. Bairstow, Herbert Howells, Charles V. Stanford, Percy Whitlock, and Healey Willan (who moved to Canada in 1913). A 1925 collection of *The Oxford Series of Modern Anthems* featured the same composers, with additional anthems by Norman Cocker, Alec Rowley, Harold Darke, Leslie Heward, and William Harris. In English translation, the 1923 catalog of choral music offered fifty-three chorales, sixteen cantatas with parts for "hire," two motets, and twenty-two arias by J.S. Bach.

A 1931 catalog divided the holdings into anthems by "Old Composers" and "Modern Composers." The "Old" were restricted almost entirely to the early English—John Blow, William Byrd, Orlando Gibbons, Pelham Humphreys, Henry Purcell, Christopher Tye, Thomas Tallis, Samuel Wesley, and selections from William Boyce's *Cathedral Music*. Palestrina had one title and Vittoria two. Anthems by the "Modern Composers" included those cited in the 1923 catalog, plus Henry C. Ley (6), Edmund Rubbra, Geoffrey Shaw, G.E.P. Arkwright (6), Ernest Bullock (3), C. Hylton Stewart, and a litany by William Walton.

In a 1950 catalog J. S. Bach had more than thirty chorales and songs translated into both English and Welsh. W. A. Mozart's *Requiem* is listed in a translation by Edward J. Dent, and seven

"Cathedral Anthems" were also offered in octavo arrangements by Dent. Among the "Modern" composers of this date, Martin Shaw appeared with one anthem; Benjamin Britten had choral variations on "A Boy Was Born"; and J. H. Arnold, as composer or editor, had nineteen selections for the various services of the church.

The 1974 catalog revealed a recovery from World War II and an obvious growth in musical activities in the churches. The catalog included American composers Samuel Adler (5), Everett J. Hilty, and Gordon Young (2). In addition to twenty-three Bach chorales, Mozart had two titles and Johannes Brahms three. The remainder were English, and indicated a tremendous increase in contemporary composers and the number of their titles—George Oldroyd (3); John Rutter (6); Martin Shaw (4); Ralph Vaughan Williams (22); William Walton (4); and Healey Willan (14). The service music was, for the most part, music of earlier periods, except for a few settings by Vaughan Williams, Walton, and Willan.

The same catalog offered a large selection of historical cantatas and oratorios by J. S. Bach, C. P. E. Bach, J. C. Bach, Handel, Mendelssohn, and Heinrich Schutz (7). Major contemporary works were listed by Vaughan Williams (6) and William Walton (3).

The continuing growth of Oxford's holdings in church music is represented in the 1983-84 catalog. There are five collections of anthems, one *Oxford Book of Tudor Anthems*, and two books of *Anthems for Men's Voices.* Recordings of carols and the Tudor anthems are also available. The historic literature is dominated by William Byrd (15) and Thomas Tallis (15). The modern English composers listed most are William Matthias (18); John Rutter (13); Ralph Vaughan Williams (18); William Walton (5); Healey Willan (7); and a large catalog of works by David Willcocks. Modern American composers are limited to Adler, Hilty, Lovelace, and G. Young. Oxford University Press has remained committed to traditional and contemporary English choral music. It has also maintained a significant influence upon American church music through the Episcopal

Church of America and through the concert choirs of colleges and seminaries throughout America.

Through this cursory examination of the music and materials available to the contemporary minister of music, one can understand the difficulties in selecting the best music for each ensemble. The minister of music can attend music reading clinics and church music workshops. He is the target of the aggressive marketing of scores through examination packets of scores, most with recorded performances, and many with taped instrumental accompaniments. Undoubtedly, in the near future cantatas will come completely choreographed and dramatized on a videotape.

Some denominational publishing houses offer an all-level catalog of music to which the director can conveniently subscribe. Other independent organizations and publications offer significant aid in the search for appropriate literature. *The Choral Journal*, published by the American Choral Directors Association in Lawton, Oklahoma, reviews sacred literature from all major publishers. Two additional independent publications, designed especially for the minister of music, are *Creator*, "the bi-monthly magazine of church musicians" from Wichita, Kansas, and *Church Music World* of Grapevine, Texas. They feature reviews of new music and helpful articles on problem areas in the music ministry.

Ed Spann has given us a thoughtful approach to this musical dilemma:

> A philosophy of church music is really the bottom line in consideration of the dilemma of church music selection for the local church musician. After having a thorough education in the field, giving much prayerful consideration and judicious thought to the purpose of the music, and knowing where certain types of music can be purchased, the dilemma will be less severe.[2]

In any case, the sorting of the musical options for the contemporary minister of music will continue to be the most time-consuming facet of the total ministry.

19

Hymnody

The twentieth century inherited a large body of hymns and tunes from the eighteenth and nineteenth centuries, many of which have remained as a central focus of Protestant hymnody. The eighteenth-century hymns of Watts and the Wesleys, plus the Reformation chorales, have become an educational cornerstone of twentieth-century hymnody. The English hymns of the Oxford Movement and many gospel songs of the late nineteenth and early twentieth centuries have likewise found their place in most contemporary hymnals.

The musical settings of our hymns during the early part of this century were dominated by the German and English style of four-part harmony with a soprano melody and by the Romantic ideal that the music should express the mood and message of the text. This created an inviolate relationship between the music, text, and harmony. This was an interesting parallel to the custom setting of each new gospel song, which hardly had such noble esthetic intentions, but sought, instead, a simple and memorable carrier of the text. Under the influence of the singing school movement or the singing conventions of Lowell Mason, these gospel tunes became as "correctly written" as their hymnic counterparts, but with much slower harmonic progressions. During the 1930s the gospel songs became much more "soloistic" in design and adopted the more chromatic harmonic style of the big bands and the musical theater. At the same time, the shaped-note books of the singing schools, with their simplistic harmony and peppy "afterbeat" rhythms, were adopted by the small rural churches—and became the object of disdain among the more serious church musicians.

During the 1940s World War II created a democratic tolerance of the religious music of others, and our musically academic hymns and gospel songs were both influenced by the indigenous folk hymns and spirituals of the South. Early acceptance constituted the use of tunes that were reharmonized according to major and minor key standards, then used as solos or choir "specials." John Jacob Niles and Virgil Thomson did many beautiful settings of these and published them as octavos for the choir. The spirituals appeared in hymnals in their basic refrain-stanza structure and often retained the simple harmonizations of their original arrangers and publishers. They were heard more often, however, as TTBB arrangements for men or in special SATB arrangements for the choir.

The short congregational chorus so popular in the 1930s and 1940s was almost abandoned until the 1960s. Then a new style known as the "Scripture-verse" chorus appeared and has been widely used in many congregations and among the youth. Its return may have been aided by the fact that after 1950 congregational singing became a source of great concern, rather than the heart of Protestant worship. Within the hush of acoustic ceilings, deep carpets, cushioned pews, and the indispensable air conditioning, the vigor of reverberating voices was lost. Only the organ, the amplified choir, and the pulpit singer or speakers were heard by everyone. A fairly recent move to encourage the congregation has been the use of a small group of instruments with the congregation. An additional and worthy motive has been the involvement of more musicians already trained in our public-school orchestras and bands. A similar device to encourage more congregational participation has been to lower the key of the hymn, then encourage unison singing of the tune.

In spite of the positive efforts of the Hymn Society for half a century, the literary hymns gained little acceptance. The clergy lost interest in a poetic expression of their theology or wrote in a stilted literary style, without appealing poetic imagery. The composers then spent their efforts on anthems or cantatas, using Scripture texts or familiar religious poetry. The most prolific output of religious song was left to the writers of popular gospel solos or quartets.

A dramatic turn in recent years has been billed as an "explosion" of hymn writing, notably by members of the English clergy. *The Hymn* devoted its April 1984 issue to the writing of hymn texts and tunes. Brian Wren, a clergyman at Oxford, England, and a currently well-known writer of hymns, suggests:

> You must first question yourself (What do I know? What do I believe?) and find your own words to express that. . . . A hymn writer also needs to think in picture language. You try to give the reader a vehicle to ride in . . . which gives a fresh view of the way and destination. Next, you need to control the picture language you use so that it is consistent and theologically sound.[3]

Writing from the vantage point of a college professor, a translator of German hymns, and as a judge of "thousands of hymns for the new Lutheran Book of Worship and for the Hymn Society of America hymn contests," Gracia Grindal also writes about the hymn as a poem.

> A hymn is one of the most tightly structured poems in the tradition. . . . Few poets these days have learned the skill of writing such formal verse. . . . To speak naturally about God, one's emotions, and one's ultimate concern in tight restrictive poems is not something modern or post-modern poets do well. An even further restriction on this form is that these hymns, after they are written, are no longer the property of the poet: they have become the property of the pious. Hymns are not only personal statements; they are also statements of the community.[4]

Grindal also suggests that the inability of the Romantic and modern poets to express themselves "without a signature, a personal voice" is a basic problem, and that congregations do not want to sing the personal politics or theology of any writer which are not commonly held by the congregation. She reflects upon reading so many hymn texts that "have been too theologically correct, while being fairly mediocre poems"[5]—a basic conflict of form and content. She may have diagnosed very well the continuing twentieth-century reversion to the poems of Watts, the Wesleys, and the gospel songs of Fanny J. Crosby.

A summary analysis of many "survivor" hymns might yield some helpful guidelines for a new generation of hymnists:

1. Their texts are consistent with elemental religious thought and concerns which are common to the disciplined intellectual as well as the uneducated.
2. They address God in an appropriate recognition of His being and work as Creator, Redeemer, and Lord.
3. Their role and element of instruction is through an effective poetic parable, an image of a biblical truth, or a personal religious experience that should be understood and available to all.
4. They portray an honest religious response to God's love and a missionary concern for others.
5. They maintain a musical integrity of style consistent with the content of their texts—either providing emotional support for a subjective text or an uninvolved carrier of the more objective congregational expressions of praise or worship.

The writing of tunes for the new literary hymnody of the twentieth century has experienced a resurgence of interest and serious efforts in recent years. After a long period in which the writing of tunes was almost the total domain of the gospel song, the new "explosion" of hymn writing has finally called for new tunes to express the depths of contemporary poetic thought. The composers have recognized a unique challenge in writing "a simple tune of short duration, sung by everyone and repeated four or five times [which] has many advantages over a large scale work in communicating an 'inspirational' idea."[6]

In sharp contrast to the writers of tunes in the nineteenth and twentieth centuries for the gospel songbooks, there has been no mass production of tunes which have a congregational "character" equal to many of the fine texts that are now available. A parallel might be the astonishing symphonic output of Haydn and Mozart to Beethoven's nine symphonies and Brahms' only four. The musical abilities of the composers should not differ greatly—just the tremendous increase in the musical resources available and the corresponding responsibility to deal with them judiciously. Sankey, Bliss, Towner, and others worked within simplistic parameters. The contemporary composer has resources undreamed of a half-century ago. Our survey of hymnals has pointed out the extensive incorporation of folk tunes, spirituals, and many "traditional" tunes from varied hymnic backgrounds. Many of these tunes have been treated with fresh academic harmonizations—assuming an accompaniment to be necessary for the unison tune. Aware of the modal origin of many of these tunes, the modern writer resorts to

> modal material to achieve the freshness I want and revert to the more familiar major and minor tonalities at crucial spots, like cadences, to keep it friendly. . . . I find modes extremely useful in giving me many ways to go with simple material.[7]

All of the composers who discussed the writing of tunes stressed their concerns for the rhythm of the text, the climactic words or lines, the parameters of range and melodic movement, and (most discussed) the element of mood or color. The melody itself can accommodate each of the concerns except for complications which arise when different stanzas have differing lines of climax or of mood. These factors are, admittedly, more in the realm of harmony than melody. More and more, the composers are favoring the unison hymn tune over the four-part setting. This allows for a stronger harmonic coloration in the free accompaniment, but the unison settings are receiving mixed reactions from the congregations. If the four-part setting is used, greater care must be given to the movement of each individual voice line as the harmonic structure becomes more complex. A proper doubling of a voice part is not nearly so important to the singer as the logical movement of his individual vocal line.

With the Romantic, modal, folk, and contemporary melodic and harmonic resources at hand, "once in a great while, that experience may result in a hymn tune which endures beyond the immediate present, that may enrich the song of the Church for years—or even generations—to come."[8]

20

Choral Innovations

Although the anthem has maintained a fixed position in Protestant worship, the hymn has been a very important element of this music literature. The hymn-anthem assumed a dual musical character. One was an original musical setting of a well-known hymn text, and this was already a standard practice at the beginning of the century. These represented a major segment of the catalogs of the Lorenz and Presser companies.

These original settings were within the rigid nineteenth-century harmonic and structural patterns. Each stanza was often given a different voicing, harmonic setting, or even a new melody in order to intensify the message of the text. Other hymn-anthems used both the familiar text and its familiar tune. These achieved textual enhancement through solos, harmonic intensity, and limited polyphonic imitation. An artistic example of this might be F. Melius Christiansen's arrangement of "Beautiful Savior."

The popular appeal of these latter hymn arrangements continues to provide the choral contribution to a majority of Protestant worship services and has created an enormous market for records and tapes. They have thus provided the material for many sustained radio programs such as "Hymns We Love"—a two-hour program each Sunday morning over KRQX (WFAA), Dallas, and hosted by Norvell Slater since 1951. Another program, "Sunday Hymns" hosted by Ted Strasser from WJR, Detroit, has had an almost equal run. These arranged hymns were the standard fare of the smaller church choirs. The Church Music Department of the Baptist Sunday School Board in Nashville adopted this type of hymn anthem (1950) as one of the selections in its monthly magazine *The Church Musician* and used it as an incentive to increase congregational knowledge of a "Hymn-of-the-Month." The Choristers Guild also has a series of hymn arrangements for children's choirs called "Hymn Studies."

Hymn arrangements have become even more prominent since the many technical advances in audio and video recording. Videotapes have now made possible the commercial packaging of religious programs for television, similar to the electric transcriptions of the 1940s and 1950s. The technology has also created a huge market for taped orchestral accompaniments for choirs or gospel soloists, accommodating the smallest church choir or the most amateur soloist.

The standard anthem with Scripture text remains a major choral feature of American Protestant worship, but it has undergone many changes in musical style. The nineteenth-century quartet anthem became the prototype, with prominent solo passages and four-part harmony for the quartet. It was adapted to the volunteer choirs of the 1930s and 1940s by the use of a soloist or an entire section on the solo part and the full choir on the quartet sections. The voice ranges were often prohibitive, but the publishers quickly provided anthems in a similar style that were well within the ranges of the amateur choirs. The trend then became four-part choral with organ accompaniment. The new electric organs came in the 1930s and brought a satisfactory imitation of the sounds of worship in the large urban churches. But the technical skills of the performers limited the literature to simpler organ arrangements and accompaniment styles.

These early electric organs were built upon an adjustable harmonic (overtone) series for any fundamental tone. This adjusted tone then is set for each note in the pitch range of the keyboard or pedal board. This introduced a new synthetic (but acceptable) sound to the congregation, even though it was in sharp contrast to the change in the harmonic structure of each individual note in a rank of organ pipes. The result became theatrical in effect—an exchange of influences between the church and the world—and an exaggeration of the theatrical design of early twentieth-century pipe organs. Hardly any small church was without one of these organs by the middle of the century, and later refinements and comparative economy have assured its permanence in the Protestant sanctuary.

Recent technology in the improvement of the quality of the sound as well as the mechanics of its performance foretell the eventual precise duplication of every tone of a large pipe organ, and at a fraction of the cost and maintenance. This is only one other facet of the semiconductor "chip" which is currently used to its greatest proficiency in the commercial synthesizers, but will eventually be transferred to the church organ. In all of these electric organs, the total dynamic gradation at all times is one of the more attractive facets of the instruments and adds a stronger neo-Romantic quality of wide-range dynamics to the choral performances.

With a strong assist from the sustaining sounds from the organ, the choir's anthem began to assume a more important role in the Protestant worship service. However, its musical style has been as full of contrasts as the ethnic and musical diversity of our society. The general adoption of our inherited German music theory, the Romantic ideology, and the common practice of their four-part harmony all combined to produce a musical stability for the first quarter of the century. At this point, the new academic discipline of musicology contributed a vast treasure of historical church music. The most immediate impact was from the music of J. S. Bach, made possible through the publication of his complete works by the Bach Gesellschaft. These harmonic, polyphonic masterpieces became the models for a series of new textbooks on counterpoint, supplanting the traditional discipline of "Strict Counterpoint." The Baroque techniques of Bach became the most idealized harmonic and polyphonic models for all students of church music. The choral influence of Bach was extended directly from Leipzig through the performances of the Saint Olaf and Westminster Choirs.

A growing intellectual aversion to the emotional excesses of the Romantic composers found a refuge in the strictly disciplined style of Bach's masterful balance of harmony, form, and polyphonic development of the traditional chorale tunes and texts. Among the large sacred forms, the oratorios of Bach and Handel remain as standard fare of the better twentieth-century church choirs.

Our musicological heritage was soon extended to the music of the Renaissance, especially the church music of Palestrina. Many subscribed to the Romantic idealism of Palestrina's biographer, Guiseppe Baini (1775-1844), and declared the modal polyphony of Palestrina to be the purest form of church music and the complete fulfillment of the musical standards prescribed by the Council of Trent. Even the Latin language was envisioned as a universal and ecumenical language of Christianity. The diatonic modality of the sixteenth century appeared as the antithesis of the chromatic excesses of Romanticism and the most perfect vehicle for worship and spiritual contemplation. Choir directors, and many composers, believed sixteenth-century polyphony to be the ideal choral medium for the new a cappella tradition. The Westminster Choir concerts always opened with a group by sixteenth-century composers. The a cappella performance of this modal polyphony found limited use in the actual Protestant worship service because of the vocal and musical limitations of the volunteer choirs, ineffective transcriptions, and the difficulties incurred when transferring a liturgical text to an evangelical worship service.

The most important influence of Renaissance polyphony upon our churches was not from a direct adoption but in its new perspectives for a new generation of composers. They received a new awareness of the validity of the modal system, of the modal origins of our own folk music, and the validity of many of our musical traditions more basic than the major and minor key systems of Baroque and Romantic music. The common practice of sixteenth-century polyphony became the basis for new studies in counterpoint which were pioneered by the Eastman School and is now a common theoretical discipline for almost all students of church music. The young composers found new rhythmic freedoms grounded upon plainsong and the natural rhythmic flow of text, besides a new basis for tonality beyond a major dominant triad progressing to a major or minor tonic.

The rapid growth of higher education in music after World War II was phenomenal, and the techniques of composition were expanding in their complexity. Each "school" of thought was attempting to establish a dominant trend or style. Theorists were trying to categorize each new movement as it seemed to relate to an earlier practice (for example, neo-Baroque, neo-Classical, or neo-Romantic). The distinct techniques practiced by each group were identified as quartal harmony (tetrads), twelve-tone serialism, dissonant bass, or aleatory.

Again, a stabilizing force was a two-volume German text (1937 and 1939) on counterpoint/composition by Paul Hindemith and translated into English as *The Craft of Musical Composition* (1941 and 1949). Hindemith treated tonality as a composite of melodic movement, counterpoint, and vertical harmonies. His analytical study of melody includes all possible movements within the twelve tones of our octave scale and emphasizes melody's independence from harmonic generation or control. The vertical sonorities (not triads) are treated as combinations of consonant and dissonant intervals, essentially derived from the natural harmonic series. Each sonority has a root tone, which is determined by its strongest component interval. The progression of these root tones then determines a harmony-based tonality in a near traditional manner.

The two became standard textbooks in contemporary counterpoint/composition, even at the undergraduate level. Hindemith himself taught at Yale University, 1940-1953, before retiring to Switzerland. He wrote many operas, solo songs in both English and German, and the often-performed choral work *Apparebit Repentina Dies* for chorus and brass.

The direct influence of sixteenth- and eighteenth-century music upon our twentieth-century church music has not been a massive use of the music itself. And the music of Paul Hindemith, even though much of it is religious, does not lend itself to the worship service. The techniques and ideals of each of these textbook styles have been incorporated into the fiber of original sacred works by hundreds of American composers of living music for a living twentieth-century church. Some of these composers are writing for highly skilled musicians and semiprofessional college, concert, and church choirs. To these performers and their musically sophisticated congregations, an intensely academic musical setting of a Scripture text often provides the only adequate understanding of its spiritual content. This enormous group of composers and performers are creating musical literacy, stability, and dreams for the future spiritual maturity of church music and church musicians.

The foundation for an American church music tradition was carefully in place, but because of the democratic nature of each congregation, an effective church music ministry was by nature an "art of the possible." It must begin at the existing capacities of the people and then build upon the musical capacities of the director. Emphasizing the latter, Noble Cain often said, "Your choir can sing anything that you [the director] understand." Seldom have I found this to be false. Unfortunately, many choirs are restricted by the musical limitations of the director.

The first half of this century was plagued by a scarcity of appropriate anthem literature. The choices were usually Barnby, Buck, Harker, Roberts, Rogers, Shelley, or Stainer—or, perhaps, a chorus from an oratorio of Mendelssohn or Gounod, or even an adaptation of something from Richard Wagner. Such extractions from their dramatic musical context were often attractive, but seldom seemed quite appropriate for the worship needs of the hour. The academic music world had abandoned the sanctuary in favor of the professional concert world of oratorio and symphony. The churches were not equal to Arthur Honegger's *King David,* William Walton's *Belshazzar's Feast,* or even Randall Thompson's *The Peaceable Kingdom.* And serious academic composers dared not risk their personal compositional ideals in order to accomplish the "possible" in church music. Some could become ecstatic over a monophonic Gregorian plainsong, but did not dare attack the same restrictions for a children's choir. A notable exception was Leo Sowerby, who could write with equal care for the boys at the Wa-Li-Ro music camp as for the choir at the Washington Cathedral.

The historic literature of the *Concord Anthems* from E. C. Schirmer or the *Master Choruses* from Oliver Ditson almost became standard literature for the large urban churches—but America was growing her own in music schools all across the land. The discipline of composition within limitations became a challenge, and now two generations of young composers are writing their own texts, tunes, and anthems especially for next Sunday's worship service. The 1986 convention of the Southern Baptist Church Music Conference meeting in Atlanta featured solo recitals, children's choirs, church choirs of other denominations, men's choirs, and college and seminary choirs. The groups performed 126 solo or choral numbers and only 29 of these were from the historical choral literature. There were sixteen composers in original or arranged scores: J. S. Bach, Beethoven, Dvorak, Gabrieli, Gibbons, Gounod, Handel, Haydn, Lotti, Mendelssohn, Mozart, Parry, Praetorius, Purcell, Schubert, and Schutz. The remainder were from the twentieth century and almost entirely American.

The graded choir programs which grew so rapidly in the 1950s and 1960s created an immediate demand for new choral literature suitable for children and adolescents. Special organizations were established to publish these materials and to provide leadership in the training of teachers and conductors. The Choristers Guild, a nonprofit organization, was formed in 1949 by Ruth Krehbiel Jacobs, and she was its president until her death in 1960. The Guild was chartered in Tennessee in 1953, and the national headquarters is now in Garland, Texas. Other distinguished church music educators who have served as executive directors include her husband, Leslie Jacobs, Federal Lee Whittlesey, John S. C. Kemp, Cecil E. Lapo, and John T. Burke. The Guild's monthly publication, *Choristers Guild Letters*, features helpful articles, news about workshops, new music, and a "Director's Forum" on music education for children. The Forum contains the best from Orff, Kodaly, and contemporary child psychologists.

The 1982-83 catalog of music issued by the Guild lists thirty-two anthems for Advent and Christmas; eighteen for Palm Sunday, Lent, and Easter; and almost one hundred "General Anthems" which include seventeen arrangements of choral masterworks. Except for these arrangements, the remainder of the works are by contemporay composers, and many incorporate handbells and/or Orff instruments in the accompaniments. The catalog also contains cantatas, collections of anthems, books, more than seventy "Hymn Studies" for children, and thirty-nine handbell selections. The composers featured most are Austin C. Lovelace, Hal H. Hopson, and Natalie Sleeth. The Choristers Guild catalog of music is also distributed by the Lorenz Company.

A recent organization designed to assist directors with the special problems of the adolescent changing voice is the Cambiata Vocal Music Institute of America. Founded in 1979 by Don Collins, it is also a nonprofit organization of music educators and church musicians. The Institute is an outgrowth and extension of the work of a distinguished Canadian music educator and longtime professor at Florida State University, Irvin Cooper. His college textbook, *Teaching Junior High School Music*, became an original source for the movement, and his choral arrangements for boys' voices were released by at least ten publishers. These arrangements established guidelines for later composers of music for adolescents.

The Institute's own *The Cambiata Concept* comprises a "Comprehensive Philosophy and Methodology of Teaching Music to Adolescents" and the textbook for the basic focus of the organization: "to train music educators."[9] The Cambiata Press, located in Conway, Arkansas, became the musical outlet for the Institute, with more than 150 special arrangements for Soprano, Alto, Cambiata, Bass; SSCB; SSACB; SC; SCB; SSC; CCB; and CCBB. These include choral classics of the sixteenth through the nineteenth centuries, spirituals, and many original works by contemporary composers in both sacred and secular octavos, and ranging in difficulty from easy to difficult.

The Actual Pitch is a biannual newsletter publication of the Institute, which is circulated to approximately 100,000 church and public-school educators. The magazine contains articles of interest and help for teachers, composers, and conductors, and informs them of workshops, festivals, new music, and current teaching methodology.

From the 1960s, a major portion of church music literature

has been designed for youth choirs, about fifteen to nineteen years of age. At this age the voices can be divided into male and female registers or even four-part SATB. However, since the voices are still light in timbre, a typical SATB voicing is still lacking in resonance and color, especially in an a cappella performance. In large choirs, composers and arrangers compensate for this by a further division of parts into SSAATTBB. This adds richness and maturity to the ensemble through its density of harmonic texture. Since the youth choirs in most churches are seldom chosen by vocal auditions and musicianship, another practical alternative is a two-voice or unison (actually octaves between the male and female voices), with a more complex harmonic and rhythmic accompaniment. This becomes an effective compromise which compensates for the innate lack of vocal color, as well as acoustical problems which are common to most sanctuaries. A two-voice texture allows for an imitative form, which adds interest and challenge for the choir. The organ then provides the harmonic framework (either traditional or contemporary), and both choir and congregation share a stimulating musical performance. This latter style has almost become a common practice.

One of the more valuable books on the youth choir and its music is *The Youth Choir* by Austin C. Lovelace, published by Abingdon Press. Lovelace includes a bibliography of important writings on youth and children's choirs during the 1950s and 1960s and an eight-page listing of 155 anthems, 22 cantatas, and 8 choral collections for youth. The publishers of these collections are E. C. Schirmer (unison anthems); Westminster Press, edited by W. Lawrence Curry; Shawnee Press, edited by Roy Ringwald; Neil Kjos, edited by Peter Tkach; two from Concordia, edited by Paul Thomas and Healey Willan; Abingdon Press, edited by Samuel Walter; and Broadman Press, edited by Walter Ehret.[10] The historical composers represented in these are Bach, Buxtehude, Handel, Lasso, Mendelssohn, and Vittoria. The list of anthems, however, is predominantly twentieth-century English and American. Lovelace's enormous catalog of youth music comprises more than twenty-five unison, two-part, and SAB anthems. Other composers listed comprise an impressive roster of active church musicians and composers of church music in America during the 1950s: Joseph Clokey, Katherine Davis, Archibald Davison, George Lynn, Jane Marshall, Lloyd Pfautsch, Frank Pooler, Richard Purvis, Carl Schalk, Robert Shaw, Leo Sowerby, David McK. Williams, and Carlton Young.

One of the most widely publicized stylistic developments in twentieth-century church music has been the deliberate use of contemporary jazz idioms by serious musicians—and with the encouragement of many members of the clergy. The first experiment and public endorsement was from Geoffrey Beaumont, an English clergyman who wrote a *Twentieth Century Folk Mass* in 1960. His rationale was to entice young people back to the church. The event was widely publicized. After reading about the performance, one of my colleagues at Southwestern Seminary and I wrote to Beaumont and asked if a tape of the performance were available. Shortly thereafter we received the tape and promptly played it for a large class of church music majors without introduction or comment. The response was a bit of a surprise—not the style or liturgical content, but, being accustomed to a sophisticated American jazz, the students were more interested in the performance itself. Nevertheless, some of the tunes have survived in a few hymnals, and three hymn tunes are listed in the 1983 Novello catalog—CHESTERTON, DEAN STREET, and GRACIAS.

Some very notable American religious works followed in a very solid jazz idiom with Edward Kennedy (Duke) Ellington's sacred concert, *In the Beginning God*, Lionel Hampton's *King David Suite*, and David (Dave) Brubeck's oratorio *The Light in the Wilderness* and two cantatas, *The Gates of Justice* and *Truth Is Fallen*. The importance of these carefully scored works by masters of the style has been their patronage, their worldwide audiences, and their influence upon other American composers of anthems and service music.

Of particular importance have been the "sacred concerts" of Duke Ellington. Documented in his book *Music Is My Mistress,* Ellington presents a thoughtful and profound approach to music as the utmost expression of worship and personal interpretation of a scriptural theology. He does not use the word *jazz* as a style description of his music, saying: "We stopped using the word in 1943, and we much prefer to call it the American Idiom, or the Music of Freedom of Expression."[11]

Ellington's move into the "sacred concerts" came in 1965 when he was

> invited by Dean C.J. Bartlett and Reverend John S. Yaryan to present a concert of sacred music in Grace Cathedral, San Francisco, as a part of a year-long series celebrating the completion and consecration of that great Episcopal Cathedral atop Nob Hill. I recognized this as an exceptional opportunity. "Now I can say openly," I said, "what I have been saying to myself on my knees."[12]

His primary concern was to present his music honestly, because "every time God's children have thrown away fear in pursuit of honesty—trying to communicate themselves, understood or not—miracles have happened."[13] He was also convinced that all people pray to God in their own language, and there is no language that God does not understand.

The premiere of *In the Beginning God* in September 1965 exceeded all expectations. The same was true at the December performance at Fifth Avenue Presbyterian in New York City. The following year it was performed in many cities from "Cambridge, Massachusetts to Cambridge, England," including the rebuilt Coventry Cathedral. A climactic performance occurred in the Cathedral of St. John the Divine in New York City in January 1968, which Ellington considered "the most important thing I have ever done" and included the routines and lyrics in full. The program outline of *In the Beginning God* follows:

INVOCATION
ORGAN PRELUDE
OPENING THEME: PRAISE GOD featuring solo instrumental-
    ist
SUPREME BEING the choir, orchestra and solo instrumentalist
SONNET OF THE APPLE (Solo recitative for Little Boy)
SOMETHING ABOUT BELIEVING featuring soloists from the
    choir in speaking roles

ALMIGHTY GOD featuring solo vocalist
THE SHEPHERD (WHO WATCHES OVER THE NIGHT
    FLOCK) featuring solo instrumentalist
HEAVEN featuring solo vocalist and instrumentalist
FREEDOM the choir, Orchestra and solo vocalists

(INTERMISSION)

MEDITATION featuring the composer at the piano
THE BIGGEST AND BUSIEST INTERSECTION featuring the
    percussion section (A fire-and-brimstone sermonette)
T.G.T.T. (*Too Good to Title*)
DON'T GET DOWN ON YOUR KNEES TO PRAY UNTIL YOU
    HAVE FORGIVEN EVERYONE featuring solo vocalist
FATHER FORGIVE vocal soloist and the Choir
DON'T GET DOWN ON YOUR KNEES TO PRAY UNTIL YOU
    HAVE FORGIVEN EVERYONE (Reprise)
PRAISE GOD AND DANCE by the entire company and featur-
    ing vocal soloist[14]

Over seven thousand people packed St. John's for the performance, "and their excitement as two companies of dancers
swung down the aisle in the finale, 'Praise God and Dance' was
Tremendous."[15] At a later performance in Minneapolis, the
audience joined in a "hand dance" during the finale.

Another movement with a greater impact upon the musical
message of American Protestantism since the 1960s has been
the widespread use of "Folk Musicals" by youth choirs of the
churches. They were probably stimulated first by the popular
television show featuring folk music, "Hootenanny." In the
mid-1960s, a group of young people working as "staffers" at the
Glorieta Baptist Conference Center, near Santa Fe, New Mexico, put together a group of original songs with guitar accompaniment. These were then compiled and edited by Bob
Oldenburg and published by Broadman Press as a folk musical
entitled *Good News* (1967).

The immediate acceptance of the music by young people
ushered in a musical style which was created and dominated by
the amateur musician. In this sense it might be termed "folk,"
since both text and music were generally created by nonpoets
and nonmusicians. Its texts and music captured the social and

religious ferment of the period, and the professional authors and composers quickly picked up the style and the trend. Among the most successful of these early "musicals" were *Tell It Like It Is* by Ralph Carmichael and Kurt Kaiser; *A Christmas Happening* by John Wilson; and *Celebrate Life* by Buryl Red and Ragan Courtney.

This popular form fostered a new wave of Christian artists performing and recording "Christian Music," which followed the rapidly changing styles of their secular counterparts. Hustad in his book *Jubilate!* cites a list of 106 of these soloists or performing groups which were promoted in four issues of the *Christian Bookseller* in 1979-80.[16] Another measure of the scope of this new choral literature for youth is found in current catalogs of church music. In just four of the 1983 catalogs (Broadman, Choristers Guild, Lorenz, and Word), ninety-three youth musicals are offered. These musicals are often presented as a drama, but in concert form they are the centerpiece for a choir tour, a mission trip, or special music camps or retreats.

The choral literature of twentieth-century Protestantism is more diverse now than at any time in the history of Christianity. At one end of the spectrum college and adult church choirs are performing anthems and oratorios in the academic harmonic idioms of Paul Hindemith, Howard Hanson, Halsey Stevens, Leo Sowerby, Benjamin Britten, or John Rutter. The same choirs present cantatas by J. S. Bach or Dave Brubeck. Large churches are creating and presenting musical dramas or choreographed oratorios and original outdoor pageants to celebrate Christmas and Easter. Handel's *Messiah*, J. S. Bach's cantatas and oratorios, and many standard oratorios of the nineteenth century are still common repertoire among most larger church choirs. Many twentieth-century composers have written oratorios on commission or for special events, but few have received sufficient acceptance to be classified among the standard literature of contemporary church music.

If there is a stylistic mainstream in the total choral literature of the church, it would probably lie in a neo-Romanticism or Impressionism—a style reminiscent of the musical scores for the spectacular movies of the 1950s. The universality of the highly developed electric organ and the increasing use of a live (or taped) instrumental accompaniment afford a dramatic content, a powerful climax, and intensity of emotion. Within a multiplicity of compositional techniques, all of these effects are sought (and available) in the most simplistic of youth music and the most complex harmonic techniques of the academic composers. This subjectivity in church music is a normal religious expression when the church is in a period of reexamination of its heritage and its academic as well as its practical theology. It is doubtful that any musical "common practice" will ever occur again in the foreseeable future. Our music is a free religious expression, even in the most rigid denominational structure. Many churches are not even using their "official" hymnal, and choral music is completely free to follow the taste and musical proficiencies of the choir and congregation.

This musical environment might appear to be self-destructive; but historically, the opposite has often been true. When we remember the Christian church as a living organism, our performances of our historic literature have great genealogical value—to remind us of when and where we were in our Christian pilgrimage. But music is a living expression of a living faith, and we must create honest contemporary expressions of our own, in every medium available to us as composers, performers, and participants in the corporate worship and proclamation of the gospel. For, in the final analysis, the effectiveness of a ministry of church music will be determined by the residue of music literature in the minds of the people in the choirs and in the pews. No hymnal committee, no minister of music, and no pastor can determine the precise time or condition under which any particular person will experience a divine confrontation in the text or tune of a hymn or an anthem. A person's first encounter is always at his own intellectual, emotional, and musical capacities—the parables of Jesus ranged in imagery from the "lost sheep" to the abstraction of a "new birth."

The ministry of music is to see that these encounters continue and increase in depth and spiritual perception. The music literature learned should be retained as a foundation for growth limited only by one's willingness to study and learn. A listener can experience the mind and soul of Bach or Brahms or, even better, the less skillful work of some contemporary soul who shares the same fears, doubts, and searching spirit of the pilgrim, but who can honestly communicate a living musical expression of his own faith through text and music.

21

Anthem Composers

The use and development of the strictly choral anthem took place in the well-established churches along the Atlantic seaboard and in the larger cities of the Midwest. Leonard Ellinwood cites an extensive survey by Harold W. Thompson in 1923, which included 104 directors from "all parts of the country" who listed the anthems which they found most useful. Almost half of the churches were Episcopal, and the remainder were mostly Presbyterian and Congregational. In these 104 churches, 32 used mixed adult choirs, 22 used a quartet and mixed chorus, 18 used quartets only, and 22 used choirs of boys and men.

The anthems which received the most votes were "Souls of the Righteous"—Noble (29); "Ho, Everyone that Thirsteth"—Martin (22); "Hail Gladd'ning Light"—Martin (22); "Fierce Was the Wild Billow"—Noble (17); "How Lovely Is Thy Dwelling Place" (*Requiem*)—Brahms (13); "Psalm 150"—Franck (13); "In Heavenly Love Abiding"—Parker (13); "The Lord Is My Light" —Parker (12); "Fear Not Ye, O Israel"—Spicker (12); and "Still, Still with Thee"—Foote (11). Six are by American composers. Of the twenty-five favorite composers listed, more than half were American. The three top favorites were Horatio Parker, George C. Martin, and T. Tertius Noble.[17]

In a similar poll of thirty-seven "leading choirs in the country" (27 Episcopal, 4 Presbyterian, 2 Roman Catholic, 2 Lutheran, 1 Methodist, and 1 Moravian) taken for the years 1949-1953, the ten favorite anthems were "God Be in My Head"—W. Davies (18); "Greater Love Hath No Man"—Ireland (17); "Jesu, Joy of Man's Desiring"—J. S. Bach (16); "The Lord Is My Shepherd"—Brother James' Air (16); "There Shall a Star" (*Christus*) —Mendelssohn (15); "With a Voice of Singing"—M. Shaw (15); "How Lovely Is Thy Dwelling Place" (*Requiem*)—Brahms (14); "God So Loved the World" (*Crucifixion*)—Stainer (12); "O Saviour of the World"—Goss (11); and "Hallelujah" (*Messiah*)— Handel (11). The six most favored composers were J. S. Bach, Healey Willan, T. Tertius Noble, Handel, Mendelssohn, and Leo Sowerby—the three contemporaries were active organists/ directors in Canada, New York, and Chicago, respectively.[18]

Ellinwood also did a significant compilation of the service music and anthems performed at the Washington Cathedral during the years 1941-51. The trend toward early polyphony at this mid-century decade is noted in seventy-seven services and anthems from composers of the fifteenth through seventeenth centuries. Twenty-seven eighteenth-century works were dominated by J. S. Bach and Handel. Thirty-five nineteenth-century works were performed and featured Samuel S. Wesley (5) and Brahms, Franck, and Mendelssohn with three each. The most significant trend first appears in the works from the early twentieth century. There were thirty-eight services and anthems by American composers. T. Tertius Noble had fifteen, David McK. Williams eight, and Horatio Parker four. The English composers of this period retained a dominant position with sixty-one works, primarily from Vaughan Williams (10), C. V. Stanford (6), Charles Wood (6), and Bairstow (5). The music from mid-century composers was predominantly from the Americans, led by Leo Sowerby with fifteen, Richard Dirksen with seven, and Paul Callaway with five. Sixteen other American composers were also programmed in this pivotal decade.

An important facet of this survey is the active role of the composer/organists Callaway, Dirksen, Noble, Sowerby, Willan, and Williams—all organist/choirmasters of major Episcopal churches. The more important significance of the survey is in the extension of the repertoire to include seventy-seven selections from the Renaissance and in the adoption of a major segment of literature by contemporary American composers. The stylistic development of the twentieth-century anthem literature after World War II was diverse and prolific. The foundations were already established in the works of Carl Mueller as early as the 1930s and 1940s. His anthems were in traditional harmonic style, carefully part written, and included nearly a hundred listings in the G. Schirmer catalog. As early as 1934 Schirmer published Mueller's eight-part arrangements of J. S. Bach's harmonizations of "Now Thank We All Our God," and shortly thereafter "A Mighty Fortress Is Our God." His arrangement of "Now Thank We All Our God" used the four-part women's chorus on the first stanza, and the men's chorus is featured on the second. As a climax he wrote a short fugue on a theme derived from the chorale tune, then concluded with an eight-part restatement of the first phrase. These arrangements were designed for the rapidly growing a cappella choral groups in colleges and high schools. The density of the harmonic texture was a compensation for the normal instrumental accompaniment in its original form and assisted the singers with the inherent problems of intonation.

Mueller's early recognition of the musical potential of graded church choirs brought several special works, usually for Christmas or Easter, combining children's choirs and adult choirs. He compiled several special collections of SA anthems for junior choirs and SAB collections suitable for youth or small church choirs. Mueller also did arrangements of Romantic choral classics, including the quartet anthems of American composers Harry Rowe Shelley and J. V. Roberts.

Two interesting series of anthems by Mueller (1950) were *Sayings of Jesus* (6) and *Sayings of the Prophets* (5). The style was almost purely through-composed, devoting a section to each verse or fragment of Scripture text, with a final restatement of the first text and theme at the end. Each section had its own structure, either imitative or antiphonal reiterations of themes. Probably his most universally performed anthem has been "Create in Me a Clean Heart, O God" (1941), which is still in the G. Schirmer catalog, along with eighteen other selections.

The Christiansen a cappella choral inheritance strongly influenced the developing anthem through the work of L. Stanley Glarum. The a cappella choir afforded Glarum an ideal medium for the coloristic text interpretations of Impressionism. This technique was shown in "The Beatitudes" (1947, Hall & McCreary). The rhythmic flow of the music followed the natural flow of the text, and the choral harmonies are delicately balanced in register and color in order to give prominence to the principal line or to establish the mood of the text. He used humming for the harmonic accompaniment of solo lines, and his harmonic textures were continually changing from unisons to four or eight parts. He used seventh chords freely, voicing them for a balance of the choral sound and resolving them according to the flow of the principal voice line or for the parallel planar flow of the harmonies.

A new musical dimension for choral text interpretation was now in place for one of the major contributors to the anthem literature of twentieth-century Protestantism, Jane Marshall. An active organist and choir director and member of the faculty of the School of Music and Perkins School of Theology at Southern Methodist University, she was attracted to profound theological prose and poetry for many of her lyrics. These proved to be demanding but appealing material for the color and speech-rhythm of impressionism. Among these sources were the nineteenth-century Christina Rossetti ("None Other Lamb," 1954, Carl Fischer); the medical missionary, musician, and theologian Albert Schweitzer ("He Comes to Us," 1957, Carl Fischer); Edward Caswell's translation of an early Latin text ("My Eternal King," 1954, C. Fischer); and a Winfred Douglas translation of Paul Gerhardt ("Awake, My Heart" 1958, H. W. Gray), which was the prize-winning anthem of the American Guild of Organists. As expected, Scripture texts were almost the norm for her anthems, but for many of her works for children's choirs, she penned her own lyrics; used contemporary religious poetry for children by Mary Elizabeth Montgomery; and chose selections from such books as *Tell Me About Prayer* by Mary Alice Jones.

From her earliest works for Carl Fischer, Jane Marshall revealed an unusual sensitivity to text and its musical interpretation. "None Other Lamb" used the organ extensively for dramatic and coloristic accompaniment and added a cello obligato for greater emotional intensity. A cappella sections were also framed by the instruments. The vocal sections used characteristic antiphonal repetitions and rapid changes of texture from unisons to divided parts. Polyphonic imitation was not employed beyond canonic structures, and these only in more energetic and less subjective lyrics. As in the works of Glarum, she used seventh and ninth chords in a variety of voicings, for both color and richness of choral sound. Her part writing was quite free, but used thoughtfully in order to strengthen the flow of text and the harmonic progressions.

A cappella anthems were not frequent, but her setting of Lauchlan L. Watt's "I Bind My Heart This Tide" (1957, Carl Fischer) is an early example. It begins with an accompanied solo, with the choir joining with a humming accompaniment. The choir then has a middle section in four parts, a cappella. A third stanza is also an accompanied solo, but then the work returns to the a cappella choir for the climactic fourth stanza, "I Bind Myself to Peace."

An unusual ending for an anthem, with a spark of inspiration, occurs after a sensitive setting of the lines from Albert Schweitzer's book *The Quest of the Historical Jesus*, "He Comes to Us":

> He will reveal himself in the toils, the conflicts, the sufferings which they shall pass through in His fellowship, and, as an ineffable mystery, they shall learn in their own experience who He is.

Discussing with me her own feeling that the anthem was incomplete, Mrs. Marshall added an affirmation from J. S. Bach's harmonization of "O Morning Star" (Catherine Winkworth, Tr.) with her own *allargando al fine* at the end.

From such musical complexities, she turned easily to the limitations of the child voice and wrote easily memorized SA anthems to teach basic biblical truths. An equally sharp contrast to the large Impressionistic works was her "Awake, My Heart," which almost became a prototype of an entire genre of literature for church choirs. A driving rhythmic choral unison with a strong organ background gives way to a contrasting harmonic middle section performed a cappella, then returns to the original theme with a multiple-voice climax. This ABA form is almost typically a two-voice canon when the "A" section returns, with the organ adding density and color to the final cadence.

Jane Marshall brought a more empathetic congregational participation in worship through both the text and music of the anthem. Her music turned the focus of mind and spirit upon its message rather than the musical performance.

Another pivotal influence in the development of the contemporary anthem was the work of Leland B. Sateren. His solid Christiansen heritage is seen in *The Redeemer* (1958, Schmitt, Hall & McCreary), a choral cycle based upon a six-stanza poem by Thomas W. Wersell, the stanzas subtitled "Promise," "Birth," "Death," "Resurrection," "Ascension," and "Return." The strongest impression received from his "Resurrection" is the feeling of balanced choral sonority and a strong feeling for text interpretation. A striking technical feature is his carefully crafted cadences, using all of the elements of counterpoint, dissonance, and harmony.

One particular three-voice cadence, which treats the words *death* and *hell*, approaches the final minor triad with three chords built upon a perfect fourth, perfect fifth, and perfect fourth between the tenors and altos, resolving to the minor third of the final minor triad. The sopranos have three successive tritones above the perfect fourths and fifth, finally resolving downward a minor third to the fifth of the cadential minor triad. After this extreme dissonance in the sopranos, the resolution to the minor triad is an outstanding cadential repose. His five-voice triadic harmonies, at another point, using only a single common tone progress through a series of major chords from F to D-flat to A to C and finally to A-flat major.

A melismatic passage moves in four-voice parallel triads, with the third of the chords in the tenor, and the parallel octaves and fifths are in the SSA parts. This planar movement gives mass to the a cappella sonority and interpretive strength to the text "All is well, all is well." The final cadence is a harmonic progression of an E-minor triad in first inversion to the penultimate seventh chord b,d,f,a, then to an A-major triad. The seventh chord is voiced from f in the bass upward to d', a', b' and d". The final chord is a,c#',e',a',c#",e". The words are "All is well!"

A 1962 anthem "They Follow Me" (John 10:27-28, Augsburg) is a more interesting study of a more contemporary choral technique. In this a cappella work, Sateren limits himself to four voice parts and moves often between octave unisons (SA and TB) and two-, three-, or four-voice textures. Counterpoint assumes a more important role, not as an imitative technique but as a structural bass line to counter the main soprano lines, support the vertical harmonic sonorities, and inject an element of form by restating the main theme in its inversion at the end. The cadences are of special interest in that they avoid any strong finality until the end. The final cadence is plagal, with a IV-7 (a,c,g) plus a dissonant d" in the soprano, which resolves down a minor third to b' of the tonic E Major. A frequent semicadence chord is a minor triad plus a minor seventh, but voiced with the seventh in the bass and forming a perfect fourth with the third of the chord in the tenor, then the altos have the fifth of the chord and the sopranos the root placed a perfect fourth above the altos. A minor seventh would thus be voiced g,c',e',a'. The sonority is balanced, easily tuned, and an excellent harmonic pause. This anthem provides a more sophisticated and valid academic harmonic idiom for contemporary worship.

The most useful anthem literature of the twentieth century has been created by active ministers of music and teachers associated with seminaries or church-related colleges. Another of these composers is Gordon Young. A competent organist and former college professor, he has served many years as organist-director of the First Presbyterian Church of Detroit. Many of Young's early works were hymn-anthems for the Theodore Presser Company: "Oh, for a Closer Walk," "Jesus, the Very Thought of Thee," and the Oliver Wendell Holmes text "Build

Thee More Stately Mansions" (1959). The organ assumes a
dominant role in the total musical structure. The choir sings
stanza 1 in unison; stanza 2 is a two-part canon with the women
leading; stanza 3 is also a two-part canon with the organ adding
chromatic harmonies in consecutive 6/4 chords; and stanza 4 is
a musical restatement of stanza 1, but with a canon added.

In 1960 the hymn-anthems continued for Galaxy Music with
Henry F. Lyte's "God of Mercy, God of Grace." The first stanza
is in unison SA, the second is unison TB, and the third is two-
part ST and AB. The organ has a major role again, and the right
hand is playing three-voice chords in perfect fourths. These
tetrads add mass to the total ensemble and tend to neutralize
harmony as the controlling force behind melody and form. In
much the same format the same year was a setting of Isaac
Watts' "From All That Dwell Below the Skies." Three years
later a setting of a text by Henry H. Milman, "Ride On! Ride
On!" began with an octave unison SA and TB with an organ
ostinato pedal line and the hands playing more sustained triadic
harmonies, then left and right playing triads in contrary motion
to introduce the four-part middle section a cappella. The third
section is a return to the theme and unison texture of the first
section. This formal pattern had at this date almost become one
of "common practice."

The appeal of Young's work brought many special commis-
sions from many churches from the Detroit area to La Jolla,
California, the Mormon Tabernacle Choir, Oklahoma, and
Texas. His publishers soon included Abingdon Press, Broadman, Harold Flammer, Heritage Music Press, Sacred Music
Press, Augsburg, Neil A. Kjos, Oxford, and Word, Incorporated.
The organ always plays an important role, but there are at least
two anthems written for a cappella performance. These are in
traditional tonalities, and the settings are syllabic throughout.
The "Litany for Easter" (1964, Abingdon) is a one-measure
isorhythmic setting of the text "Allelulia! Christ Is Risen, Allelulia!" in continuous four-voice texture. A short middle section is a slower setting of the text "Jesus Christ Is Risen Today!
Allelulia!" The third section is a repeat of the first. "Jesus, Thou
Blessed Name of Mercy" (1967, Sacred Music Press) is on an

original text by Young and is scored for SSATTB. It is alternately antiphonal between the men and women and then combined in six-part harmony. A middle section is an unaccompanied octave unison (SA and TB) melody in the parallel minor, which closes with five "Amens" in six-part harmony. The third section is a repeat of the first.

"God Is My Shepherd" (1974, Harold Flammer) is inscribed to the Mormon Tabernacle Choir. The first section is for a "solo or all voices" and gives the organ a continuous triadic accompaniment in triplets. At the verse "Yea, though I walk . . ." it is scored unison and four-voice a cappella. At "Thou preparest . . ." the women sing in unison with a chordal accompaniment in the organ. "Surely goodness . . ." brings the organ triplet accompaniment while the men and women sing a two-voice canon. The climactic SSATB harmonic cadence moves from a subtonic C-major to a D-major tonic, all in parallel motion.

Despite Gordon Young's enormous production, probably his most universal and memorable anthem is one of his earliest—"Now Let Us All Praise God and Sing" (1956, Galaxy). The mixed rhythms in threes and twos in the organ; the driving unisons of the first and third sections; and the four-voice a cappella middle section have all combined to become one of the most familiar anthems to Protestant choirs and congregations all over America.

The anthems of Gordon Young are a representative catalog of the dominant trends in recent choral literature for the church. They are, at the same time, examples of the "art of the possible" for volunteer church choirs. With much unison and two-part writing, the nonprofessional can effectively participate in a gratifying musical worship experience. Even the customary a cappella sections are unisons or part written in simple harmonic progressions.

The current profusion of composers of music for the church is unprecedented. Many of these serve as ministers of music who are thoroughly capable of writing their own anthems and hymn arrangements. With the technical advances in copy machines, we could well be returning to a minister of music who is also a "composer in residence." Already a large number of church musicians in large and small churches are adapting printed scores to the specific choral resources of their own congregations.

This abundance of composers has sprung from a great educational heritage of scholarship and instruction at our colleges and seminaries. These institutions have developed high levels of skills in music theory, composition, and style analysis. These, in turn, have produced the ability to create, select, and perform church music from all historical periods.

A study of contemporary church music, then, would not be complete without ample recognition of many teachers who have instructed so many others in the mastery and consistency of musical style through their classes in performance, musicology, and composition. Although the original works of many of these are not primarily in the field of church music, the skills and understanding which they have imparted deserve the highest recognition. The Christiansens, Leo Sowerby, Normand Lockwood, Roy Harris, Bernard Rogers, Archibald T. Davison, Howard Hanson, John Finley Williamson, Paul Hindemith, Clarence Dickinson, and Isham E. Reynolds have already been mentioned in relation to their particular institutions.

Other great scholars, composers, conductors, clinicians, and teachers who have been a part of this great educational heritage of contemporary church music must include Samuel Adler, Warren Angell, Morris Beachy, Charles Hirt, Lara Hoggard, Allen McHose, Daniel Moe, Carl Parrish, Lloyd Pfautsch, Paul Pisk, Euell Porter, Robert Shaw, Halsey Stevens, and Randall Thompson.

This analysis of a representative group of twentieth-century anthems should reveal that our musical practices in worship have been diverse and in continuous transition in style and contents. The diversity of texts is striking. At the beginning of our century, anthem texts were uniformly from the Scriptures or familiar hymns. These sources are still in the majority, but with some variations:

1. There are more translations of historical texts from early Latin and Greek texts.

2. More recently, there are many new hymn texts by contemporary poets which speak to current issues and are being used as anthem lyrics as often as familiar hymns.

3. Many composers, as in contemporary hymnody, are writing their lyrics to anthems for all levels of the graded choirs.

4. The themes of the new texts tend toward ecumenical themes, but at the same time greater subjectivity is exercised in the musical settings.

5. Anthems with a highly specific social or doctrinal message are not being used extensively. Even the patriotic themes seldom extend beyond "America the Beautiful" or the choral arrangement of the "Battle Hymn of the Republic."

6. The highly academic texts in contemporary musical settings have not become a prominent feature of Protestant worship.

In most respects, the music of our anthem literature has been subjected to more external influences, consequently experiencing more change than the texts. Any period of great technical change in a single aspect of an art form almost requires that other elements remain simple or traditional. Musicological research, mass communications, and theoretical experimentation had little effect upon the style content of church music until after the advent of graded choirs, electric organs, and a high level of music education in our secondary schools and colleges. A general summation of the musical development of the twentieth-century church anthem might conclude that:

1. The musical styles maintained a high historical context, preserving much of our folk heritage and a continuing use of the musical forms and harmonic styles of our Baroque and Romantic foundations.

2. The anthem has been revitalized through the use of the harmonic techniques of early twentieth-century Impressionism.

3. In addition to the poetic flow of text-rhythm, strong elements of syncopation have become commonplace.

4. A modal influence upon harmony and cadential formulae has emerged from our study and performance of sixteenth-century music. One that is particularly noticeable is the use of

a pseudo-mixolydian mode through the use of a subtonic triad instead of the diminished triad on the vii chord. Another is an increasing use of counterpoint and dissonance in effecting cadences, rather than the totally harmonic patterns of traditional harmony.

5. A new musical concern for the clear enunciation of text has become evident in the melodic and rhythmic settings of the basic thematic materials. This has become more essential, since the contemporary anthem normally contains more text and cannot indulge in a lengthy baroque polyphonic setting of two or three phrases of text.

6. The organ has become a more basic component of the contemporary anthem. Since limited rehearsal time often prescribes an anthem which is built upon unison or antiphonal text setting, a rich harmonic background from the organ is essential. In the absence of an adequate organ, many smaller churches are resorting to recorded accompaniments by small orchestras or synthesizers.

As a focal point in the drama of worship, the anthem will surely maintain its position and function, but many recent developments foretell greater experimentation in its style and presentation. Video recordings of professional choirs are even a possibility. However, it is doubtful if they would help attendance, contribute to corporate worship, or supplant the need for a personal expression of praise and proclamation. Another probability might be the addition of a projected background for the music—either abstractions, visual illustration, or actual dramatization.

The technology of the future can be both exciting and disturbing. When talking movies first came out, many thoughtful people predicted that we would soon be going to our community church on Sundays to hear America's greatest preachers from a silver screen. Only when it can enhance the individual's opportunity for a personal encounter with his Creator through worship and commitment will a videocassette recording ever transcend the gift of personal praise to God in song. Worship is impossible for spectators, and church music is the ultimate involvement of an individual in spiritual development through the fellowship of song.

22

Evaluations and Philosophies

The first half of this century was marked by the writings and struggles of Daniel B. Towner, Isham E. Reynolds, John F. Williamson, and Clarence Dickinson to establish a viable ministry of music in Protestant churches and to provide adequate education in music and theology to make the ministry effective. Once their institutions had adopted their plans, many conflicts arose in the areas of curricula, worship, missions, evangelism, hymnody, and choral music. The most immediate and persistent of these were centered around the gospel song, the hymn, and worship. Many of these problems have persisted, and many have become even more complicated. However, the romantic optimism of American Protestantism refused to see anything but the brightest future for the newly established ministry of music. Even in the depths of the Great Depression, Winfred Douglas could write:

> an ever increasing company of religiously-minded musicians is not only spreading their [historic traditions] effective use in our Parish Churches and Cathedrals, but also composing new and worthy music in the devotional spirit of the old, but in idioms of our own time. . . . We can thank God that he [sic] has led us so far toward a pure worship when prayer will sing and music will pray; where each member of the Mystical Body of Christ will be taken up into heavenly worship and actively participate in it with heart and mind and voice.[19]

With the establishment of the volunteer choir and the graded choir system, attention was quickly focused upon the planning of unified worship services, with interrelated hymns, Scriptures, anthems, and sermon. Carefully planned "Sermons in Song" were the frequent format of the Sunday evening services and might have a unified theme or be in segments with varied emphases. The overwhelming body of church publications, then, dealt with techniques of instruction in conducting, leadership, vocal and choral techniques, administration of the choir programs, hymnody, and music literature for all branches of the music ministry.

Worship was not entirely forgotten. The denominational hymnals always spoke the official attitudes of the hymnal committees toward music, hymns, and their roles in the corporate worship of the church. A few teachers, pastors, and musicians also voiced strong opinions on the subject. Probably the most outspoken in his attacks upon churches that failed to "pay due respect to dignity, order, and beauty" was Archibald T. Davison. His first book, *Protestant Church Music in America,* appeared in 1920 (revised in 1933) and a second book, *Church Music: Illusion and Reality,* in 1952. The latter book did not in any way renounce any positions taken in the first because "certain issues are fundamental, and though a number of these found a place in the previous work they are, of necessity, recapitulated here."[20] He spoke from his position as an organist and choirmaster "of long experience in a variety of churches" and stated his musical creed thus:

> no man to whom the God he worships is perfect with a perfection that transcends human imagining could be held sincere did he not, to the utmost, maintain toward church music the most inflexibly purist ideals reinforced by every critical faculty he possesses.[21]

As choral director at Harvard and Radcliffe, he performed the polyphonic music of the sixteenth century and visualized this as the "purest" music for worship. He compiled a list of sixty-nine suitable anthems by twenty-six composers—mostly from the sixteenth century. Only four of his contemporaries made the list—one American, one Canadian, and two English. His stylistic requirements for suitable church music were:

> a rhythm that avoids strong pulses; a melody whose physiognomy is neither so characteristic nor so engaging as to make an appeal in its own behalf; counterpoint, which cultivates long-breathed eloquence rather than instant and dramatic effect; a chromaticism which is at all times restricted in amount and lacking in emotionalism; dissonance, used only when it is technically necessary or in the interest of text emphasis; and modality which creates an atmosphere unmistakably ecclesiastical. . . . The stylistic principles which, in the sixteenth century, set sacred music apart from secular are so intrinsic in musical expression that their validity is subject neither to time nor to circumstance.[22]

He chose to ignore the fact that Roland de Lassus, one of the greatest composers of the Renaissance, used his contrapuntal style indiscriminately for secular madrigals, chansons, German lieder, and sacred motets.

An eloquent spokesman to the philosophical and theological issues involving church music in recent years has been the English scholar, musician, and theologian Erik Routley. As a frequent guest lecturer and teacher, he came to know and understand our American church music. He wrote in 1964:

> The vitality of American church music is abundant, and the prospects are of a considerable surge forward in an environment where the professional musician is highly regarded and where scholarship is enjoying an increasing status.[23]

This was written soon after Father Geoffrey Beaumont's *Folk Mass* (1960) and the formation of the Twentieth-Century Church Light Music Group in England. Routley described the organization as "a sophisticated, articulate and self-conscious movement. I am, indeed, going to describe its most impressive practitioner [Beaumont] as an artist writing 'in dialect.' "[24] Other works followed, imitating Beaumont's experiment, which Routley reported as derivatives of the "big musical" rather than jazz or pop. He added that those which it sought to evangelize have neither filled the churches nor abandoned the adulation of their pop idols. A major impact of the *Folk Mass* was the shock to conservatives and an awakening of "the minds of church musicians to quite a new situation and a series of quite new questions."[25]

This was also written only six years before the release in England of a controversial recording (1970) of the music for Andrew Lloyd Webber's *Jesus Christ, Superstar*. The later stage and movie versions in America were even more controversial— and more successful. The rock "pop" score included the synthesizer as a part of the orchestra as another signal of things to come. The team of Rice and Webber had successfully removed Jesus Christ "from the stained-glass windows," but His biblical image was somewhat tarnished by their lyrics and music.

The incursions of more recent "pop" and experimental sounds (or their imitation) have brought more stringent responses from other scholars and church musicians. Paul Wohlgemuth contends that "we are now at a time in the life of the church when the mood of experimentation and change is so dramatic, so intense, that a constant reevaluation must take place."[26] He cites a lecture by Donald Hustad on the efforts of most evangelicals toward more meaningful hymns and anthems: "We had just started going uphill, when we met the competition coming down, playing guitars and singing folksongs."[27]

The difficulties with contemporary rock stem from its textual associations more than the technical characteristics of the music. As long as the sounds of the music are a reminder of the textual contents of the song, the use of the rock idioms will remain a source of controversy. The use of a new generic term "contemporary gospel" has become sufficient justification for youth groups within the church, the principal programming for Christian radio stations, and "star" performers to fill stadiums and civic auditoriums for their "Christian" messages. All of this has prompted Wohlgemuth to ask:

> (1) If the medium is the message, could it be that rock music is inherently incapable of providing mature Christian messages?
> (2) Will our less cerebral and more experience-oriented music have a long-term debilitating effect upon the spiritual and musi-

cal life of the believing community? (3) Is the Church abdicating its role to teach the music of witness and worship to meet the total ministry of the church for all of its people?[28]

Even more severe criticism of the use of "pop" musical idioms is developed at length by Calvin Johansson because it is easy to consume; it is entertainment; it is success oriented; it has elements of Romanticism; it is inhospitable to quality; it capitalizes on sensationalism; and it is the epitome of transience.[29] He excludes folk and jazz from his "pop" categories because in their origin they were a distinct part of human culture—a particular culture, with unknown origin and with a complete absence of commercialism. Folk music is "of the people and not foisted upon the people. It is part of the evolutionary process of culture. The integrity of the music lies in its faithful mirroring of common usages."[30] Jazz has developed into a serious musical art form at the expense of its popularity. Originally an art based upon improvisation, it was the "chamber music" of illiterate musicians and practiced by and for the performers. The "progressive" development of jazz by the big bands transformed an art of spontaneous creativity into a very complicated musical art. Johansson says, "Good jazz is compatible with the gospel because it is good art, having musical worth, and has a place in the church's musical expressions."[31]

Routley approaches the "popular" in a different manner:

> All music which self-consciously adopts a style is like a person who puts on airs. It is affected and overbearing. I am afraid that in the experience of most of us this affectation is called "popular." That has come to mean the productions of the Light Music School in England and of many groups in America associated with the young. . . . Not infrequently they are put up to it by trendy clergy, but the fact is that the movements are often associated with youth.[32]

After a rather lengthy treatment of the problems and values of pop music, traditional church music, and Romantic music, his summation appears as a theological plumb line for twentieth-century church music.

> Our music and music-making should aim at being conformable

to a gospel which tells of a crucified and risen Redeemer, and which lays on us all the duty and delight of losing our lives that we may save them.[33]

Many other intrusions of external and internal forces upon the rapidly growing ministries of music have necessitated a rethinking of our concepts, practices, and philosophy of music and worship. In recent years reevaluations have been occurring regularly in denominational publications, but more openly from independent writers and publishers. The more common issues in church music have arisen from many inherent conditions—too much success too quickly; false recruitment techniques; failure to achieve spiritual goals; a lack of musical enrichment on the part of the minister of music and his choirs; a failure to effect creative solutions to worship and ministry; and an inundation of popular religious music which has almost usurped control of the music selection process.

Perhaps the most immediate concern in the literature of church music is a quest for effective corporate worship among the free churches. Wohlgemuth approaches the problem from two points of view—the attempt at a Topical (or Unified) service and a Mood service. The Topical service follows a singular focus throughout, but the Mood service follows the pattern of Isaiah 6:1-8 and would thus serve the multiple functions of Praise, Confession, Forgiveness, and Dedication.[34] The latter is closely related to the major liturgical services but often inserts additional elements peculiar to each denomination. This will continue to be a very open issue.

Since the 1950s, charismatic worship has found expression in almost all Protestant denominations. The emphasis here is upon dynamic worship, where

> a common freedom and excitement of praise is often found. . . . Their service draws expressions and participation, not only from the worship leaders, but also from the worshipper. Thus, the action of worship firmly takes place from within the worshipping congregation. A type of "guided spontaneity" prevails, in which events in the service are anticipated but not prescribed or predicted.[35]

This spontaneity almost approximates Kierkegaard's true drama of worship, "when worshippers in the congregation are the actors, the preacher and the choir are the prompters, and God is the listener."[36]

Since the music of the worship service is our primary concern, a major problem for the twentieth-century minister of music has been the choice of music literature. The simple gospel song and hymn controversy in the first half of the century has been compounded by the stylistic adoptions of ethnic music, contemporary gospel, complex harmonic techniques, and myriad electronic sounds undreamed of just decades before. These new sounds have brought problems of acceptance and performance. The spiritual has been caricatured for so many years that it is difficult for choirs and congregations to feel its drama and ecstasy. The performance can easily become an act of patronage. Many anthems in a more academic harmonic style are difficult for many choirs to give more than a perfunctory performance, and that with an unwilling sensitivity to its emotional content. Anthems with an element of jazz are already a more acceptable style to both choir and congregation, since it has become a distinct art form and far removed from its origins.

Any use of pop rock is still divisive. Its current lyrics are too strongly associated with the musical medium. Consequently, the medium is a constant reminder of lyrics so crude and vulgar as to invite high-level legal investigations. Its present fragmented motives are not compatible with a text with syntax, much less with a scriptural context. The overpowering beat is, of itself, static, hypnotic, and without counterpoint or anticipated harmonic or melodic progression. The "Christian gospel," designed especially for the unconverted, is currently at the top of the charts and features lyrics of religious experience usually unknown to the performers and unavailable to the listeners. All of this has become an extreme dilemma for the minister of music, since the church is completely involved with the world through Christ, and the gospel "is as fastidious as the man seeking a goodly pearl and as hospitable as the dragnet."[37]

An attempt to establish a total ministry of music based upon the "dragnet" would be pragmatism at its extreme. Music would thus be valued only for its effectiveness in producing some desired result, and "the gospel is stripped of its full integrity and power, and manipulating selling technique supplants the work of the spirit."[38]

Another factor which often serves as a basis for a ministry in church music is an emphasis upon the esthetic. The first premise of estheticism must be a concrete musical standard by which any music can be deemed worthy for use in the worship of God. As an example, for many years the polyphonic music of the sixteenth century was romantically acclaimed as the only "pure" church music, and Palestrina was hailed as its "savior." In reality, it was written for a musical clergy and for the adornment of the Roman Liturgy. Its approval by the congregation was neither sought nor considered necessary. A regular fare of sixteenth-century motets in contemporary worship would minister only to ardent disciples or performers of vocal chamber music. Since beauty is a product of individual contemplation and impossible to categorize objectively, the end result would be the worship of a style of music rather than the living God. Fortunately for us, God is sovereign and often uses even our disobedience to accomplish His purposes.

> Moses was instructed to speak to the rock for water to quench the thirst of the children of Israel; instead he disobeyed and smote the rock with his rod. Water still came—he got the desired result.[39]

But Moses was not allowed to enter the Promised Land. As ministers of music, "Our methodology must have the qualities of that which we hope to accomplish. . . . But more than that, it must be an indication of a right and obedient stand before God."[40]

All of these authors reflect the historical dilemma of church music—a general misunderstanding of the mysterious art of music and a continuing quest for "good" church music. Throughout the history of Protestantism, the definition of the "good" has been left to each congregation, within certain theological boundaries, and with as many differing solutions as there were churches. Often many committees have drawn up official guidelines for their churches, but with so many generalities that the technical "manuals" became meaningless and the churches were left to their own tastes and resources. As we have seen, the scholars and theologians have been equally ambiguous or narrow in their standards, except in terms of their own musical knowledge and experience.

A very widely accepted definition of "good" for many years has been "function." Music that fulfills its teaching, worship, or evangelistic "function" well for the congregation is "good." This has been a working code for church musicians for many years of diversified musical ministries and has produced just as many different musical practices. Such lack of proper perspectives, or even confusion, often arises because we look for our solutions from the wrong direction—we begin with the music. Since the basic concern of a music ministry is unalterably founded upon a textual concept which can be verbalized effectively for the congregation, we must begin our evaluations with the text. The integrity of our entire ministries is founded upon the message of the *Word*, and the music can be evaluated only in terms of its effective presentation of this biblical message. This is a more basic concern than "results," which can often usurp the authority of the Holy Spirit.

Once the text is validated as Scripture, or scriptural message, we can approach the music with well-established standards for textual presentation. This is really an area of multiple solutions, depending upon the musical abilities of the performers and the effectiveness of the musical setting. Given the multiplicity of historical and contemporary styles, we can make reliable musical judgments based upon established styles and techniques. The manner in which our varied historical styles have presented scriptural texts provides us varied and acceptable standards for general musical response and understanding of text/music relationships.

If the text is biblical, and not a subject for theological or subjective interpretation, a neo-Renaissance or neo-Baroque choral treatment would be quite effective. The typical structure would be similar to the sixteenth-century motets, J. S. Bach's chorale cantatas, or the dramatic oratorios of Bach and

Handel. One must remember that the scholarly polyphonic motets of the sixteenth-century masses and motets were designed for the adornment of the liturgy and under no circumstances could be considered as the composer's interpretation of the text. In fact a sacred motet was often the transcription of a secular work. In either case, the words were assigned to the printed music by the performers, but according to strict rules as set forth in Zarlino's theoretical treatise, *Istituzioni armoniche.*

It was much the same in the choral music of the Baroque. In the choruses of Handel's *Messiah,* a line of text is presented with its musical theme, then is multiplied, compounded, and transposed until it is indelibly inscribed upon the memory of the performer and listener. Bach uses the same choral techniques in his large choral works, but frequently interrupts the dramatic flow of events with the syllabic setting of a familiar chorale in four-part harmony. These choral techniques are still valid in a traditional or contemporary harmonic idiom for the declamation of a basic Scripture or a hymn text of corporate worship and praise.

In spite of this complicated but basically objective choral style of the Baroque, the story line is given to a solo "evangelist," and the drama is portrayed intensely by the solo aria. This use of the solo voice for the narration (Recitative) and the dramatic aria was the essential beginning of opera. Its harmonic structure stemmed from a bass line (Continuo) with figured consonant intervals (8s,6s,5s, and 3s) to indicate the upper voice parts to be filled in by the keyboard. The outline of the solo narrative was in sketchy speechlike rhythm, leaving much to the improvisation of the soloist. The solo aria was intentionally quite subjective. Throughout his cantatas based upon chorale tunes and texts, Bach "framed" his solo stanzas with accompanying interpretive motives or themes. Some of these ("Jesu, Joy of Man's Desiring") constitute some of our most treasured church music to this day and represent volumes of solo arias and organ chorale preludes. The contemporary choral composer has these same techniques available for the development of his textual ideas, and the traditional forms will support the validity of his style.

The greatest contribution to church music in the eighteenth century was the English hymn. The harmonized Lutheran chorale also became a central element of Lutheran worship. The hymns of Watts and Wesley gradually replaced metrical psalmody in England and America, and they remain the most numerous hymns in all of our twentieth-century Protestant hymnals in America. When arranging or writing a choral setting of any of these traditional hymn texts, the composer can safely use the Baroque style. Any subjective Romantic development of these hymn texts would be a distortion of the theological ideologies of both Watts and Wesley.

Another most productive period for church music was the nineteenth century. The new freedoms in religious life and the raging fires of evangelism in England and America were strongly supported by stylistic changes in the music. The new theories of harmony changed the accompaniment function to an interpretive relationship between the music and text. The poets had proclaimed music the most romantic of all the arts, and capable of expressing meanings beyond the power of words to suggest. Early in this century, I heard one of the greatest American symphony conductors introduce a fugue by J. S. Bach as being music "so profound as to only suggest its true meaning to our finite minds." Nineteenth-century composers accepted this high status and found the "inexpressible longing" of Romanticism to be an ideal medium for the subjective interpretation of Scripture as well as the Romantic hymn and gospel song.

Toward the end of the nineteenth century, Romantic hymns became linked to a tune which attempted to express solely the mood of its text. The tune then became a symbolic statement of the hymn itself. This also presupposed that any choral arrangement of the hymn must retain its original rhythm and harmonic outlines. However, intensification, even to excess, could be effected through a contrapuntal obligato, through density of choral texture, or through chromatic harmonic functions. Harmony controlled the outline of melody as well as the flow of text and rhythm. Dissonance became "non-chord tones" instead of an interval-relation with the bass line and added another dimension to subjective interpretation. The most intense choral expression of this pathos occurred when the non-chord tone was given to the soprano line instead of an inner part. This pattern was used extensively by Wagner; and even though he did not write functional church music, many of his orchestral and operatic excerpts became favorite choral transcriptions with sacred texts added.

The other choral alternative to the hymn arrangement became the hymn-anthem, with the composer's original setting of the familiar hymn text. These took on many of the characteristics of the quartet anthem—intensified solos, changes of key, and a new theme to better interpret each new stanza.

The decline of Romanticism brought many new musical resources to the twentieth-century anthem. These included the folk element, modality, impressionism, a wide range of textures from unisons to SSAATTBB, and a more complex role for the organ. These have allowed the composer to inject a wider variety of moods into the text settings. The text can have a mystical modality; the indifference of a folk setting; the coloristic quality of impressionism; an abstract traditional polyphony; an intense contemporary harmony; or even a reversion to a subjective Romanticism. The breadth of these resources demands a thorough grasp of the text with its clear meanings and subtle subjective implications. The choral director has an equal responsibility to recognize and evaluate the work of the composer. At the same time he must keep one ear tuned to the musical resources in his choirs and on the organ bench.

The subjective pathos of Romanticism has moved from the gospel song and the spirituals to an unprecedented Christian music which has created its own lyrics and a theology of benign religious clichés with some biblical imagery, but is always the personal testimony of new religious experience. The music is always in a distinctive popular idiom which demands a performance style as personal and professional as the best of the popular entertainers.

Never before have composers and ministers of music had so many musical resources at their disposal, and never before so much responsibility for their use. The message of the texts has never changed, but it is often altered to make it easier or more comfortable. Also, there are frequent changes in emphasis of denominational priorities or current social issues. These, too, are the responsibility of the composer and minister of music. The message is so vital and so varied that it must be planned for weeks in advance—either according to the church year or by seasonal emphasis in the individual church. The message is singular—*redemption!* The facets are so many—the virgin and a baby; shepherds and the heavenly choir; the sermon and the parables; the women and children; the sick and the dead; the hungry and bereaved; the Last Supper and Gethsemane; crucifixion and resurrection; ascension and Pentecost; and imminent return. What treasures of truth and wells of living water! Texts which avoid these in order to talk *about* them or to tell of our personal experience *with* them are irresponsibly neglecting "the way, the truth, and the life" (John 14:6).

Once the texts are confirmed, the musical sensitivity of the composer and minister of music must respond with the most convincing musical carrier of the message. The objective and subjective qualities of the text and the musical resources available for the performance will then dictate the proper musical response.

Notes

1. Personal correspondence from Neil A. Kjos, Jr., June 24, 1983.

2. Spann, Ed, "The Dilemma of Selecting Church Music Material," *Southern Baptist Church Music Journal*, Hugh T. McElrath, ed., Vol. 2, 1985, p.54.

3. Eskew, Harry, "Writing Hymn Texts and Tunes, an Interview," *The Hymn*, Harry Eskew, ed. (Fort Worth: Hymn Society of America), Vol. 35, No. 2, April, 1984, p.71.

4. Grindal, Gracia, "On Writing Hymns at the End of the Century," *Church Music 79*, Carl Schalk, ed. (St. Louis: Concordia Publishing House, 1979), p.25.

5. Ibid., p.26.

6. Eskew, quoting Calvin Hampton, p.87.

7. Ibid., quoting Jane Marshall, p.89.

8. Ibid., quoting Carl Schalk, p.93.

Evaluations and Philosophies   **265**

9. Collins, Don L., *The Cambiata Concept* (Conway, Ark.: University of Central Arkansas, n.d.), p.3.

10. Lovelace, Austin C., *The Youth Choir* (Nashville: Abingdon Press, 1964).

11. Ellington, Edward Kennedy, *Music Is My Mistress* (Garden City, N.Y.: Doubleday & Company, Inc., 1973), p.309.

12. Ibid., p.261.

13. Ibid., p.261.

14. Ibid., pp.270-279.

15. Ibid., p.280.

16. Hustad, Donald P., *Jubilate!* (Carol Stream, Ill.: Hope Publishing Co., 1981), p.324.

17. Ellinwood, Leonard, *The History of American Church Music* (New York: Morehouse-Gorham Company, 1953), pp.134-135.

18. Ibid., pp.138-139.

19. Douglas, Winfred, *Church Music in History and Practice* (New York: Charles Scribner's Sons, 1937), pp.271-272.

20. Davison, Archibald T., *Church Music; Illusion and Reality* (Cambridge: Harvard University Press, 1952), p.vii.

21. Ibid., p.ix.

22. Ibid., pp.37-38.

23. Routley, Erik, *Twentieth Century Church Music* (New York: Oxford University Press, 1964), p.90.

24. Ibid., p.152.

25. Ibid., p.167.

26. Wohlgemuth, Paul W., *Rethinking Church Music* (Carol Stream, Ill.: Hope Publishing Company, 1981), p.76.

27. Ibid.

28. Ibid., p.86.

29. Johansson, Calvin M., *Music and Ministry; a Biblical Counterpoint* (Peabody, Mass.: Hendrickson Publishers, Inc., 1984), pp.52-53.

30. Ibid., pp.59-60.

31. Ibid., p.61.

32. Routley, Erik, *Church Music and the Christian Faith* (Carol Stream, Ill.: Agape, 1978), p.89.

33. Ibid., p.137.

34. Wohlgemuth, pp.56-57.

35. Ibid., p.65.

36. Ibid., citing Soren Kierkegaard, *Purity of Heart* (New York: Harper & Brothers, 1956), pp.177-184.

37. Routley, CM&CF, p.68.

38. Johansson, p.6.

39. Ibid., p.58.

40. Ibid., p.59.

Bibliography

Alexander, Helen C., and MacLean, J. Kennedy. *Charles M. Alexander*. London: Marshall Brothers, Ltd., n.d.

Armstrong, Ben. *The Electric Church*. Nashville, TN: Thomas Nelson Publishers, Inc., 1979.

Ayres, Lew, Personal Correspondence, April 17, 1976.

Baker's Biographical Dictionary of Musicians, 5th Edition. New York: G. Schirmer, 1965.

Baptist Hymnal, W. Hines Sims, ed. Nashville, TN: Convention Press, 1956.

Baptist Hymnal, William J. Reynolds, ed. Nashville, TN: Convention Press, 1975.

Baptist Standard, Presnall Wood, ed., Vol. 96, No. 21.

BCTN Magazine, Walter E. Cranor, ed., Vol. IV, Nos. 2 and 4.

Benson, Louis F. *The English Hymn*. Richmond, VA: John Knox Press, 1962.

Blake, Manfred Nelson. *A Short History of American Life*. New York, NY: McGraw-Hill Book Company, Inc., 1952.

Brown, Alfred. "Wanted, A Chair of Tent-making," *The Atlantic Monthly*, Vol. LXXXIV, December 1899. New York, NY: Doubleday & McClure Co.

Butterfield, Roger. "Homer Rodeheaver," *Life*, September 3, 1945.

Calman, Charles Jeffrey and Kaufmann, William I. *The Mormon Tabernacle Choir*. New York, NY: Harper and Row, 1979.

Carman, Harry J., Kimmel, William G., and Walker, Mabel G. *Historic Currents in Changing America*. Chicago, IL: John C. Winston Company, 1942.

Coffin, Henry Sloane. *A Half Century of Union Theological*

Seminary, 1896-1945. New York, NY: Charles Scribner's Sons, 1954.

Coleman, Lucien. "The Southern Baptist Convention and the Media," *Review and Expositor*, Vol. LXXXI, No. 1, Roy L. Honeycutt, ed. Louisville, KY: The Southern Baptist Theological Seminary, 1984.

Collins, Don L. *The Cambiata Concept*. Conway, Ark.: University of Central Arkansas, n.d.

_____ *Principles and Practices Prevailing in Church Music Education Programs of Selected Protestant Churches of America*. The Florida State University, 1970.

Darden, Bob. "Gospel Lectern," *Billboard Magazine*, October 5, 1985.

Davison, Archibald T. *Church Music; Illusion and Reality*. Cambridge, MA: Harvard University Press, 1952.

Dean, Talmage W. "Congregational Singing: a Historical Perspective," *Southwestern Journal of Theology*, Vol. II, No. 1, October 1959.

_____ ed. *Source Readings in the History of Church Music*. Fort Worth: Southwestern Seminary Press, 1964.

Diehl, Katherine Smith. *Hymns and Tunes-an Index*. New York: The Scarecrow Press, Inc. 1966.

Douglas, Winfred. *Church Music in History and Practice*. New York: Charles Scribner's Sons, 1937.

Downey, James Cecil. *The Music of Revivalism*. Ph.D. Dissertation, Tulane University, 1968.

Dwight's Journal of Music, Vol.XLI, No. 104, April 23, 1881. Boston: Houghton, Mifflin & Company.

Ellington, Edward Kennedy [Duke]. *Music Is My Mistress*. Garden City: N.Y.: Doubleday & Company, Inc., 1973.

Ellinwood, Leonard. *The History of American Church Music*. New York: Morehouse-Gorham Company, 1953.

Fant, Clyde E., and Pinson, William M. *Twenty Centuries of Great Preaching*, Vol. VIII. Waco, TX: Word Books, Inc., 1971.

Ennis, Michael. "Onward Chris Christian-rock soldier," *Texas Monthly*, December 1985.

Eskew, Harry. "Writing Hymn Texts and Tunes, an Interview,"

The Hymn, Harry Eskew, Ed., Fort Worth: Hymn Society of America, Vol. 35, No. 2, April 1984.

Fink, Fred W. *Graduate Music Curricula in Protestant Theological Seminaries of America.* M.M. Thesis, Southern Methodist University, 1952.

Fleming, Jo Lee. *James D. Vaughan, Music Publisher, Lawrenceburg, Tennessee, 1912-1964.* S.M.D. Dissertation, Union Theological Seminary, 1972.

Foote, Henry W. "Recent American Hymnody," *The Papers of the Hymn Society of America,* Lindsay B. Longacre, ed. New York: The Hymn Society of America, 1952.

_____ *Three Centuries of American Hymnody.* Cambridge: Harvard University Press, 1940.

Fuller, Daniel P. *Give the Winds a Mighty Voice.* Waco, Tex.: Word Books, 1972.

Gallo, William K. *The Life and Church Music of Dudley Buck (1839-1909).* Ph.D. Dissertation, The Catholic University of America, 1968.

Garcia, William Burres. *The Life and Choral Music of John Wesley Work (1901-1967).* Ph.D. Dissertation, The University of Iowa, 1973.

Getz, Gene A. *MBI, The Story of Moody Bible Institute.* Chicago: Moody Press, 1969.

Glass, James W. *The Sacred Art Song in the United States,* 1869-1975. D.M.A. Dissertation, Southwestern Baptist Theological Seminary, 1976.

Grindal, Gracia. "On Writing Hymns at the End of the Century," *Church Music 79,* Carl Schalk, Ed. Saint Louis: Concordia Publishing House, 1979.

Harvard Dictionary of Music, 2nd Edition. Cambridge: Harvard University Press, 1964.

Hooker, Gordon, Personal Interview, November 19, 1984.

Hooper, William Loyd. *The Master's Degree in Church Music in Protestant Theological Seminaries of the United States.* Ph.D. Dissertation, George Peabody College for Teachers, 1966.

Hustad, Donald P. *Jubilate! Church Music in the Evangelical Tradition.* Carol Stream, Ill.: Hope Publishing Company, 1981.

Hymnal, The, Clarence Dickinson, ed. Philadelphia: Presbyterian Board of Christian Education, 1933.

Hymnal, The, Bishop Henry Judah Mikell, Chairman of the Joint Commission. New York: The Church Pension Fund, 1940.

Hymnal 1982, The, The Church Hymnal Corporation. New York: The Church Pension Fund, 1985.

Hymnal, Army and Navy, The, Ivan L. Bennett, ed. Washington: U.S. Government Printing Office, 1941.

Hymnal Supplement, no ed. Carol Stream, Ill.: Agape, 1984.

Hymnbook, The, David Hugh Jones, ed. Philadelphia: John Ribble, Publishing Agent, 1955.

Ives, Charles E. *Essays Before a Sonata.* New York: The Knickerbocker Press, 1920.

James, William. *The Varieties of Religious Experience.* New York: Collier Books, 1961.

Johansson, Calvin M. *Music and Ministry; a Biblical Counterpoint.* Peabody, Mass.: Hendrickson Publishers, Inc., 1984.

Johnson, Albert Rykken. *The Christiansen Choral Tradition: F. Melius Christiansen, Olaf C. Christiansen, and Paul J. Christiansen.* Ph.D. Dissertation, The University of Iowa, 1973.

Jones, Raymond D. *Leo Sowerby: His Life and His Choral Music.* Ann Arbor, Mich.: University Microfilms, 1973.

Kasten, Seth, Personal Correspondence, November 30, 1985.

Kjos, Neil A. Jr., Personal Correspondence, June 24, 1983.

Lang, Paul Henry. *Music in Western Civilization.* New York: W.W. Norton and Company, 1941.

Lanterman, Walter F. "Broadcasting," *Encyclopedia Britannica,* Vol. IV. Chicago: Encyclopedia Britannica, Inc., 1952.

Leckie, Robert. "Tarawa: Conquest of the Unconquerable," *Illustrated Story of World War II.* Pleasantville: The Reader's Digest Association, Inc., 1969.

Lehmann, Arnold Otto. *The Music of the Lutheran Synodical Conference, Chiefly the Areas of Missouri, Illinois, Wisconsin and Neighboring States.* Ph.D. Dissertation, Western Reserve University, 1967.

Litton, James. "An Episcopalian Looks at the *Lutheran Book of*

Worship," Church Music, Carl Schalk, ed. Saint Louis: Concordia Publishing House, 1979.

Lorenz, Ellen Jane. *Glory, Hallelujah!* Nashville: Abingdon Press, 1980.

Lorenz, Edmund S. *Practical Church Music.* New York: Fleming H. Revell Company, 1909.

_____, ed. *The Choir Leader,* 1900, 1915, and 1930. Dayton: Lorenz Publishing Company.

_____, ed. *The Choir Herald,* 1900, 1915, and 1930. Dayton: Lorenz Publishing Company.

_____, ed. *The Volunteer Choir,* 1915 and 1930. Dayton, Oh.: Lorenz Publishing Company.

Los Angeles Times, May 29, 1983.

Lovelace, Austin C. *The Youth Choir.* Nashville: Abingdon Press, 1964.

Lutheran Book of Worship, Inter-Lutheran Commission on Worship, Eugene Brand, director. Minneapolis: Augsburg Publishing House, 1978.

Lutheran Hymnal, The, The Evangelical Lutheran Synodical Conference of North America. Saint Louis: Concordia Publishing House, 1941.

Maier, Paul L. *A Man Spoke, A World Listened.* St. Louis: Concordia Publishing House, 1980.

Malone, Bill C. *Southern Music, American Music.* Lexington: The University Press of Kentucky, 1979.

Marsh, J. B. T. *The Story of the Jubilee Singers; with Their Songs,* Revised Edition. New York: Negro Universities Press, 1969.

McDougald, Worth, and Stewart, Lynda. *Welcome South Brother, Fifty Years of Broadcasting at WSB.* Atlanta: Verlan Industries, Inc., 1974.

Methodist Hymnal, The, Carlton R. Young, ed. Nashville: The Methodist Publishing House, 1966.

Moody, Michael Finlinson. *Hymnody in the Church of Jesus Christ of Latter-day Saints.* Ph.D. Dissertation, University of Southern California, 1972.

Murray, Harold. *Sixty Years an Evangelist.* London: Marshall, Morgan & Scott, Ltd., 1937.

Neve, Paul E. *The Contributions of the Lutheran College Choirs to Music in America.* Ann Arbor: University Microfilms, 1967.

New Hymnal, The, Cortland Whitehead, Chairman of the Joint Commission. New York: The Church Pension Fund, The H. W. Gray Company, 1916.

Parker, Thomas Henry. *Homer Alvan Rodeheaver (1880-1955), Evangelistic Musician and Publisher.* Ed.D. Dissertation, New Orleans Baptist Theological Seminary, 1981.

Peattie, Elia W. "The Artistic Side of Chicago," *The Atlantic Monthly,* Vol. LXXXIV, December 1899. New York: Doubleday & McClure Company.

Pollock, John. *Billy Graham.* McGraw-Hill Book Company, 1966.

Redden, Sally Jean. *A History of the School of Music at New Orleans Baptist Theological Seminary* (1919-1966). M.C.M. Thesis, NOBTS, New Orleans, 1968.

Reynolds, William J. *Companion to Baptist Hymnal.* Nashville: Broadman Press, 1976.

_____. *Hymns of Our Faith.* Nashville: Broadman Press, 1964.

_____, "10 Years Later, Reynolds Pleased with Hymnal," *Southwestern News,* Vol. 43, No. 8.

Rodeheaver, Homer. *Twenty Years with Billy Sunday.* Nashville: Cokesbury Press, 1936.

_____, "Wrecking the Service with the Wrong Song," *The Choir Leader,* E. S. Lorenz, ed., Vol. XXXVIII, No. 8.

Rosewall, Richard B. *Singing Schools of Pennsylvania, 1800-1900.* Ph.D. Dissertation, University of Minnesota, 1969.

Routley, Erik. *Church Music and the Christian Faith.* Carol Stream, Ill.: Agape, 1978.

_____. *Twentieth Century Church Music.* New York: Oxford University Press, 1964.

Schwarz, Jack, Personal Correspondence, April 25, 1983.

Siepmann, Charles A. *Radio, Television and Society.* New York: Oxford University Press, 1950.

Singing Church, The, no ed. Carol Stream: Hope Publishing Company, 1985.

Smith, Gipsy. *Forty Years an Evangelist.* New York: George H. Doran Company, 1923.

_____. *Gipsy Smith, His Life and Work.* New York: Fleming H. Revell Company, 1906.

Sowerby, Leo. *Ideals in Church Music.* Greenwich, Conn.: Seabury Press, 1956.

Spann, Ed. "The Dilemma of Selecting Church Music Material," *Southern Baptist Church Music Journal,* Hugh T. McElrath, ed., Vol. 2, 1985.

Spigener, Tommy R. *The Contributions of Isham E. Reynolds to Church Music in the Southern Baptist Convention between 1915-1945.* M.C.M. Thesis Southwestern Baptist Theological Seminary, Fort Worth, 1962.

Stevenson, Robert. *Protestant Church Music in America.* New York: W.W. Norton & Company, Inc., 1966.

Stewart, Roger D. *The Contributions of Edmund S. Lorenz to American Church Music.* M.C.M. Thesis, Southwestern Baptist Theological Seminary, 1967.

Time, Vol. LIV, No. 19, November 7, 1949.

_____, Vol. LIV, No. 20, 1949.

Washington, Booker T. "The Case of the Negro," *The Atlantic Monthly,* Vol. LXXXIV, November, 1899. New York: Doubleday & McClure Company.

Weisberger, Bernard A. *They Gathered at the River.* Boston: Little, Brown and Company, 1958.

Wehr, David A. *John Finley Williamson (1887-1964): His Life and Contribution to Choral Music.* Ph.D. Dissertation, University of Miami, 1971.

Westminster Choir College, Catalog for 1982-1984.

Wohlgemuth, Paul W. *Rethinking Church Music.* Carol Stream, Ill.: Hope Publishing Company, 1981.

Index